Potpourri OF Nostalgia

Potpourri OF Nostalgia

A COLLECTION OF STORIES
BLENDING THE "SPICES" OF LIFE

BONNIE HUGHES FALK

BHF MEMORIES UNLIMITED

WHITE BEAR LAKE, MINNESOTA

Published by BHF Memories Unlimited
3470 Rolling View Court
White Bear Lake, MN 55110

Distributed by Adventure Publications, Inc.
P. O. Box 269
Cambridge, MN 55008

Library of Congress Cataloging-in-Publication Data

Falk, Bonnie Hughes, ed. 1945-
    Potpourri of nostalgia, a collection of stories
    blending the spices of life.

    1. United States--Social life and customs--
        anecdotes, facetiae, satire, etc.

    PN6162.F186   813.F186   90-081795

ISBN: 0-9614108-2-5

Cover and book design by Bonnie Hughes Falk
Edited by Bonnie Hughes Falk
Typography: Macintosh Plus, Microsoft Word 4.0, LaserWriter II
Printed by Sentinel Printing, St. Cloud, MN

Printed in the United States of America

To Tom
my husband and best friend

and

To Scott and Andy
the greatest sons in the
whole wide world

ACKNOWLEDGMENTS

This book is the culmination of a dream I have had for some time, and I put my whole heart and soul into its production. There were many frustrations along the way, and without the support of my family and friends, I never would have made it. A great big thank you is in order to everyone who helped make my dream a reality. Following are some of those special people:

My husband, Tom, and sons, Scott and Andy, who many times did not have a table to eat on, since my things were spread out on every flat surface available; my mother, Mae Kjos, and sisters, Norma Schlichter and Shirley Selzer, for assisting me in so many different ways; Aunt Selma for her help and concern; Karen Kuehn for sharing her computer knowledge and proofreading the manuscript--a lifesaver; Vicki Johnson, Cindy Lerfald, Carol Petronack, and John Schell, who acted as my "sounding board" and helped with the proof-reading; Leslie Dimond and Mary Coughlin for their graphics expertise; the Minnesota Historical Society Audio-Visual Library staff for providing photographs; the Lakewood Community College Computer staff and the guys at Kinkos in Maplewood for their technical assistance; and Marv Bauer for guiding me through the printing process.

A very special thank you to all those contributors who took the time to send me their stories. Without them, this book would not have been possible. Although I have not met each of them personally, I now consider them my friends.

I wish to thank the following for granting me permission to use their work:

Borden, Inc. for permission to copy the Cracker Jack® boy and prizes.
St. Paul Pioneer Press for permission to use three stories on SPAM
      ("SPAM Saves the Day," "Everything's Coming up SPAM," and
      "Alfreds"); and "Fellow Americans Looked So Good!"
Mankato Free Press for permission to use an excerpt from "Country Doctor
      Retires After Busy Half Century," by Stephen C. Bakken.
Mankato Free Press and Roy B. Moore for permission to use excerpts from
      "Family Portrait" and "Catalog Gifts Filled Our Christmases."
Roy B. Moore for permission to use "Ballad of the Left and Right," from
      Kindly Frost and Other Rime, 1982, by Roy B. Moore, and "The Finish
      Line," from *Sparks from the Embers*, 1976, by Roy B. Moore.
Lake Crystal Tribune for permission to use "Letters from Santa."
Minnesota Historical Society for use of photographs.
Art Fleming for use of photographs.
Rod Furan for Farmfest illustration, page 11.
Jeanette Starr for Tomten illustration, page 167.
Marilyn Olin for rosemaling illustration, page 167.

CONTENTS

PREFACE

ANCESTRY 1
    Exploring My Roots 2
    The Family Farm 8
    Grandmas and Grandpas 12

FAMILY LIFE 17
    Family Time 18
    Daily Chores 24
    Porches, Cellars, and Outhouses 27
    Family Trips 32

CUSTOMS AND CELEBRATIONS 35
    Milestones 36
    The Community 49
    Fairs and Festivals 53

GROWING UP 57
    Adventures of Youth 58
    Games We Played 64
    Earning Pocket Money 67
    Looking Back 70

SCHOOL DAYS 75
    The One-Room School 76
    The 3R's and Much More 80
    Extra-Curricular Activities 87

FASHION AND FUN 91
    What We Wore 92
    What We Did For Fun 101

HOLIDAYS 107
    New Year's Day 108
    Valentine's Day 109
    Easter 110
    Fourth of July 112
    Halloween 114
    Thanksgiving 116
    Christmas 121

ADVENTURES ON WHEELS 127
    Bicycles 128
    Automobiles 129
    Trains 134

Streetcars... 137
Airplanes 139

ANIMAL TALES... 141

FAVORITE FOODS.. 151
From Homemade Ice Cream to Spam 152
From Ravioli to Lutefisk 159

TREASURES 163
Heirlooms, Collections, and Hobbies.................. 164
Places to Browse and Dream 169

SPORTS AND LEISURE 173

HARD TIMES... 185
Mother Nature... 186
The Depression.. 189
War... 192

THIS 'N' THAT.. 201
Unforgettable Characters.................................... 202
Do You Remember? 205
Reflections 209

CONTRIBUTORS 211

PREFACE

There are many fill-in-the-blank memory books on the market to-day; unfortunately, a great number of them remain blank, waiting for the "author" to find the right moment, the right pen, or just the right words to write. Consequently, many "life stories" never get recorded.

On the other hand, as these same individuals read books on the subject of memories, nostalgia, etc., I have often heard them say, "I could have written that!" Then, they proceed to tell their own stories; however, if those stories are not recorded orally or in written form, they are lost. Also, most families have photographs which record specific events important to that family, but the stories that go along with those photographs are not usually recorded. Therefore, they, along with many other priceless treasures, are often meaningless to those who later uncover them from their secret hiding places.

I am trying to encourage as many people as possible to record their stories and identify their keepsakes before it is too late. *Potpourri of Nostalgia* is a start. One hundred individuals--men and women, young and old, rural and urban--shared with me, orally or in written form, anywhere from one to thirty stories each. These stories span nearly a century of living--from the turn of the century to the present.

Obtaining these stories was not an easy task, for people are all so busy today. Also, there were a number of procrastinators in the group! Many initially thought they didn't have anything to write about, that their stories wouldn't be of interest to others, or that they couldn't write well enough. But when they sat down and gave it some thought, they surprised themselves, and the words began to flow. However, I'm sure many of them are glad to see this book completed, so that I will quit "pestering" them for stories.

I've always been a saver. I have everything--from the dried flowers of my first corsage--to the sugar packet from the first "expensive" restaurant I ate in! All this, and much more, has a permanent home in one of my many scrapbooks. I realize that not everyone is a "saver," but I do think it is important that each of us leaves some part of our-selves behind, in whatever form.

Potpourri of Nostalgia is a combination of many elements. Yet, they all seem to blend well together, forming the "spices" of life. Therefore, the word "potpourri" seemed appropriate. There are stories about ancestors and family life; growing up and school days; fashion and fun; customs and celebrations; the "good" and the "hard" times; and many, many more. Each story represents a significant event in someone's life, and is, therefore, important.

Hopefully, you will be able to relate to some of these stories, and as you read through the book, you will say, "I remember that," or "I have a better one than that to tell," for the goal of this book is to get YOU to record some of YOUR lifetime memories, either in oral or written form. It is important to get something down in some format. You can always rewrite it later. Therefore, I suggest that as you read this book, you have a notebook or scrap of paper with you to jot things down as you remember them. If you think you will do it later, nine chances out of ten you will forget what you were going to write by then!

So sit back, relax, and enjoy reading these stories and writing your own. Hopefully, the stories, photographs, and other memorabilia in *Potpourri of Nostalgia* will stimulate you to dig out your old photo albums, diaries, scrapbooks, or other "treasures" from the trunk, attic, or wherever those long dormant memories lie--unveiling some images from your past. NOW is the time to record those lifetime memories!

Bonnie Hughes Falk

Note: At the end of each story, you will find the contributor's name, where the story took place, and the approximate year or decade. I wrote a short introduction at the beginning of some of the sections, after which you will find the notation (BHF).

ANCESTRY

THE BEN D. HUGHES FAMILY

EXPLORING MY ROOTS

TO FORGET ONE'S ANCESTORS IS TO BE A BROOK
WITHOUT A SOURCE, A TREE WITHOUT A ROOT.
(Chinese Proverb)

Grace James Hughes
1844-1892

I developed an interest in researching my roots several years ago. Looking through my family history, I discovered that several of my ancestors were also interesting in preserving their heritage. Therefore, the groundwork had been laid; I am merely carrying on a tradition which began many generations ago.

--My great, great uncle, Reverend Peter S. Davies, edited and published a temperance paper, "The Shining Light," in the 1870s.

--My great grandfather, Reverend Thomas E. Hughes, was one of four individuals who compiled and edited the *History of the Welsh in Minnesota*, published in 1895.

--My grandfather, Benjamin D. Hughes, a Minnesota State Legislator in the 1940s, wrote a history of the Horeb Church in Cambria in the 1930s.

--My uncle, David Wendell Hughes, wrote and compiled a history of his father's family (Hughes and James) and his mother's family (Davies and Evans) in 1969.

Hopefully, after reading this section about my ancestors, you will be inspired to explore your own roots.

(Note: The first three excerpts are taken from biographies written in the *History of the Welsh in Minnesota*, edited by Revs. Thos. E. Hughes and David Edwards, and Messrs. Hugh G. Roberts and Thomas Hughes. The Free Press Printing Co., Mankato, MN, 1895. (BHF)

REVEREND DAVID DAVIES (my paternal great, great grandfather)

Reverend Davies was born at Tirgwyn, Llandysiliogogo, Cardiganshire, Wales, July 12, 1789. He was a son of Evan and Elizabeth Davies, and brother of Reverend Samuel Davies and Reverend Jenkin Davies, the latter being a very noted Calvinistic Methodist minister. His father was a prominent elder of the church of Pensarn, located on his farm. The family tradition is that the late distinguished Dr. Samuel Davies, president of Princeton College, was a member of the same Davies family. The subject of our sketch also prepared himself for the ministry, though his educational advantages were few.

Reverend Davies emigrated to Bloomfield Township, Jackson County, Ohio, in 1837. There he preached to the Welsh settlers. In America his ministerial connection was with the Presbyterian church, but he ministered mostly to Congregational churches. Being a strong Abolitionist, he became a member of the Underground Railroad. In May 1856, he removed with his family to Blue Earth County, Minnesota. From 1856 until his death in 1861, he preached in Blue Earth and LeSueur Counties.

Dr. Davies (as he was generally called from his having studied medicine) was a great reader, a close thinker and a sound reasoner. A man of strong convictions and of unswerving loyalty to his principles. A fast friend of all that was right and a firm foe to all that was wrong.

REVEREND THOMAS E. HUGHES (my paternal great grandfather)

Reverend Hughes was born at Clynnog, Carnarvonshire, North Wales, June 27, 1844. He is the first born of eight children. He came with his parents to the United States in the summer of 1845. The family settled in Columbus, Wisconsin, where Mr. Hughes received his education in the common schools of the day and at Wayland University, a Baptist institution not far from his home. He served in the Union Army for about three years--from August 1862, to July 1865--in Company G, Twenty-third Regiment, Wisconsin Volunteers. He commenced preaching in 1866 in Columbus. From 1868 to 1873 he was engaged in mission work among the Freedmen in the states of Arkansas and Missouri, under the auspices of the American Missionary Association and the Welsh Presbyterian Synod of Wisconsin. In 1874 he accepted a call to the Williamsburg and Welsh Prairie churches in Iowa, where he served as pastor for fourteen years. In 1888 he removed to Minnesota, accepting a pastorate in Blue Earth County.

Rev. Thomas Evan Hughes
1844-1921

BENJAMIN DWIGHT HUGHES (my paternal grandfather)

(Note: My grandfather was elected to public office continuously from 1908 to 1947. He was serving his fourth term as a Minnesota State Representative at the time of his death on April 4, 1947. Following is an excerpt from an article which appeared in the *Mankato Free Press*.) (BHF)

"It is hard to reconcile one's self to the fact that Mr. B. D. Hughes is no longer with us. "B.D.," as we familiarly called him, was a man who was well-known throughout this county, and whose friends were legion. He had served long as a public servant, and had served well. The fact that he received such a fine vote each time in his district proved that he was well thought of among his constituency. His untimely death ended more than a quarter century of virtually continuous, faithful, and valuable service to his home community, to Blue Earth County, and to the state of Minnesota.

It was his dependability, his quiet, thorough, painstaking work, his devotion to his home community and to the agricultural territory which he represented, that made him one of the outstanding members of the lower house of the legislature, where he had served continuously since 1941. Blue Earth County, and the state as a whole, will miss him sorely over the years ahead. One of the crying needs of the nation

BEN. D. HUGHES
The NOMINATED CANDIDATE *For*
State Representative
BLUE EARTH COUNTY, MINNESOTA
Your FRIENDLY EXPERIENCED LEGISLATOR
UNFRIENDLY TO HIGH TAXES

today is more "grassroots politicians" with the sympathetic understanding of the public, and the sane, balanced outlook on government, that was held by Ben Hughes."

<u>ALICE DAVIES HUGHES</u> (my paternal grandmother)
(Note: Sometimes we only know a grandparent through stories we hear about them or by reading their obituary. Such is the case with my paternal grandmother, who died five years before I was born. It saddens me that I did not have the opportunity to know this special person.) (BHF)

ALICE DAVIES HUGHES

Funeral services were held Wednesday afternoon, October 30, 1941, for Mrs. B. D. Hughes. Mrs. Alice Hughes was born on January 15, 1881, in Brown County, Minnesota. She was one of eleven children of David S. and Rachel Davies. On March 30, 1899, she was united in marriage to Ben D. Hughes.

The services were large, and a loud speaker was extended from the church to the nearby schoolhouse, which was also filled to capacity, with as many outside as were housed in both church and school. This was a clear indication of the high esteem in which the departed was held by her neighbors and all within reach who knew her. The deceased was an ideal wife and mother. However, she did not confine her usefulness to her home only, but shared her life with the church and community. She was willing to help in religious and civic works of the community and held the love and esteem of her friends to the end. Mrs. Hughes was a deeply spiritual woman and consecrated her whole life to the Service of the Master.

(Note: The following three stories are about my maternal ancestors. The first two are written by my mother, and the third is taken from a *Mankato Free Press* article about her cousin.) (BHF)

REMINISCING

Our heritage and ancestry become a very important part of our retiring years. It is good to stop the world occasionally and reminisce about how we got where we are. I have been doing just that recently while going through boxes of scrapbooks and other memorabilia. It is good for the soul!

My father came by boat to this country from Norway when he was six months old. He came with his mother and six other children. His father had come before them in pursuit of work and shelter. It must have been extremely difficult, but somehow they managed. They had ten children and three others who died in infancy. They were a handsome family--seven boys and three girls--and they enjoyed much family togetherness. In spite of all the adversities, my grandparents celebrated their sixtieth wedding anniversary and both lived to be ninety years old.

As for my mother and father, an extreme change took place during their lifetime. As I look back to my own childhood and compare that to the conveniences and extravagances we have now, it is unbelievable. I can't conceive of another generation possibly experiencing as much progress.
(Mae Hanson Hughes Kjos--Lake Crystal, MN)

AUNT BETTY

As we gather to celebrate your ninetieth birthday, many thoughts go through my mind as I think of your active, full life. There have been so many times in all of our lives when you, Aunt Betty, were there to listen, to help, and to care. Your love of God and intense faith has made a lasting impression on your big family of relatives.

We all marvel at your alert mind, good attitude, perseverance, and determination, even through adversity. You are a talented lady with many interests. Everyone knows of your great love of flowers, sewing, birds, gardening, canning, carpentry, and crafts of all kinds. There just isn't anything, it seems, that you don't know a clever way to make or remedy. Your love of cooking is still a part of your every day--trying all the new recipes and some favorite old ones. We've all sampled your pies, cookies, rolls, fried chicken, and sauerkraut and dumplings, to name a few.

Going to your house is like coming home for all of us. There is always an open door and a warm welcome. You have love, understanding, and compassion for all. We love you, Aunt Betty.
(Mae Hanson Hughes Kjos--Lake Crystal, MN--1985)

ELIZABETH GAPPA JUHL

COUNTRY DOCTOR RETIRES AFTER BUSY HALF CENTURY

After 3,000 deliveries, five doctor bags, and a century of housecalls, Lewis Hanson is calling it quits. A disciplined, organized, general practitioner who tackled every barrier in the most direct way possible, "Doc" Hanson set and maintained an exhaustive daily pace for fifty-one years. "Believe it or not, I used to see 80 patients a day--sometimes as many as 110 a day if they knew I would be going on vacation," Hanson said. His practice covered a sixty-mile radius of Frost, Minnesota.

"He never kept any written records or charts and never sent out any bills," recalled Kay Lloyd, the first--and only--nurse to serve under Hanson. His fees were always within the patient's ability to pay. He once accepted a gasoline engine in lieu of money for a call. "He also never went by appointment. People just came into his waiting room and Doc Hanson would come out and ask, 'Who's next?'" Lloyd said.

"I was honest," said Hanson. "People could trust me. I limited myself to what I could do well and I was a good

5

6

diagnostician." Dr. Marcus Keil, an Albert Lea internist who has known Hanson since 1948, said, "Louie is implicitly honest, humble, and has a perception in quickness of diagnosis."

If marathon days and fees based on ability to pay were trademarks of his intense medical career, so were house calls. "I never quit making them," Hanson said. "When you go into a house, you see a lot and learn something besides medicine from that family." He claims about seventy percent of the patients he attended at home never really needed to see a doctor, but "my presence was a real consolation to them." Despite the dozens of daily, diverse consultations, Doc Hanson knew every patient like the back of his hand. He has treated three and four generations of some families.

Hanson has many stories to go with the 3,000 plus babies he has delivered. "Once, my Chevy broke down and I had to trudge a mile through rain to reach a farm. When I got there, the expectant father loaned me his good Sunday suit because my own clothes were drenched. And that's what I wore to deliver the baby."

But if deliveries performed with his huge hands were among the doctor's best times, they also were among his saddest. "I once sat with a tiny leukemia victim in my lap. That baby was bleeding from her nose. She was vomiting and passing blood," he said with his eyes misting and his voice slowing. "And you sit holding this child....and you can't do a damn thing....that really gets you."

Doc Hanson's concern for newborns may stem from personal experience. He was born with a hair lip and cleft palate and had six operations before he was a year old. "Because I was smart and had confidence in myself, I never let it interfere with me one bit." In reflecting on his life, the doctor said, "A lot of people get sorry on life. I have nothing to be sorry about. For somebody who was born handicapped, from a family of very moderate means, I've done pretty well. In fact, I wasn't given a middle name because they never thought I was going to live," he said with a smile. "But I sure fooled them!"

(From an article in the *Mankato Free Press*, by Stephen C. Bakken)

THE JOHN GAPPA FAMILY

MARY GAPPA HANSON

THE HANSON BROTHERS

CHRIS HANSON

DOUBLE WEDDING-DELMAR & MATILDA FANNING-RUSSELL & MAE HUGHES

MAE HANSON HUGHES

THE FAMILY FARM

GROWING UP ON THE FARM

I have many wonderful memories of growing up on a farm in southern Minnesota. Since there were no boys in our family, I helped my dad in the fields. I loved the wide open spaces, particularly driving the tractor on a sunny day, singing at the top of my lungs! I started driving our small tractor (a 1948 Ford) when I was still in grade school, and later advanced to the Allis Chalmers and Farmall. The Ford tractor was always my favorite though, and it was still going strong in 1978 (after thirty years of dedicated service) when it was sold at our farm auction. How sad I was to see it go.

Every summer, my family spent countless hours walking the bean rows--pulling cockleburs, corn, and weeds. This was a hot, dirty, seemingly endless job. At the end of the day our muscles really ached, but since it was a job that needed to be done, we all pitched in and helped.

It seemed there was always something adventurous to do on the farm--chasing pigs that got out; climbing up the silo (seeing how high you could go before "chickening" out); searching for newborn kittens in the dark crevices of the haymow--just to name a few.
(Bonnie Hughes Falk--Lake Crystal, MN--1950s-60s)

WATKINS MAN

My dad used a team of horses and wagon to go from farm to farm with his Watkins business. Everyone looked forward to his visits, and every farmer in the county knew and loved him. Since there were no radios or newspapers, he brought them the news. He also brought the children gum and candy, so that made them happy.

When dad was far from home, he would stay overnight at various places. For his meal and bed, he would help with the chores or whatever else needed to be done. When people couldn't pay their bills, he would trade for vegetables or meat, so he would bring big tubs of them home to be canned. Since we had no freezer, everything had to be preserved by canning. We canned chicken, meat balls, and all kinds of fruit. When company came, a meal could always readily be served.
(Beatrice Salberg--Berlin, ND--1920s-30s)

THE ARRIVAL OF ELECTRICITY

Living on the farm, I remember when electricity (REA) arrived in 1952. Actually, our farm was quite modern in that we had a home generator that ran off big glass-sided batteries. The wind charged them, or if there was no wind, a motor, so we had lights in every room and switches to turn them on. However, when the electricians wired the WHOLE house, this was REALLY modern!

We got a television set in about 1956; only one station, of course! Some programs were pretty good, but the local broadcasts were pretty bad. However, since we only had the one channel, we watched whatever was on. I remember that the local weatherman had a grease pen and one map on which to do the weather.
(Wayne Feller--Groton, SD--1950s)

THE "MAGIC MILK FACTORY"

When I was growing up on a farm, I was intrigued by our "magic milk factory." I noticed that a cow ate lots of green grass and drank lots of water out of a big water tank. From these, she produced lots of white milk which was squeezed out of her "four faucets."

I wonder how much children of today know or think about the milk they are urged to drink every day. They know it comes all nice and cold out of a carton in the refrigerator and it was purchased at the store, but there's a fascinating story behind that glass of milk. Fortunate are the children who know about it or have been on a farm to see where and how it begins!
(Selma Anderson Hughes--Watonwan Co., MN--1910s-20s)

THRESHING TIME

Threshing time was always exciting for us kids. We watched eagerly for the big lumbering steam engine to pull into the field, followed by the cook car--where the crew ate, and the bunk car--where they slept. There were usually two cooks who worked from before dawn until after dark, preparing three huge meals for the crew, as well as a mid-afternoon lunch consisting of thick meat sandwiches, cake, and gallons of hot coffee.

The high straw-stacks were used for bedding in the barn during the winter, and some farmers even fed it to their stock, but it was very poor feed. On the flat North Dakota plains, the straw-stacks filled an unusual role. In the winter when they were covered with snow, they were a substitute hill for sliding.
(Mae F. Hardin--ND--1920s)

DAD LET US BLOW THE WHISTLE

In the middle 1920s, my dad ran a steam engine threshing machine, with a crew of about twenty men who put the shocks into the thresher. Each hayrack had an extra man, called the "spike pitcher." The straw came out a blower and the grain

10

went into wagons. My mom and another lady cooked for the crew three times a day. The men slept in the farmer's haymow, and the women, plus myself, slept in the cook shack. The thrill of the day was when Dad let us blow the whistle. After about three years, a tornado came and demolished everything, so that was the end of our threshing services.
(Lucille Blair Johnson--Groton, SD--1920s)

GOOD APPETITES AND JOVIAL NEIGHBORLINESS

Threshing was something neighbors looked forward to. It was hard work, but the stories, kidding, jokes, and tricks that went on during the work made it fun. Everyone looked forward to lunch each morning, huge dinners of chicken, roast beef, pie, etc., at noon, lunch again in the afternoon, and a big supper at night. About twelve men would be seated around a big table--good appetites and jovial neighborliness! It seemed as though each lady tried to outdo the others. The men had to report each night on the kind of meat and pie that was served, so it would not be the same the next time. Then combines took over, and neighbors never worked together in quite the same way. These times were missed. If a neighbor is sick or in need today, there still is a "bee" of farmers helping out, but nothing can quite compare to the threshing bees of old.
(Mae Hanson Hughes Kjos--Lake Crystal, MN--1940s)

FARM AUCTION

OWNER HAS DISCONTINUED FARMING AND RETIRED TO LAKE CRYSTAL; THEREFORE THE FOLLOWING LIST OF TRACTORS, TRUCK, HARVESTING EQUIPMENT, FARM MACHINERY AND MISCELLANEOUS WILL BE SOLD AT PUBLIC AUCTION LOCATED 3½ MILES WEST OF LAKE CRYSTAL, MINNESOTA ON STATE HIWAY #60 AND TWO MILES SOUTH ON BLUE EARTH CO. RD. #32 OR SEVEN MILES EAST OF MADELIA ON STATE HIWAY #60 AND TWO MILES SOUTH ON BLUE EARTH CO. RD. #32 (WATCH FOR AUCTION ARROWS) ON

SATURDAY - OCTOBER 21 - 12:30 P. M.

DAN'S LUNCH ON GROUNDS

HARVESTING EQUIPMENT

1. John Deere 55 Combine w/13½' header, Love sickle, Hume reel, skour kleen, and chopper. A good running combine.

2. IHC 2 PR pull type two row corn picker.

3. Kewanee 44 ft. model 600 Daubee chain elevator w/P.T.O. drive.

4. Three 5 ton rubber tired wagons w/steel flare boxes and bolster hydraulic hoists.

TRACTORS

1. 1963 IHC 560 gas tractor w/wide adj. front axle and fast hitch (This unit is extra nice).

2. 1952 IHC Super "M" w/wide adj. front axle and two way hydraulic. (Another tractor in A-1 condition)

3. 1948 Ford 8N tractor in good condition w/good rubber and Dearborn standard loader, manure fork, snow bucket, and dirt plate.

TRUCK

1970 Ford 3/4 ton 250 w360 V8 engine, automatic transmission, radio, step bumper, and only 53,000 actual miles. This is an excellent well taken care of pickup.

FARM MISCELLANEOUS

300 gal. fuel tank and stand, clipper fanning mill, band duals for IHC 560 or M, 4 bottom plow trash rake, two sets 28" tractor chains, two heat covers for IHC, two hyd. cyls. w/hoses, A.C. single acting cylinder, tractor radio, A.C. tractor rear wheel weights, narrow front for IHC "M" and WD Allis tractors, DE Laval cream separator, category two new tractor top link, 11.22x5 tractor tire and rim, Best cattle oiler, hog oiler, portable air compressor, ½" electric drill, small anvil, bench vise, oils and greases, grease guns, oil and grease pumps, log chains, wedges, clevises, drawpins, hand and farm tools, oil measures, house movers jack, mechanical jack, 5 ton, Hydraulic jack, tarpaulin 8'x10', used lumber includes 2"x6"s and 2"x10"s, two 5 ft. step ladders, 24 ft. extension ladder, 16 ft. single ladder, wheel barrow, garden cultivator, approx. 40 treated fence posts, large asst. of steel fence posts, fence wire, snow fencing, crib ventilators, cultivator sweeps, electric motors, asst. of bolts and nuts, misc. hardware, asst. of scrap and welding iron, plus more.

...ipment, truck, and misc. has always had the best of care and ... Be sure and attend the auction for good clean tractors, etc.

HUGHES - Owner
LAKE CRYSTAL, MINN.
507-726-2517
4008
67-3159

Usual Auction terms
Not responsible for accidents
No property to be removed before settlement.

...al Bank of Lake Crystal, Minnesota

Lake Crystal
Minnesota
Sept. 13-19, '76

R.F.DRAN

FARMFEST '76

America's Bicentennial Salute to Agriculture

GRANDMAS AND GRANDPAS

GRANDMA'S ATTIC

My fondest childhood memories are of the summer vacations I spent at Grandma's house. How I anxiously looked forward to these "special" visits with Grandma in her big majestic house, with its stately roof-top gables. This huge, white, wooden structure on the crest of a hill in rural Iowa is still an outstanding landmark in northwestern Iowa.

My favorite room in Grandma's house was the attic. In this large, airy, enchanting tidy room, Grandma stored countless family treasures, heirlooms, and antiques. It was like visiting a historical museum! I was overwhelmed! I often found myself rummaging through the attic hour after hour on a hot summer day; frequently, I left the room in complete disarray.

The keepsakes that I found to be especially fascinating were my aunt's fashionable Charleston dresses, the high-buttoned shoes, and the colorful hats and purses. How I loved dressing up and parading around in these traditional costumes of the '20s. Special heirlooms stored in Grandma's attic included my dad's World War I Army uniform and the impressive German family Bible (dated 1884-85). Also, I remember the many boxes of books/textbooks that belonged to my aunts and uncles; the several player piano music rolls; the numerous family portraits/photo albums; and the valuable collection of family letters, cards, and other memorabilia.

The years have passed and Grandma's house is now gone. However, some of the nostalgic "keepsakes/heirlooms" from "Grandma's attic," which were so much a part of my heritage and childhood years, are now treasures in my own home.
(Darlene Lonneman Philiph--Little Rock, IA--1930s-40s)

GRANDMA'S KITCHEN

My grandma's comfortable, inviting home was a continuous "open house," with family and friends coming from near and far to visit. Therefore, she spent endless time in her kitchen. Grandma worked long, tireless hours over the hot, wooden cook stove, preparing homemade bread, pies, cakes, and fried chicken. Her meals were like banquets. I can still smell the pleasant aroma of all the homemade food. I especially remember Grandma's tasteful, delightful angel food cake, topped with fresh, juicy, homegrown strawberries. I often helped Grandma pick and stem these berries while I was visiting her during my summer vacation.

Everyone loved going to Grandma's house; they loved her generous hospitality and her delicious food. I have many wonderful memories of Grandma's country kitchen.
(Darlene Lonneman Philiph--Little Rock, IA--1930s)

The Midway Cafe, as the name implies,
stands at the center of town.
And daily its doors open wide to our world
and to anyone who happens around.

Flour-covered apron, over cotton-print dress,
the belt stretching far as it can.
The daily attire of the woman inside,
who runs this place like a man.

Wisps of white hair escape from her bun,
encircling her head like a crown.
The laughing eyes and the wrinkling face
are never known to frown.

Thick, heavy arms, dusted with white,
rhythmically roll to and fro.
Work-worn hands gently caress
the pin that flattens the dough.

Apple, cherry, and blueberry pie;
lemon and butterscotch, too.
Amber meringue, as high as the sky,
jeweled with golden dew.

Odors of baking wind through the door,
inviting all through the day;
To this heaven on earth that Grandma has made,
here at the Midway Cafe.
(Susan M. Grace--Groton, SD--1940s-50s)

GRANDMA'S SHOES

Grandma was a petite woman, not more than five feet one or two inches tall. She was most proud of her feet, a 4 1/2B or a 5A, the size called "sample shoes,"--the ones salesmen carried in their cases to show prospective buyers in the shops.

Grandmother walked in short, quick steps, with her feet al-ways encased in the latest sample shoes from her salesmen friends. I can remember Grandmother sitting in her big wicker armchair by the bay window, trying on various shoes, turning her foot this way and that, as she admired the latest possibili-ties. All the shoes laced across the instep; shoes without laces were called dancing slippers. Shoes would not stay on the foot for any serious walking unless they were firmly laced on.

The shoes were usually browns, greys, and blacks in various shades. Some were smooth leather with fancy cutouts or en-graved designs on them; I liked to run my fingers over the de-signs. Others--dress shoes--were suede leather, and they had to

14

be brushed with a fine copper bristle brush. They must never, never get wet, for that would stain the leather and ruin the looks. The heels were the stylish height for women, not high heels, and certainly not flats, but called "cuban heels." They lifted you up nicely so the back stayed straight and the stomach stayed tucked in.

I admired Grandmother's shoes for years and hoped that one day I, too, could wear such pretty things. However, by the time I had completed eighth grade, my feet were bigger than Grandmother's, so I knew I could not save money buying "sample shoes." When I was a senior in high school, my feet hurt me dreadfully, and I was sent to a shoe store for some good, sensible shoes that would support my feet and arches. The shoes were black, cuban-heeled, and laced tightly across the instep. They felt good, but they didn't look like a smart, up-to-date high school senior at all; they looked like Grandma's shoes and I hated them! They sat on the closet floor many years before I threw them away.
(Florence H. Carr--Faribault Co., MN--1930s)

THE DIFFERENCE BETWEEN MOTHERS AND GRANDMOTHERS

Grandmothers are most often distinguished from mothers by the generous padding on numerous parts of a grandmother's anatomy--the soft, cuddly spots and the super-soft lap for snuggling. Moms will work hard to avoid these cozy spots by jumping, jogging, playing ball, or doing those difficult exercises called aerobics. Grandmothers prefer gentle rocking and sipping tea; these "gentle" exercises can be accomplished while soothing a restless little one.

Mothers deserve a special day just for them, but setting aside a day for grandmothers was totally unnecessary. Any day is a grandmother's day when a little one plants a sticky lollipop kiss on a wrinkled cheek, or a tall teenager says, "Hi, Grandma!"
(Margaret Seeger Hedlund--Pope Co., MN--1960s)

LETTER FROM GRANDMA TO GRANDSON

Your grandpa, grandma, and you, Andy, are excited tonight, for we are getting ready to leave for the airport, where your mom, dad, and brother will be returning from their trip to Florida. Since you are only ten months old, they didn't think you would enjoy the trip, so Grandpa and I came to stay with you.

For eight days we have fed, bathed, and diapered you, played with you, and answered your every whim. We have been exhausted by night, and at times are at our wits end wondering just how to answer your needs and demands for the long day, and again keeping an open ear during the night. But, oh, the delight of such a happy smile and hearty laughter. You have been a charmer, and without speaking a word, have conveyed your messages and let your wants be known. We've called you a little "tiger" for the mischief you get into and the way you take tumbles without a whimper and go right back for more. You aren't one to be cuddled and rocked for very long; you must be "on the go." You cry very, very little, but do a lot of grunting and coaxing. You've been real strong and steady on your feet and take a step, but decide it's faster on all fours. You are very alert to everything and don't miss much.

It has been a fun week and we will miss our little "bundle of joy." We haven't laughed so much in a long time!
(Mae Hanson Hughes Kjos--written to Andy Falk--1975)

JOHN OTTO JOHNSON

At age seventeen, my grandfather was a fireman aboard a small whaling ship. At age eighteen, he used his savings to go to America. He sailed on the Thingvalla of the Scandinavian-American Line, leaving Oslo on November 9, 1893, at a cost of 183 Krone. The emigration records in Oslo listed him as Johan O. Johansen, an eighteen-year-old seaman from Horten, Norway.

When he got off the boat in New York City, he had to go through immigration. As he walked through the building, one of the barbers called for him to come over and told him that he was required to get a haircut. That cost him twenty-five cents. A little farther along, a different man tried to require another haircut! By now he was smarter and said, "No."

Grandfather traveled on a train, with only a loaf of bread, his accordion, and a couple of dollars. His ticket got him only as far as Chicago. After walking around the railroad yards, a Scandinavian trainman said he could ride to St. Paul with him in a caboose on a freight train. So he came to White Bear Lake and worked at Amundson's Boat Works for a couple years. He also worked for Peterson, another boat builder, whose daughter Mary became his first wife on November 10, 1896. His job at Amundson's Boat Works paid seventy-five cents a day. Times were hard and his pay was later reduced to fifty cents a day, so he decided to quit and find other work. When he got married at age twenty-one, he had twelve dollars. The license cost two dollars and he gave the minister a dollar. After buying dishes and a few housewares, there was only forty-five cents left.

While working at Amundson's, he got some ideas for a new design for a sailboat. At first nobody would listen to him. Then he found a sailor who agreed to fund the building of the boat. In 1896, in a shed, he built his first sailboat for two hundred dollars. The boat won its first race easily, and he started his own business. In the winter of 1899-1900, he built the first "Inland Lake Sailing Scow," a thirty-eight foot, Class A, sailboat named the "Minnezitka." This design became the standard for

16

the fast scow type sailboats of today. A model of the "Minne-zitka" is in the Smithsonian Institute.

My grandfather also invented the first rotary snowplow in 1924. He wanted the roads usable in the winter so that he could use his car year round. The snowplow became a very successful venture.
(John W. Johnson--White Bear Lake, MN)

N. R. ALLEN, SR.

I remember my grandfather as a great figure of a man--readily touched by others and tenderhearted with children. Several of his favorite pleasures were daily walks through town, his newspapers, reading in his comfortable green leather chair, or a good cigar. He equally enjoyed both visiting with the "boys" over a game of cards at the local mens' clubs, and the quiet luxury of home life.

Although Grandpa proudly renewed his driver's license when necessary, he never owned a car, or even entertained the idea of purchasing one that I can recall. All of his traveling was accomplished by train, bus, or riding with others.

Grandpa was an expert when it came to the bakery business. He managed many federal bakeries in different locations before settling down in Charles City, Iowa, with his own "Spic & Span Bakery." A deadly tornado swept through town in 1968, destroying the bakery. At the time, Grandfather was eighty years of age, and was acknowledged as the oldest businessman on Main Street. He was admired and respected by all who knew him.
(Jill Allen Cunion--Charles City, IA)

N. R. ALLEN, SR.
N. R. ALLEN, JR.

MY GRANDPA

My grandpa was born in 1914. His name was Russell Hughes. He was a farmer, and indeed a good one. He lived on a farm outside of Lake Crystal, Minnesota, and farmed 240 acres.

He grew up and was raised outside of Cambria, Minnesota. He went to a country school. I think they only had one classroom. That means all grades in one room. They probably had a wood stove in the middle. It was pretty hot sometimes. They needed it though in the winter especially. He went to that school for eight years; then he quit. He had good grades, but good grades aren't everything. He had a lot of friends--I mean a lot! My grandpa was smart. He was also a good, obedient child.

Grandpa didn't get into fights. He was peaceful and kind. He wasn't poor, but he wasn't rich either. He was normal like most of us. He didn't go on big trips, but mostly stayed at home. My grandpa lived sixty-four years, and then he died of a heart attack.
(Ben Selzer--Spencer, IA--written at age 10)

FAMILY LIFE

MUNSON AND ANDERSON FAMILIES, ca. 1914

FAMILY TIME

THE BEST PICTURE SHOW

It was the warmth of his arms and the love in his voice that the little girls would always remember. Every Sunday as my father was enjoying the Sunday paper, my cousin and I would attack him in the large leather armchair and beg him to read the funnies to us. Patient as always, he would lay aside the front page and invite us to sit on his lap. My cousin, with her short, curly, red hair and rosy cheeks, would snuggle in the crook of his right arm, and I, blond like Shirley Temple, would snuggle in the crook of his left arm. As soon as we were comfortable, my father would open the brightly-colored comic section, holding it so we could both see the pictures and follow along. Encircled thus, we entered the magic kingdom of make-believe.

The best picture show around captured our complete attention. My father's voice was very expressive and the occasional sound effects were the perfect accent. We would roar with childish laughter at the crazy shenanigans of the Katzen-jammer Kids. Maggie and Jiggs could always be counted on for a domestic squabble--usually ending with Maggie clobbering Jiggs over the head with a rolling pin! Then we would move on to the adventures of Alley Oop and his cavemen friends. The Bumsteads--Blondie, Dagwood, their children, and dog named Daisy--reflected the ups and downs of life in the late thirties and early forties. Dagwood was always being caught napping on the sofa when he was supposed to be washing the windows or minding the kids! Of all the comics we loved to hear, our favorite was Nancy. We were loyal fans of Nancy, Sluggo and Aunt Fritzie Ritz; like dessert, we always asked to save that favorite for last.

Great literature they were not! However, we learned a little about life and a lot about the importance of reading to our children. In reflection, what a great cover for *Saturday Evening Post* we would have made, if only Norman Rockwell could have observed us.
(Clare Hibbard--MN--1930s-40s)

"YES! WE HAVE NO BANANAS"

"Yes! We Have No Bananas" was the first song I ever heard on the radio. In the 1920s, we were living on a farm in southern Wisconsin, when a traveling man came to conduct some business. On the back seat of his Model T Ford touring car, was a large radio set with several tuning dials and soft rubber earphones. We were invited to listen to his radio. It was then that I heard that song for the first time, and I've never forgotten it.
(Ole Schelsnes--WI--1920s)

Before TV "soaps," there were radio serials--"Portia Faces Life," "Young Dr. Malone," "Jack Armstrong, the All-American Boy," to name a few--and the sickeningly sweet "Ma Perkins." Whole families gathered around the radio every weeknight to listen avidly to the fantastic adventures of "Little Orphan Annie." Later, we enjoyed the shivers as we listened to the creaking door of "Inner Sanctum," "The Shadow Knows," or "The Green Hornet." "Grand Central Station" and "Lincoln Highway" were favorite programs, and "Jack Benny," "Fibber McGee and Molly," and "George Burns and Gracie Allen" were popular comedies. The Saturday night "Hit Parade" had many faithful listeners.
(Mae F. Hardin--ND--1920s-50s)

ARTHUR GODFREY

We didn't have TV right away. Our neighbors had one, so they used to invite us over to watch the "Arthur Godfrey Show." Of course, he made the Hawaii tourist trade what it is today! It was all so very beautiful--dreamlike--and everyone wanted to see it. My trip there in 1972 was a real thrill, but I think I expected too much of the area. Today, it is so commercialized!
(Mary E. Strong--St. Paul, MN--1952)

DRIVE-IN MOVIES

When our children were small, one of our favorite outings was to the drive-in movie. We bathed the children, put them in their sleepers, and loaded the car with pillows, blankets, a big bag of popcorn, and a jug of water. What a simple way to see a good movie! If the children fell asleep, they could be tucked into bed when we got home. Television was the death of the drive-in movie.
(Mary Simonson Thompson--Aberdeen, SD--1940s-50s)

SATURDAY NIGHT BATH

Most West St. Paul families followed the time-honored system of the Saturday night bath. A round galvanized washtub was placed on the floor in the middle of the kitchen, and water was heated in teakettles and pails on wood-burning or kerosene-burning stoves. First, the water had to be pumped by hand from the outside well. In the winter this part of the job was a sizable chore in itself.

Families with just two or three kids usually worked out the bath situation without any particular problems. However, in

larger families, it became more complex. It just was not practical, especially in the wintertime, to heat enough water to bathe each child separately. It was, therefore, a common practice to bathe two or three kids all in the same water. Mothers usually started bathing the littlest kids first, reasoning that the smaller skin area would tend to contaminate the water the least. By opposite reasoning, the smallest kids were usually the dirtiest!
(Allan Degnan--West St. Paul, MN--1920s)

BROTHER AND SISTER

Two faded notes tucked away by Mother read as follows:
Dear Mother (or Dad),
I hope you will notice Tommy's socks on your bedroom floor. You will find holes in the bottoms. They are from his cowboy boots. If I were you, I'd burn the boots the minute I had a chance. Love, Alice
P.S. Tom moved his socks after reading this note. The socks were only five days old. You will find the socks sometime.

Dear Mother and Dad,
Alice is a big tattletale. Don't read the note she gives you in the morning because it is a lie. Tommy
P.S. Don't burn my cowboy boots until I get a new pair.
(Alice and Tom Hughes--Alden, MN--1950 (Ages 10 and 7)

ALICE AND TOM HUGHES

LOST CHILD?

When our sixth child, a daughter, was about four or five years old, we forgot her at church! We didn't miss her until the pastor called to tell us. We had eight children at that time, and I guess we forgot to count! After that incident, whenever we got in the car, we took a head count.
(Ada Ronnei Pederson--Pope Co., MN--1946)

I WAS SO PROUD, I NEARLY BURST

May I tell you of one of the happiest memories I have of my mother, who was a very able actress and speaker. I have no idea how the people in our town knew about her talents, but, sometime in the middle of the long and dreary winter, she was asked to give a humorous reading at the monthly community program.
When the big night arrived, both of my little brothers were sick with colds. Because hired baby sitters were unheard of in those days, it was my father's responsibility to stay home with them. I got to go, however, and when we arrived at the school auditorium, I went down close to the front so I wouldn't miss a thing.

I was so totally absorbed in this great thing that was about to happen, that I have no idea what took place before they announced my mother's name. Then, suddenly it was very dark. The curtains slowly opened, and there was my beautiful mother in her black velveteen dress with the little lace collar, and around her waist was a shiny, silver, link belt. The stage lights shone down on her from above and the footlights from below, and she began to speak and move about the stage, gesturing and smiling. The people laughed and laughed. When she had finished, she bowed and walked off into the wings. The people kept on clapping; finally, she came back on stage to smile and wave her hand. I was so proud I nearly burst into a million pieces!

On the way home, we held each other's hands and swung along together, just savoring the triumph of her moment. It was the one and only time I ever saw her play a part on stage, because the following year she died of a virulent flu. But that one happy night will never be forgotten. A tangible reminder in one of my dresser drawers is a shiny silver belt--the one she wore on that night so long ago.
(Dawn Blair Gullikson--SD--1930s)

TREATS FROM DAD

Because my sisters, brothers, and I grew up in the Depression, there was never much money for us, but we always had good meals and a secure, loving home. When we went to town on a weeknight to take our cream can to the railroad depot, my dad would always get all eight of us children ice cream cones. Or, if he had to go to town for parts for his machinery, he would always bring home a bag of candy as a treat. On Saturday night, we would each get a dime, or maybe a bit more, if we were going to the movie.

My dad had a game he would play with us sometimes. He would take the loose change from his pocket and say, "I have eight pieces of money. Who can guess how much it is?" If we happened to guess the exact amount, we got the money! The number of coins varied, of course. I can remember one time when I guessed correctly and received over a dollar's worth of coins. I felt very rich!
(Mary Simonson Thompson--Groton, SD--1930s)

WARM, WONDERFUL MEMORIES

I cannot think of growing up without remembering the wonderful aromas coming from the kitchen--the cinnamon rolls my mother made just about every Saturday, the great homemade chicken noodle soup, and all the other good homemade food that we miss today. My two sisters and I also benefited from our mother's seamstress skills; she always had the sewing

NORMA HUGHES SCHLICHTER

machine set up, with some dress in progress for one or more of us.

Those memories still give me a warm, secure feeling as I rush around in this busy world.

(Norma Hughes Schlichter--Lake Crystal, MN--1950s)

THE BALLROOM

My grandfather had twelve children. In order to hold wedding dances for them, he had a ballroom built onto his farmhouse. This very large room was also used for other activities during the year. Any large family gathering or party was held in this room. I can remember Uncle Frank playing the accordion and Aunt Annie strumming on a guitar, although she never did know how to play one! I also remember Uncle George standing on his head in the middle of this room.

In the fall, the family would gather in this room to husk corn. Those gathering corn from the field would throw the ears of corn in the window; the family would then husk the corn and throw the cobs back out the window to be taken to the corncrib. In the winter, the room was used to store butchered pigs. Because the room was not heated, it was cold enough to keep the pigs frozen.

My parents, Louis and Lucie, had their wedding dance in this room. They also lived in the farmhouse for awhile after their marriage; in fact, this is where my older sister and I were born. When the farm was sold, Grandpa had the ballroom detached from the house and moved into town. This building was divided into apartments and is still standing today in Cumberland, Wisconsin.

(James Zappa, Sr.--Cumberland, WI--1920s-60s)

QUARANTINE

Just about forgotten now are the "Quarantine" signs which appeared every winter, announcing the presence on the premises of one of the communicable illnesses--measles, mumps, chicken pox, smallpox, scarlet fever, and diphtheria were the common ones. When a doctor (they made house calls in those days) found evidence of one of these illnesses, he was required to report it to the county health officer, who would then send someone to tack the proper sign on the front of the house. This meant that those in the house were to remain there for the duration of the quarantine period, and no outsiders were to enter. The only exception was the bread-winner of the family, who was permitted to go back and forth to his job. The quarantine period usually lasted about ten days.

(Allan Degnan--West St. Paul, MN--1920s)

Every August for the past sixty-eight years, there has been a Kjos-Reishus Reunion. I have no idea how it got started; however, I am sure of the year it started because there was a large picture taken of everyone attending. My father is holding me in the picture, and I was born in February of that year.

In the early years, it was a very big deal, with about 150 people attending. Family members would come from all over--North Dakota, Iowa, Wisconsin, and many places in Minnesota. In the later years, some have come from as far away as California.

The Kjos and Reishus families were early settlers in the town of Rushford, Minnesota, in about 1860. They were both big families and many marriages took place between the two families--Kjos brothers and sisters marrying Reishus brothers and sisters, etc. Of course, some married into other families, also, and both families grew.

In the early years, the reunion was held at farm homes or in a big park in Lanesboro. In later years, we have met at a park in Rochester and along the lake in Winona. The last several years have been at a community hall in Rushford. Like everyone else, we do not like the heat so now we go to an air conditioned place to meet.

The numbers are decreasing, with forty or forty-five attending last year, and not many young people come anymore. I guess it is like everything else; the young people have so many other things to do. But I hope we can keep it going for a few more years yet. There are some people that I wait all year to see.
(Al Kjos--Rushford, MN--1922 to present)

KJOS-REISHUS REUNION, 1935

DAILY CHORES

NO RESPITE FROM DAILY CHORES

I learned early that the dairy farm doesn't provide for respite from daily chores, even though the calendar shows Christmas holiday time. During the first several days of school vacation, I remember working ahead fervently--cutting with a hay knife and loosening enough hay and straw for a week's use (that was before bales); digging out extra silage that was often frozen to the silo walls; carrying wood from the shed to the woodbox until it overflowed; and doing whatever I could to make more prime family time possible, especially between Christmas and New Years.

Even though we couldn't work ahead feeding, bedding, and milking the cows (by hand), cleaning the barn, or gathering eggs, more time was still salvaged for playing games, such as checkers, cards, and mill, one of my father's favorite games. There was also more time to read (by lamplight), sometimes sitting on the bear rug next to the wood stove. I'd urge my father to tell once again how my grandfather and he wounded a bear that had attacked my grandfather. That bear rug hangs on my rec room wall, often leading me to retell that same story.
(Ruben F. Schmidt--Shawano Co., WI--1920s-30s)

"PUMP" JOBS

There was a time when turning a little handle which caused water to appear was really a miracle--and a luxury bestowed on a chosen few. Our water came from a deep, dark well and a black iron pump, usually located closer to the barn than to the house.

There were many trips to the pump every day to get water for drinking, washing dishes, cooking, and casual washing. Then, there were the special times when we would get bath water, usually pumped in the morning so that it would warm slightly by evening. It was made more tolerable by adding just enough hot water from the teakettle.

The big "pump job" came on Sunday evening when we had to pump water for the Monday laundry. Every available container had to be filled--two or three washtubs, a copper boiler, and several pails. Clothes had to be washed on a scrub board, rinsed, and put through a hand wringer; many of them had to be boiled. Hanging them on the outdoor clothesline had to be done according to a certain system--the newest and whitest articles had to be hung closest to the road; the older, darker, shabbier things were hung where they could dry without being seen by a possible passerby!
(Ida Posteher Fabyanske--Ramsey Co., MN--1920s)

How I hated Mondays! My job was to wash the long black stockings on the scrub board, or wash board, as it was also called. It was a board with corrugated lines which was placed in a tub, and then held up by the stomach. Away you scrubbed! Blistered knuckles were common. I think I must have washed a million black stockings in my early days, as even the boys wore them!

In the summer, the washtubs were set up out in the yard. We also had a hand-wringer attached to the rinse tub.

Go back to the olden days? No way! I'll take my automatic any day.
(Mary E. Strong--LeCenter, MN--1915-23)

TUESDAY WAS IRONING DAY

Tuesday was ironing day. During the colder seasons, the flatirons could heat on the kitchen wood stove all day, if necessary. Not so during the hot summer months! The ironing had to be done while the stove was heating for some other purpose, such as baking, cooking, or heating water for bathing, dishwashing, etc. It was important to do as many things at one time as possible, so that the fire could burn out and the temperature in the kitchen could become more tolerable.
(Ida Posteher Fabyanske--Ramsey Co., MN--1920s)

THOSE "GHOSTLY" LOOKING THINGS

For many years, my mother had to do laundry for eight people. She would pump the water the night before she planned to wash. Some wells had a lot of iron in the water, so in the morning she would skim off the iron, and then put the water on the old wood stove to heat. She would do the wash on a wash board, using a bar of homemade soap or Fels Naptha. Both were very hard on the hands.

In the wintertime, she would hang the clothes outside on the clotheslines until they froze. After they froze, she would bring those "ghostly" looking things into the house to thaw. The mens' full suits of underwear were the funniest looking things! In the summer, it was very pleasant to be outside hanging clothes and enjoying the day.
(Gail Bishop--Cloverton, MN--1940s)

LIFE WAS HARD IN THE "GOOD OLD DAYS"

The "good old days" weren't all that good sometimes! It was a hard life. We didn't have running water when I was in grade school. Every drop was pumped from a trusty pump across the yard, next to the horse pasture. It was very good spring water. We carried it in by the buckets (carrying one in each hand was a good balance), and out again in the slop pail. Is it any wonder that we developed such good arm muscles?! In the summer, Mom had her kitchen down in the coal basement, so we carried the water up and down the stairs.

We would also have to bring in dry chopped wood to get both stoves going early in the morning, plus a pile of briquet coal and lignite. Dad hauled the coal from town with a team and wagon--a six-mile trip. He loaded it by hand from a box car, and unloaded it through a window in the basement. You had to carry these buckets up the stairs, too, and then carry the ashes out. Next, we had to carry the milk in, separate it in the basement, carry the milk out, and then feed the calves and pigs. We didn't have electricity, a refrigerator, or indoor bathroom facilities either, and, of course, those pots had to be emptied! Up and down the stairway! Up and down the stairway!

In the summer, Dad built a cooler in our playhouse. A pulley lifted a bucket from a well that kept everything cool and fresh. We milked cows, fed pigs, butchered pigs, gathered eggs, and sold milk, cream, and eggs to the "town folks," delivering them in pint jars on Friday or Saturday.

Mom washed our clothes on a scrub board, with a hand-turned wringer. Each piece was rinsed by hand in two tubs, the second one containing blueing to help whiten the clothes. We put clothes on wooden racks and set them out to freeze in the wintertime. At night we hung them to dry by stringing lines across the kitchen, in the basement, or upstairs. In the summer, everything went on the clotheslines outside until we ran out of room; then socks and overalls went over the fence!

Life was what it was. We didn't know anything different, and we were happy. We know now that our parents worked too hard.

(Edith Tannahill Lerfald--Thompson, ND--1920s-30s)

PORCHES, CELLARS, AND OUTHOUSES

WATCHING THE WORLD GO BY

Our house was on the corner of a busy intersection. We had a great big glassed-in front porch where we would sit in the evening and watch all the traffic. People would come and go, and we would wave at everyone. It was a big social thing to sit on the porch and greet people. There were four rocking chairs on our porch, and Grandpa would sit out there for hours after he retired. Grandma would make crocheted rugs on the porch, and I would sit and sew the rags together for her. We would also play games--"Gin Rummy," "Pinochle," etc., and have coffee out there. Everything we did in the summer seemed to take place on the porch.
(Mary B. Twar--Two Harbors, MN--1930s-40s)

THE FRONT STOOP

We lived in a three-story brownstone house in Bay Ridge, Brooklyn, New York. The front stoop was quite steep, with about twenty-five brown stairs leading to a formal wooden door. There was an "airy way" in front of the house and a cellar entrance, like in your old storm cellars, with a black metal fence surrounding the airy way. The living area was on the first floor. Our back yard was cemented in after countless tons of mud had been tramped all over the house. As small children, our life outside of school was in this back yard. There was no shade, other than an old green doghouse, which was our club-house. As we grew older we were allowed out in front, and that is where the stoop comes in to play, especially in my early teen years.

In the late spring and summer, late afternoons and evenings were when a person used the stoop as the front porch. You would sit on the steps and watch the endless stickball games in the street and get to know the boys in the neighborhood. A type of courting often went on. The boys would strut their stuff while playing ball, doing all sorts of weird "boy" things to get a girl's attention.

The stoop was also the gossip place for neighbors and friends passing by and stopping to chat, just like the front porch. People's outfits, new babies, sickness, etc., were discussed and discussed. We used to do "horse ranges" in the summer, and the great accomplishment was how fast your "rope" could do the entire length of the stoop. When there were weddings or proms, the neighbors would always manage to be out on their stoops to watch the proceedings.

28

One of my uncles was a priest. He spent most of his childhood in Brooklyn on 49th Street. Uncle Gene was quite an Irishman, and a great gossip regarding family matters. He loved to spend nice evenings on the stoop, commenting and lamenting about world and family situations.

After my father's death in 1964, we moved to North Tarrytown to a rather uppity area known as Philispe Manor. Our house was quite large, with a good expanse of front lawn. There were four front steps and railings on each side--a stoop! Now, when Uncle Gene would come for a visit, he always quickly removed his collar, put on a bright sport shirt, grabbed a beer, and to the chagrin of the neighbors, parked his buns on the stoop and "played Brooklyn." Keep in mind that Philispe Manor was a rather "rich" area (how we got there is beyond me), so Uncle Gene's "playing Brooklyn" was a bit risque, but how he loved it!

Three girls had wedding and prom pictures on that stoop in "The Manor." Endless first kisses, arguments, and tears took place there. Retrospectively, those steps played a large part in the Paré story and I was sad to leave them.
(Mary Paré Falk--Brooklyn/N. Tarrytown, NY--1950s-60s)

COURAGE

It was a balmy summer evening. Supper had been eaten, the dishes washed, and there was still time to sit on the front porch before bedtime. One of my older sisters and my mother sat on chairs; I sat on the steps.

Most homes had open porches where families often gathered after the day's work was done--to visit, watch cars go by, or observe people out for an evening stroll. The streets were not well-lighted, as the incandescent lights were dim and rather far apart. They usually hung on a wire in the center of the street intersection or were mounted high on a corner post. The lighted circumference was small. Not every corner had a light, and our house in the middle of the block did not benefit greatly.

We had been sitting on the porch only a short time, when Effie noticed something near the pole under the street light. It appeared to be a large object, with a small boy crouching nearby. We became curious, so my sister and I walked over for a closer look. The little boy standing there was a bit hesitant to talk, but he finally told us why he was there.

He had gone with his mother to the Wisconsin River to gather clams. At that time, clamming was a means of earning a little extra money. They had worked several hours and had filled two large gunny sacks. Since night was approaching, they dragged the two heavy sacks from the river bank to this corner (the first one with a street light), a distance of about six blocks. The mother, realizing that she could not drag the two heavy sacks any farther, told the boy to stay there with one sack until she returned. After inquiring where the boy lived, we realized that the mother had close to a mile to drag her heavy sack, then walk back to drag the other.

My sister suggested that he come sit on the porch with us until his mother returned. Having been told to watch the bag, he was reluctant to leave his lonely post. However, after assuring him that we could all see it from the porch, he came with us. He said very little, constantly watching as the night grew darker. Some time later, the happy little boy saw his mother come into the dim glow of the street light. Then we watched as the weary mother, dragging her second heavy bag, with the small boy walking beside her, disappeared into the darkness.
(Ella M. Morse--Stevens Point, WI--1920)

THE GREATEST BACK PORCH

Grandpa and Grandma Hughes had the greatest back porch! It was big and all screened in. It faced the east, and in the summer it was so much fun to have breakfast out there as the sun came shining through the trees. Other meals were eaten out there, too. Much family living took place on that porch. There was a cot at one end to be used for a nap or a good night's sleep on a hot summer night. The washing machine also had its spot on the porch, as did the ice box. The table served as the work space for food preparation. Whatever the job, doing it out on the porch made it much more pleasant. If it could be done on the porch, it was!
(Selma Anderson Hughes--Blue Earth Co., MN--1930s)

THE TRAP DOOR

We lived in an old log house that had a cellar. There was a trap door under the dining room table, which had a ladder leading down to the cellar. There was a knothole in the door, and I remember my sister getting the leg of her chair caught in it; her chair tilted back and her feet came up over the top of the table! We all had a good laugh, but my father didn't think it was funny. He hollered at us to eat our meal!
(Gail Bishop--Cloverton, MN--1940s)

IT WAS DARK, CLAMMY, AND SCARY

I remember the cellar we had in our house when we came to St. Paul in 1923. The trap door was on one side of the kitchen floor and it opened up by a big round ring. In one corner of the cellar was a coal bin, filled with coal. The truck would back up to the cellar window and send the coal down through a chute. This process was very messy--lots of coal dust, and it had a bad smell. Very spooky!

One section of the cellar was used to pile the wood that had been chopped for the kitchen stove. In another section there was shelf space for canned goods, a potato bin, and a big barrel for apples. The eggs, squash, etc., were also kept down there. My dad had a box of sand to store carrots in for the winter.

My job was to bring up eggs, vegetables, and canned goods each day. My brothers had to haul up coal for the heating stove and wood for the kitchen wood box.

I hated that cellar! It was so dark, clammy, and scary. I never saw a mouse, but I'm sure they were there. When I got older-- about fifteen--I REFUSED to go down there. This was definitely NOT your ideal family room type basement!
(Mary E. Strong--St. Paul, MN--1923-33)

NOW WE FELT SAFE

When I was five years old, we lived in a very small house on a farm in southern Minnesota. One summer day, the sky became very dark and we feared a bad storm. Pa was in the field at the time.

My mother took her four little children outside. She lifted the big cellar door, took us down the steps, and pulled the big door closed. I can't remember what kind of light we had down there as we huddled together in fear, but I do remember the heavy noise on the cellar door just before it lifted and Pa came down to join us. Now we felt much safer.
(Selma Anderson Hughes--Watonwan Co., MN--1917)

MY NEW POCKET WATCH

When I was in the second grade, for my birthday I got a new pocket watch. Now I was really proud of that watch! I don't think many of the other kids had one. In those days, all the boys wore bib overalls to school and there was a special pocket in the bib part for your watch. Of course, in those days all the plumbing was outside.

One day when I went to the outhouse and took down my overalls, my watch fell out and went down the hole through a crack in the floor. I'm sure I started crying. I don't remember if I went back to school or to Grandpa's place, which adjoined the school grounds, but I do remember Dad and I going back to look for the watch. It was never found, and I think that was probably the saddest day of my early years.
(Clair Meredith--Cambria, MN--1934)

CLAIR MEREDITH

JOSEPH'S MITTENS

Joseph had a brand new pair of mittens, hand knitted by his grandmother. This proud little first grader showed everyone

his mittens right away when he got to school that morning. When school was called, I noticed Joseph wasn't in his place. Since he was in the habit of "curling up" with a book in some out-of-the-way corner, I assumed he would appear from somewhere as soon as I finished taking roll. However, when roll call was finished, still no Joseph. So, the next thing was to search the outhouses. Two of the boys found him there trying to retrieve one of his precious mittens that had caught on a nail when it had dropped in one of the holes!
(Amy Frederickson Meyer--Brown Co., MN--1932)

THE "WATER CLOSET"

The outhouse was also sometimes referred to as the "Water Closet." We lived in a small town in southern Minnesota, and we had no indoor bathroom. Believe me, we only made "necessary" trips to the outhouse behind our house, especially in the wintertime. We had a fancy porcelain bowl type of thing called the "bed chamber," or slop jar, for nighttime emergencies. Fun!! Toilet tissue was the Sears and Roebuck catalog. No wonder we ended up with hemorrhoids!! We moved to St. Paul when I was twelve years old and had the luxury of a bathroom and indoor facilities. I thought I was quite rich then!
(Mary E. Strong--LeCenter, MN--1911-23)

OUTHOUSE ON STILTS

Living on a farm in my early years, we always had a pump and an outhouse. One farm we lived on had previously belonged to a Finnish family. The outhouse was near the barn and built up on stilts. There must have been four to five steps before you could get into it. During the cold, snowy winters, the snow came in the cracks, so you had to brush the snow off the seat before you could sit down. The wind just whistled around below you. It was a very chilling experience!
(Gail Bishop--Cloverton, MN--1940s)

PEACH PAPERS

I remember being happy when peach-canning season arrived each year because then we would have nice, soft, pliable "peach papers" in the outdoor toilet, instead of the stiffer, glossy pages from the Sears Roebuck catalog!
(Lois Eugster--Oregon, WI--1940s)

FAMILY TRIPS

TRAVELOGUE

Early one summer morning, my family took off in our 1958 Chevy to see the sights out West (destination--sunny California). I was fourteen, my younger sister was eight, and my older sister had just graduated from high school. This was to be our family's one and only BIG trip.

I kept a travelogue of our two-week trip, detailing: names of states; places we visited; movie stars' homes; places we stayed (including a rating of each); and a summary of the most interesting sites. I've continued to keep a detailed log of each trip I've taken through the years. Sometimes I was so busy recording every detail that I hardly had time to enjoy the trip!

When our kids were small, we did a lot of camping--tent and fold-up camper--which proved to be an economical and interesting way to see the sights. Our first big trip was to Colorado and Wyoming in 1980. I remember my nine-year-old commenting as we approached home, "For once the sign says population instead of elevation!"

In 1983 we took a three-week trip out East, experiencing everything from:
--listening to the roar of Niagara Falls....to the peaceful quiet of Whitcomb's Summit.
--the simplicity of the red fisherman's shack....to the grandeur of the Vanderbilt Mansion.
--shopping in a little antique shop....to viewing works of art at the Metropolitan Museum of Art.
--taking a leisurely horse and buggy ride through Williamsburg....to driving the chaotic streets of Manhattan.

As everyone who travels knows, things don't always go as planned. We've had our share of: swatting mosquitoes all night; cleaning up spilled drinks in the car; endless questions, such as "When are we going to get there?"; and my personal favorite--getting lost! My husband always likes to take the roundabout way to our destination!
(Bonnie Hughes Falk)

THE FALK GANG

CAMPING BY THE RIVER

My husband, two boys, and I were all weary and anxious to get home as we rolled along the freeway past Chicago, on the final leg of our three-week camping trip out East. It was getting very late, and my husband suggested we stay at a motel.

What? A motel? And blow our budget? No way! Since my husband was too tired to argue, we found the nearest campground and pitched our tent (near a river) one last time.

How was I to know there would be torrential rains during the night that would threaten to wash us down this "tranquil" river?! How was I to know our tent would leak?! How was I to know the entire campground would be a quagmire of mud the next morning?! Needless to say, my husband wasn't too pleased with my attempt to "save a few bucks"!
(Bonnie Hughes Falk--IL--1983)

CAMPING UNDER THE STARS

When I was a child, the youngest of three girls in our family, it was not at all uncommon for Dad to come home at noon on a Saturday and say, "Let's pack up and go camping." There would be much scrambling and flurry as we gathered together the necessary equipment for spending the night out under the stars or in our small canvas tent. No fancy motor home, fifth-wheel, or trailer--just a beat up old tent, a camp stove, folding cots (no sleeping bags)--and just a pan and pail to put out on the picnic table for washing up, washing dishes, etc.

How wonderful it was to drive forty or fifty miles to a nearby park or wooded area and pitch camp. We girls would lie out on a blanket under the stars and pick out the "Milky Way," the "Big Dipper," and make up our own constellations, before we fell asleep to the chirping of the crickets and the hoot of an owl now and then. The good smell of bacon frying and coffee cooking woke us up in the morning, and often it was a matter of scurrying behind the nearest big tree to the "bathroom." It probably didn't cost us a dollar for the gas, and there was no charge for the campsite, but did we have fun!

Now with a nice trailer, bathroom, air conditioning, running water, and all the rest, I still love to listen to the night sounds as we settle down in an isolated campground for a good campout. There is just something about the smell of a campfire and the lapping of the water, if we're lucky enough to get a site near a lake or river, that gives me that feeling of--"God's in His heaven and all is right with the world."
(Marian Quam Stoneback--Alden, MN--1920s)

GOING TO GRANDMA'S

One set of grandparents lived near us so we saw them often at family gatherings; however, our other grandparents lived about 375 miles away, in Wisconsin, so we saw them only once a year. There were eight children in our family, so it was a big job preparing for this trip. Plus, we had a Ford Model T car, with no trunk and very little space to hold all ten of us. We did have some sort of luggage rack that my dad fastened on the running board on the driver's side, but that meant everyone had to get in and out on the passenger side. Since we didn't

have many clothes in those days, it didn't take many bags and boxes to hold our belongings.

Because of the early hour and the excitement of the trip, at least one or two of us would get car sick in the Bristol Hills. It was a very long trip and took many hours with our old car and the poor roads. We would eat a picnic lunch along the way. When my older brother Jack was small, he would be so excited about seeing the "Cities" (Minneapolis and St. Paul), that he would stand up all the way. However, by the time we got there, he had usually fallen asleep, so he missed them anyway!

Grandma was a very kind, sweet, little Norwegian lady who welcomed all of us with open arms and a full pantry. She always had lots of sugar cookies and lefse waiting for us. Her strawberry patch produced enough berries for us to have our fill--morning, noon, and night. Grandpa and Grandma had a big woods behind their barn, and because we lived on the South Dakota prairie, the woods was a delightful place for us to play and explore. In fact, as soon as we had given Grandma a hug, we were off to pick wildflowers and listen to the birds.

Our trips to Wisconsin had to be timed just right for my dad to get away from the farm for a week. When the corn had been planted and school was out, we could get away before it was time for sheep shearing and corn cultivating. But, Dad DID take the time to go visit Grandma and Grandpa, and those trips have given us precious memories that will live in our hearts forever.
(Mary Simonson Thompson--Groton, SD--1920s-30s)

GOING FOR A SUNDAY DRIVE

People didn't "go" as much in the 1950s as they do today. Sunday was always family/visiting day. During the nice summer Sundays, Mom would get us five kids cleaned up and we would go on a Sunday ride for the whole afternoon. We would stop at a drive-in--the kids would get hamburgers and the folks would get chicken-in-a-basket. We did so many fewer things than nowadays, so what we DID do really meant a lot to us.
(DeeDee Purcell Valento--White Bear Lake, MN--1950s)

SPECIAL TIMES OF TOGETHERNESS

My father was the assessor for Lansing Township in Mower County, Minnesota, for well over forty years. Some of my fondest childhood memories are of the times my mother would pack a sumptuous picnic, and she, my two sisters, and I would join Dad as he drove from farm to farm assessing the property, real estate, household goods, and holdings of the residents. Everyone knew O. P. and his family, and those were very special times of "togetherness" for all of us.
(Marian Quam Stoneback--Lansing, MN--1920s-30s)

CUSTOMS AND CELEBRATIONS

CHRIS AND MARY HANSON

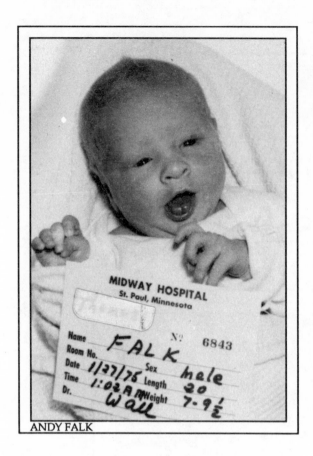

MIDWAY HOSPITAL
St. Paul, Minnesota

Name FALK N° 6843
Room No.
Date 1/27/75 Sex male
Time 1:02 AM Length 20
Dr. Weight 7-9½
Wall

ANDY FALK

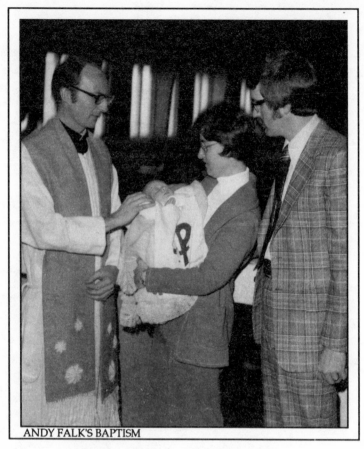

ANDY FALK'S BAPTISM

MILESTONES

JIM AND JOANN PROM

CONFIRMATION, LEWISVILLE, MN, 1931

This particular June day in 1933, the eighth-grade graduates of the rural Pope County schools were gathered on the courthouse lawn to have their picture taken. What an exciting day! My friend Mary and I had store-bought dresses, a rare treat for us girls.

On this glorious day, I had my hair "done" by a neighbor girl, firmly set with wave set made from flax seed. A handful of flax seed boiled with several cupfuls of water, and then strained, made a delightful wave set.

The sun shone warm and bright on this big day as we crowded together with our fellow classmates, while the photographer hid under his black cover and recorded this group for forthcoming generations to see. A young man standing behind me patted my hair during the picture-taking process, and remarked, "You sure have stiff hair!" My friend and I still chuckle over his remark, but he was right. As we girls knew, that flax "goo" could really hold the waves!

An eighth-grade education was a good education for those days. Going on to school was expensive, and money was hard to come by. Mary and I were both lucky to go on to normal training school, thereby making us "country schoolmarms."
(Margaret Seeger Hedlund--Pope Co., MN--1933)

"POMP AND CIRCUMSTANCE"

Walking tall, 599 soon-to-be graduates filed into Aldrich Arena and awaited the commencement of their high school graduation. Each was a little anxious about what was to be expected during the next 1 1/2 hours, myself among them. As the ominous sounds of "Pomp and Circumstance" echoed throughout the arena, a sense of disbelief overwhelmed me. Even though I had attended high school graduations before, this was a very different situation. I was the one wearing the robe this time. This was it! Twelve years of preparation was about to come to a close.

Suddenly, the principal appeared at the podium and the ceremony was underway. The guest speakers each took their turn at the podium, giving the same infamous speeches they give each year. Although I listened, I really did not hear them, for my mind was focused inside on a much busier place. My thoughts were racing about friends, the past, and the ambiguous future.

Along with the rumble of the background noise created by the speakers, I heard my name announced. It was my turn to say my piece. A sudden chill ran through my body and I clenched my fists to edge myself on. I joined the faculty on stage and faced my fellow graduates and their families. At first, the nearly 4,000 faces seemed cold and unfriendly, but as I slowly picked out those people with smiling, familiar features, I was given the strength to continue. Within minutes, my speech was over and I was given much unexpected applause. My head was swimming in all the excitement, and I could not stop myself from smiling. Soon I was back in my seat among the sea of graduates.

The minutes flew by, and before I knew it, all 599 graduates had received their diplomas, the closing remarks had been made, and we were leaving the arena. As soon as we passed through the door, there were cheers of jubilation and jumbled excitement. I tracked down my family and closest friends, and "congratulations" hugs and picture-taking followed. Tears that had been building up ever since I walked through the doorway were suddenly let loose.
(Julie Kostroski--White Bear Lake, MN--1988)

THE "EMPTY NEST"

JEFF SCHLICHTER

High School graduation for the youngest of our three sons meant the start of an "empty nest" for my husband and me. As each of our sons reached the end of high school, we could tell they were ready for college and a more independent life--but were WE ready?

After twenty-four years of nurturing and love; fevers and broken bones; hundreds of football, basketball, hockey, and soccer games; an ever-ringing phone; tons of food consumed at all times of the day and night; and multitudinous crises; yes, we thought we WERE ready for a life of independence ourselves. Until, that is, the inevitable day arrived when our youngest did leave for college. Then the "empty" in "empty nest" suddenly took on new meaning. Adjusting to an "empty nest" took time. We missed all those things that had made life so hectic and interesting, and we missed our special sons.

Then, just when we thought we had adjusted to our new independent life without kids, our son (and all his earthly possessions) returned home for the summer!
(Norma Hughes Schlichter--Northfield, MN--1988)

JEFF SCHLICHTER'S GRADUATION, 1988

Birthday parties when I was growing up were a big deal. My parents and family always made me feel that my birthday was a very special occasion. I usually received many presents. It didn't really matter that most of them were clothing of some kind; it was the "number" of packages that was important!

Besides the family birthday party, I always had a number of friends over for a party. One tradition we enjoyed was playing "Heavy, Heavy Hangover." Now, right away I have to say it's not what you think! No one thought anything of that name in the '50s. What we did was have the honored guest sit in a chair, with all the guests around her. Each girl would take a turn bringing her present up and standing behind the "birthday girl," with the present held over her head. Then they would recite the following: "Heavy, heavy hangover. Whatcha gonna do with it--eat it, wear it, or play with it?" The "birthday girl" would guess, and then we would laugh if the gift didn't fit into the category she had guessed.

If I could come up with a different name for the game, I'd introduce it to my daughter's group of friends at her next birthday party. I think it's something they would enjoy. In many ways, little girls really haven't changed that much.
(Shirley Hughes Selzer--Lake Crystal, MN--1950s)

CELEBRATING WITH LAUGHTER

I've been blessed to have a group of friends who are very creative and fun-loving. We have managed to help each other pass through our fortieth birthdays painlessly--celebrating life with laughter rather than depression.

As a group, we first pick a theme that is fitting for the birthday person, also deciding costumes we'll wear (if needed), gag gifts, and the type of birthday cake we'll make. Some of the party themes include: Four-year-old Birthday Party (with games, etc.); Complete Funeral Service (using a decorated refrigerator box for a casket); Nursing Home Resident (with wheelchair); Flashers in Trench Coats; Pillsbury's Special Cookies; Bad Taste Party; Auction; and the Famous Banana Bread Recipe. The best of these was saved to surprise my late husband and me. My husband was an avid Vikings fan, and the theme for his party on May 2, 1983, was a "Vikings Tailgate Party."

When we walked out of church on Saturday evening, to Chuck's surprise, we were greeted by crazy looking cheerleaders and men dressed in snowmobile suits. They handed him his snowmobile suit to put on and then we boarded a school bus with the Vikings mascot look-alike. We were driven to the town's football field, where the press was waiting to take our picture. In the middle of the football field were tables set for a formal dinner. Chuck was overjoyed by his friends' love and creativity!

With a group like this, you "sweat out" your approaching birthday. Since I was the youngest, I opted for a "nice party." They gave me my wish--a super boring party. However, they surprised me with my "real party" three weeks later--"Sinderella" invited to the Grand Ball held at the Royal Castle in the Glen. My royal coach was a white limo; my after-the-ball transportation was an orange Volkswagon. The court included my fairy godmother, stepmother, and a number of wicked stepsisters and brothers. They also provided me with an unusual gown, and my husband was dressed as Prince Charming.

Needless to say, we had fun. However, the topper of the evening was that my gifts were placed under a used Christmas tree--one they had saved for a year. Not one needle was left on it--just bare branches decorated with cookies! Oh yes, Prince Charming found my glass slipper under the tree.
(Konnie George Brueck--LeSueur, MN--1980s)

STILL CHIPPER AND READY FOR FUN

Ernest Falk, still chipper and ready for fun, was busy as a bee all day today--his 98th birthday--getting ready for his birthday party tonight. He said he will be disappointed if it doesn't last until midnight or later.

The big party will be held at the home of his favorite "500" partner, Otto Schmidtke. Guests will split into rival factions of "500," which is Ernest's favorite game, although he will take a whirl at "Solo" every now and then. After a few hours, the guests will partake of a midnight lunch of ice cream, home-made cake, cigars for the men, and candy for the ladies. If he functions as he did last year, Ernest will be the last one willing to go home!
(From the Fairmont, Minnesota, newspaper, 1940--Ernest lived to be 105 years old!)

FIRST KISS

I was grounded for two weeks. My mother never wanted me to stay out late. It was worth the price! The story goes like this:

We high school girls liked to parade around on balmy spring evenings and end up at Langer's Drugstore for a Dr. Pepper. It was one of those enchantingly lovely spring nights when winter had lost its hold, and the electric excitement of a new season was felt. It was like you could run around in circles and jump high in the air, higher than you ever jumped before, and not be tired. It was an evening like that.

Art J. had a pal who had a brother who had a car. On this night, the pal was allowed to drive the car, so he and his friends were out cruising around and showing off for us girls. We were showing off for them, too, acting smart and pretending not to notice that they seemed to be following us. They pulled up after a time and asked if we wanted a ride. We did, of course,--all six of us.

Anyone can figure out that six average-sized kids do not fit in the front seat of a two-seater car; in those days we called them coupes. Art and I got the rumble seat. We had to climb over the rear bumper to get in, and our feet rested on the tire pump, the jack, and the crank. I should tell you that this was a '34 Pontiac, with an expandable rumble seat.

We drove up and down the one long street in our small town many times, making sure the other kids saw that we had a car. Then we went out around the No. 1 water tank, up to the grain elevators, out to the cemetery, and back to Main Street. Every kid was in a loud and lively mood. Back in town, Mr. Rule was blinking the lights in his store, which meant that it was closing time and everyone should be ready to leave. Oh, my goodness! I had forgotten the time. Better get home quick!

We drove into the yard. Art hopped over the side to let me out, and I took the hand he offered me to climb down. Then, quickly and very unexpectedly, he gave me a big, hard, cold, damp kiss right on my lips! Then he was gone.

I ran into the house. I knew my mother heard, but I would deal with her later. I ran up the stairs and turned on the light so I could see myself in the mirror. I wanted to see if I looked the same. I did. But my face was red and felt stiff, probably from the wind. I patted my face where the kiss had landed; it was wet. I think his nose was running.

(Joy Liberda--a small town in Dakota--1940s)

PROM NIGHT

It took me several weeks to get up the nerve to ask a certain special girl if she would be my date to the high school prom. I expected her to turn me down, so when she accepted, my knees got so weak that I had to lean against a wall so I wouldn't fall down.

My mother had told me that I would be expected to pin the corsage on her dress. When I walked into her home, her mother, dad, brother, and sisters were all there to meet me. So, now we had a VERY BASHFUL farm boy, a pretty girl--who in her prom dress looked more like an angel--and her family. As I started to pin the corsage on, my hands were shaking like a leaf and my heartbeat sounded as loud as the hoof beats of a galloping horse. It took me a long, long time, but finally I thought that I had it secured to her dress. I stepped back to admire my date and the corsage, only to watch the corsage tumble to the floor! To say that I was embarrassed would be an understatement.

(Jerry Sutliff--Glenwood City, WI--1955)

Eighteen years ago today
At 8:21 a.m.
You came into this world;
What a joy! What a gem!

Weighing 6 pounds 8 ounces,
Measuring 20 inches long,
With those big blue eyes,
How could we go wrong.

When five weeks old,
You slept through the night.
Except for those "croupy" times,
When you gave us quite a fright.

Soon you started to smile;
Such a happy boy you were.
A new trick each day;
A new adventure each year.

At one you climbed on everything,
Scattering things to and fro.
When we asked, "How big are you?"
You threw up your arms just so.

At two you liked to talk a lot,
Asking what everything is.
ABC's--numbers--colors;
You were really quite a whiz.

At three your favorite expression was
"I'd 'wike' one of those."
By now you had quite a toy collection,
Along with plenty of prose.

Sandbox--swing set--
And so much more.
Down the driveway on your tractors
You and Missy would roar.

The characters of Sesame Street,
Including Oscar the Grouch,
Provided many hours of pleasure
While you rested on the couch.

At four it was super heroes;
At five dinosaurs and whales.
Then the Star Wars phenomenon,
And Mom hit all the sales.

Soon you were off to school,
And the years went flying by.
Your activities diversified;
You became quite a guy.

Indian Guides and Webelos;
You made quite a scout.
You played basketball and soccer,
And had a paper route.

You took some tumbles
Along the way.
Twelve stitches two times--
Your chin had to pay!

Now your toys are bigger;
Computers--CD's--videos galore.
You get in the "mustard truck,"
And kick it to the floor.

Your selective service card arrival
Gave us quite a jolt.
And in a few days' time
You'll for the first time vote.

Sometimes it's hard to express
The love we feel for you.
You've brought us so much joy,
And our troubles have been few.

So many words of advice
We could pass along to you,
But life's decisions will be yours
In all that you pursue.

When you're on your own,
Remember your mom and dad.
To have you as our son
Makes us so proud and glad.

Mom and Dad

(Tom and Bonnie Falk--White Bear Lake, MN--November 6, 1988)

The young people of the neighborhood thought Margaret really lucky to be dating Joe. She was a senior at the local high school, while Joe had quit school. None of this slaving over the 3R's for that young man! His father owned a farm, and he also went to a job elsewhere each day. His mother dressed nicely; she didn't seem to have to help with grain shocking, outside chores, etc. Also, she drove their car! Not many women went out driving a car in the thirties.

One evening, Margaret, Joe, and a group of young folks were out driving in Joe's car, when someone remarked that the gas tank was low. After a look at the tell-tale needle, Joe headed back to their farm to fill the tank at the FREE gas pump. He roared smartly up to the pump and began filling the tank. Suddenly, his mother appeared, pointed a shiny revolver at her wayward son, and commanded him to stop or she would shoot! Joe nonchalantly continued filling the tank, while his mother returned to the house, giving up on any attempt to discipline her son.

The young folks continued on their drive. Then, Joe stopped the car and asked Margaret to accompany him, leaving the others laughing and joking in the car. Margaret meekly followed Joe, walking amidst tall uncut weeds, to a spot behind the old country schoolhouse. Joe pressed Margaret's shoulders against the school building. Then, as a chorus of mosquitoes sang and the tall weeds softly swayed, Joe said those magic words--a girl's most waited for words--"Will you marry me?" Would I! Why not? Here was a young man asking for her in marriage--a man with a car, gas, and no work to take up his time--of course, Margaret would marry him!

Joe borrowed her newly acquired class ring so that he would know the correct size for an engagement ring. Weeks later, Margaret found out from friends that Joe's mother made him return the engagement ring, which was no doubt on her account! And so, with no ring to bind the engagement, the two began dating others, and soon the short engagement was but a memory.

(Margaret Seeger Hedlund--Pope Co., MN--1936)

LEAP YEAR PROPSAL

We lived on a ranch in eastern Oregon when I was growing up. My sister and I had our own horses; mine was named Ginger, and my sister's horse was named Nancy. Nancy always had to go first. If you got ahead of her, she would nip you "just above the saddle!"

One day when my sister and I were riding out in the wilderness looking for cattle that had strayed, we discovered a little log cabin up the canyon. We went in to explore and found that it was nearly empty--just an old stove, a bed spring with no

44

mattress, and an old dresser. We looked through the dresser and found an old tin box filled with letters, so we took them home to read.

The letters were from a lady in Ohio, probably written in the 1860s or 1870s, but since they were tucked way back in the dresser, no one had found them before. They were written to a man who had been out homesteading, and the last letter was written in Leap Year. At the end of the letter, there was a verse: "The days of Leap Year number twenty-nine; will you or will you not be mine?" We thought that was so unusual; couldn't imagine a lady proposing to a fellow!
(Eileene Barry McKee--Lake Co., OR--1920s)

QUEEN FOR A NIGHT

Miss Vernelle Sueker, an April bride, was privileged to become "Queen for a Night" at one of the loveliest and most remarkably original parties ever given in this community. It was one of those delightful affairs that can only be perpetrated where close friendships and congeniality meet in their truest form.

The members of the Huskie Hikie Club arrived early to await the unsuspecting honoree, who was prepared to attend her last club meeting as a member. Miss Sueker was presented with a lovely corsage of sweet peas, and told that she was to reign as queen over the "empire" for that night.

A two-course luncheon was then served at a large table set with blue dinnerware and pink tapers, nut cups, and bride's place cards. In the center of the table was a large blue bowl of sweet peas, which blended harmoniously with the pink and blue color scheme. Chicken salad, hot rolls, and relishes made up the first course. The highlight of the luncheon was the molded ice cream, through which was written "Vernelle" in pink, with rosebuds in each corner. The inevitable fortune telling plan was achieved by seeing who received the wedding ring (who was to be the next bride); the dime (who was to marry ruthlessly for money); and the thimble (who was doomed to spinsterhood)--all deftly hidden in the pink and white layer cake.

About this time a knock sounded at the door, and the caller handed Miss Sueker a box containing a chain of large frankfurters. A note, wrapped in wax paper, was inserted into each "frank," telling in rhyme where to find each gift. Miss Sueker proved herself a good hunter, and in no time at all she found a shower of things, each done up in butcher's paper, typifying the groom's employment in a meat shop. The little words of well wishes and love with each gift showed evidence of the high esteem and comradeship toward Miss Sueker as a thoroughbred Huskie.
(From the Lewisville, Minnesota, newspaper--1937)

CLIFF AND VERNELLE FALK

Knowing our fun-loving friends, my husband and I planned ahead for our wedding day by making arrangements with a local service garage to keep our car under "lock and key." We felt very safe and secure when the big day arrived, but when we confidently walked into the garage to pick up our car to leave on our honeymoon, there was no car to be found!

My husband's best man had somehow gotten wind of where our car was, and he had gone dashing into the garage, waving a fake marriage license, saying, "Quick, give me my car--our friends are on our trail"--and off he drove! We found our sprayed up, temporarily unworkable car a few hours later.

Our families also got into the act and visited our apartment. When we returned from our honeymoon, we found our bed short-sheeted and full of rice; also, the toilet seat was wrapped in plastic wrap! It gave us a few chuckles and made for good memories.

(Norma Hughes Schlichter--Mankato, MN--1963)

NORMA AND GARY SCHLICHTER

WAR-TIME WEDDING

I met my future husband in college, and after he was drafted into the army (1941), we had to carry on our courtship through letter-writing. Even after his medical discharge, we still wrote lots of letters, as he lived about 240 miles from me. Because of gas rationing and bad tires, we did not see each other very often. Luckily, there were still passenger trains at that time, which helped our situation somewhat.

Our wedding, in 1943, was held in a church, with only thirty relatives and close friends in attendance. Because it was during World War II, no appliances were available for purchase. Most of our wedding gifts were made of glass (Pyrex casseroles, etc.). We also received a few towels and linens. The big weddings with fancy gifts didn't happen until after the war was over. However, I acquired a refrigerator, washing machine, and sewing machine from my father-in-law when he moved out of his house. He also gave us his 1933 Ford, so we considered ourselves RICH!

(Mary Simonson Thompson--Groton, SD--1940s)

THE PARACHUTE WEDDING DRESS

My husband served in the Pacific Theater during World War II as a paratrooper. When we decided to marry, he suggested the possibility of having my wedding dress made from a parachute that he had. His sister-in-law's mother was talented in designing and sewing dresses, and she agreed to make the wedding dress. It was to be a Queen Anne style, trimmed with the shroud lines from the parachute. These were formed into a

beautiful, tight zigzag trim that was hand stitched onto the dress. This took many hours of work and patience, but it was all worth it, for it gave the dress an unusual and beautiful finish.
(Rose Grozdanich Boerboon--Minneapolis, MN--1947)

A PENNY FOR GOOD LUCK

SHIVAREE
(also spelled charivari or chivaree)

Every time we knew of a wedding, we would all go--kids, adults, everybody. We would carry old tin pans or buckets, and at the home of the bride, we would pound and yell up a storm. Years ago, the wedding usually was in church (especially Catholic) in the morning. The reception lasted all day and all night at the home of the bride's parents. We went to the shivaree even if we didn't know the bride that well. Everyone was welcome.

The bride and groom always came out on the porch or on the lawn and threw out pennies, or if they were more generous, sometimes nickles. We would all scramble to see who could get the most coins.
(Mary E. Strong--LeCenter/St. Paul, MN--1915-50)

WEDDING DANCE

I grew up in the very small town of Easton, Minnesota, where my father was the lumber dealer. The town was very predominantly Catholic, and I am the middle child of a family of thirteen.

Catholic weddings in the Easton area were always accompanied by a wedding dance the night of the wedding. Everyone went to those dances. They were free, of course, and it didn't matter whether or not you knew the bride or groom. There was also a small German Lutheran Church in Easton, but the Lutherans didn't have wedding dances. They did, however, go to them!

The bridal couple rented the hall and paid the band. No one passed a hat or pinned a dollar on the bride's veil (to pay for dancing with her), as I've seen done in the Willmar area where I live now. The wedding dance was the bridal couple's "treat" all the way.
(Loretta C. Lehman--Easton, MN--1930s--Present)

HONEYMOON TRAVELOGUE--1926

June 8--Two carloads of kids followed us as far as Lake Crystal. Left Mankato at 6:15. Ate supper by the road near Belle Plaine. Took detour out of Jordan and got lost. Went about twenty miles out of the way. Stayed at a hotel in Shakopee.

June 9--Left for Minneapolis. Went through St. Paul just fine. Visited some people there. Left for Stillwater. Went across the St. Croix River. Ate supper in a tourist camp in Wisconsin. Pitched tent and camped on the St. Croix River. Went down to river and washed our feet.

June 10--Went back to the Minnesota side. Went out to the prison and toured it. Crossed river again and started for St. Croix Falls. Stopped at Somerset for an ice cream cone. Ate dinner in a free camp at Osceola--a fine camp. Arrived at St. Croix and visited the Trout Hatchery. At Interstate Park, saw the dam. Crossed to Taylors Falls--came on Trail 35 as far as Webster. Stopped at Yellow Lake Lodge. Paid $2.00 for one room in a cottage overlooking Big Yellow Lake on one side and Little Yellow Lake on other side. Bathed our feet in Yellow Lake before going to bed.

June 11--Ate breakfast in small store along the road. Came sixty-five miles through solid woods. Had dinner at Superior. Came to Duluth and toured around. Went to the Aerial Bridge.

June 14--Went to Hibbing--certainly a fine town. Lovely tourist camp. Slept in the tourists' shelter. Visited the zoo, greenhouse, two parks, and open mine. Went to Grand Rapids and Brainerd. Went to the paper mills.

June 17--Went to Gilbert Lake, about three miles from Brainerd, to fish. Didn't catch anything. Went to the tourist camp to eat. Had a fine time and a swell lunch. Drove to the park in the evening to hear the band play. Went out toward Gull Lake to see a camp of gypsies.

June 18--Left for St. Cloud. Ate at Little Falls tourist camp.

June 19--Arrived in New Ulm at 5:45. Arrived home at 6:15. Glad to get here. Had a shivaree on Monday night.

Total car expenses for the trip=$17.13)

(Walter and Grace Meredith--Cambria, MN--1926)

WALT AND GRACE MEREDITH

DONNA AND GEORGE SELZER

For my husband's parents' fortieth anniversary, we had a big celebration. Four couples who were good friends of theirs all dressed up as clowns and told the "history" of their marriage, bringing each of their six children up on stage as the story progressed. It was a wild time, and then turned sentimental.

I wrote to everyone ahead of time and asked them to fill out a sheet that said at the top, "George and Donna, 1947-1987, I remember when...." I told them to be creative and use poems, pictures, etc. to tell their stories. I then assembled a book of all these letters from their relatives and friends. It is now one of their most treasured possessions.
(Shirley Hughes Selzer--Spencer, IA--1987)

I REMEMBER WHEN....
"Yes, we remember when it all started--and a nice young couple with a little boy came to look at the house next door. We wondered then what our new neighbors would be like. It wasn't long and we found out that they were very friendly, helpful, and always full of fun. We remember...

--The times playing "Canasta" and keeping score to see who would take who out for dinner after the "winter games."

--The 7-Up dances at the Roof Garden in Spirit Lake. Couldn't afford to go in those days, but thanks to Bud, we had enough free tickets to enjoy quite a few dances there and then take a swim afterwards, or go to Lilac Hill "where the grass is a grab and a half high."

--Donna coming over the day of Joan's wedding in Spain, which we couldn't attend due to the distance. She was a great comfort to me that day. What a friend to have!

--The time I had a flat tire and Bud took time out to run over and change it for me, even though he was leaving for a funeral. What a friend to have!

This could go on and on, but everyone who knows George (Bud) and Donna, I'm sure, will know what I mean when I say, "What great friends we have."
(Red and Betty Mart--Spencer, IA--1987)

GRIEF SHARED BY THE WHOLE COMMUNITY

Sadly to say, the death of a young child or baby was not uncommon in the days I attended school, and the family's grief was shared by the whole community. Funeral homes were not used at that time, so the visitation was always held at the family home. The teacher always spoke to the pupils about the tragedy, and then she and all the pupils would march, double file, from the school to the home of the bereaved, walk silently past the casket, and back to school. This usually took only about an hour, but it left a lifelong impression on everyone.
(Ida Posteher Fabyanske--Ramsey Co., MN--1920s)

THE COMMUNITY

COMMUNITY CLUB

In our neighborhood, we had a community club that met once a month, except during the summer. Programs would be presented by different schools in the area. Sometimes, the adults would put on a play, which would also be presented at other area community clubs. Many people were then able to enjoy the "fruits of their labors." The community hall, which had a large floor suitable for roller skating or dancing, was family oriented--the social center for everyone in that area.

We also had neighborhood card parties. The adults played "Whist," and the children played in other rooms of the house. Food was always served at the close of the evening, with each of the ladies bringing a cake or sandwiches to share. As the small children fell asleep, they would lie on the beds, covered with the coats.
(Mary Simonson Thompson--Groton, SD--1920s-30s)

BOX SOCIALS

Any little programs given by the school children were looked forward to by the whole community. Box socials were a way to make a little extra money, which was usually used for books, playground equipment, and other supplies. A program was given, and the boxes were auctioned off.

Each lady or girl packed a box with lunch for two, each trying to outdo the others. Usually the boxes contained sandwiches, fried chicken, cake, cookies, and fruit. Then she decorated the box, trying to keep her design a secret, and hoping a certain person would get it. The men and boys bought the boxes and then ate with the owner.
(Dorothea Thompson--southwest MN--1930s-50s)

MAY BASKETS

On May 1, the girls in our small town always hung May baskets on each other's door. We made them out of heavy paper, filled them with candy, nuts, popcorn, or small gift items, and usually put a bow on top. Some were very elaborate and some were rather simple, but we loved them all!
(Mary E. Strong--LeCenter, MN--1917-29)

My husband got sick and had to have major surgery at a time
when our new barn was only half built. Thirty-four neighbors
showed up and finished the job. Several neighbors' wives
brought hot dishes and cakes, and helped serve. There were
men swarming all over--like bees! They were pounding nails,
shingling, and pouring cement. We set up tables in the yard to
serve lunch and dinner, and we had a special place to wash up
outside. It was such a great feeling of warmth and generosity--a
blessing never to be forgotten.
(Edith Tannahill Lerfald--Buxton, ND--1963)

NEIGHBORHOOD CHURCH

In Berlin, North Dakota, a little town of less than 200 people,
we were the only family in town who were members of the
Lutheran church. The other families lived in the rural community. There were two other churches, and everyone respected each other's choice of faith.

In as much as we were the only members who lived in town,
it became our duty to haul the coal to the church and to clean
and dust the day before worship services. Also, my dad would
ring the first bell one-half hour before services, and the second
bell when the services started.

Services were held every other Sunday, and we always had
the pastor over for dinner afterwards. When the pastor left (he
tended three parishes), my mother would sit in various chairs
to see how things appeared from his perspective. (She did that
after any company visited!)

Today, we have the pump organ from Rolgate Lutheran
Church of Berlin, North Dakota. The church building has been
moved and now serves as a granary.
(Beatrice Salberg--Berlin, ND--1920s-30s)

BANK NIGHT

Every Wednesday night was Bank Night in Two Harbors, and
there would be a drawing for various sums of money. Sometimes, they would also give away pieces of Depression glass.
Everyone would buy tickets so that they would be eligible. I
think they cost ten cents for kids and twenty-five cents for
adults.

Then we would go to the movies (serials--to keep us coming
back each week). There were lots of westerns; I was especially
impressed with Hopalong Cassidy. The people I babysat for
didn't care to go to movies, so they would give me their tickets;
therefore, I would babysit in exchange for a show ticket.
(Mary B. Twar--Two Harbors, MN-1930s-40s)

I worked in my father's small town Iowa bakery in the 1950s. On Friday nights, especially in the summer, the town bustled with business and socializing. At 9:00 p.m. most of the stores closed, and people moved on down to Central Park, where the town band put on its Friday night band concert. There was often a guest soloist. Families and older people spread blankets and listened to the music, while teenagers mostly ignored the music in favor of laughing and flirting. Children lined up at the red popcorn wagon for ten-cent bags of hot, buttered pop-corn or peanuts in the shell.
(Merideth Allen Chelberg--Charles City, IA--1950s)

ICE CREAM SOCIALS AND BAND CONCERTS

Every Wednesday night during the summer, there would be an ice cream social and band concert in the park, which was lo-cated in the center of town. There was a band shelter (gazebo) which housed the band. It was always extremely crowded and HOT in there! Cars would be parked on the streets surrounding the park, and would honk their horns in appreciation after each song.

The ice cream social would be set up in one corner of the park. A different group would sponsor it each week (church group, band mothers, 4-H, etc.). They would serve homemade pies and cakes, ice cream, and coffee, all at very reasonable prices. Card tables with pretty little tablecloths would be set up around the area. There would also be a popcorn wagon on one corner.
(Bonnie Hughes Falk--Lake Crystal, MN--1950s-60s)

MAIN STREET

Main Street in Groton, South Dakota, was the place to be on Saturday night! People would try to get to town earlier than the rest, so as to get a good parking place. When the shopping was over, the ladies would return to their cars to visit with friends and neighbors, and to watch other shoppers as they walked by. Some of the men spent their time in the pool hall, and the young people went to the movies. I would get ten cents to spend, so that was enough for a bag of popcorn and an ice cream cone. The big decision was which to buy first!
(Mary Simonson Thompson--Groton, SD--1930s)

MY HOMETOWN

The town of Davenport, North Dakota, started as a result of two railroad lines crossing each other--the Northern Pacific line, known as the "Southwestern Branch," out of Fargo, and

52

the Great Northern, from Larimore to Breckenridge in a north/south direction. The trains brought coal in and took the locally-grown grains to market. Most of the small towns in this area were built about ten miles apart, representing the camps used to build the railroad.

The settlers in this small town of approximately 200 people came predominantly from Norway and Germany. The town had two Lutheran churches--one for the Norwegians and one for the Germans--because each couldn't understand the other's language. This nationality division carried through in school also, where each side was represented in snowball fights, etc.
(Emmett D. Salberg--Davenport, ND--1930s)

GYMANFA GANU

Twice in the past twenty years, the National Gymanfa Ganu, a Welsh hymn-singing festival, has been held in the Twin Cities. People came from throughout the United States and Canada, as well as Wales. Each Gymanfa brings me close in thought and feeling to my Welsh heritage. I will never forget sitting next to my cousin and singing with the altos at the front of the Ordway Theater in St. Paul, being part of that great congregation. For me, it seemed as close to heaven as could be experienced on this earth!
(Alice C. Hughes--St. Paul, MN--1987)

COUSINS

FAIRS AND FESTIVALS

Every year, thousands of special events are celebrated in towns and cities across the country. These celebrations often highlight the qualities that make each location special, and they are as diverse as the communities themselves. They include arts and crafts shows; polka and jazz fests; prairie and rivertown days; maple syrup, strawberry, or corn festivals; old settlers' days, and various fairs and carnivals of all types. Why not join in the fun in your community! (BHF)

LUMBERJACK DAYS

Each summer, the city of Stillwater, Minnesota, pays tribute to the industry that developed the St. Croix Valley, with the celebration of Lumberjack Days.

The festival began in November, 1934, in the depths of the Depression. People were encouraged to appear downtown in the attire of the late 1880s. Children donned fake beards. More than fifty men, who had spent countless years in the woods, registered at Lumberjack headquarters. So successful was the first celebration, that it was scheduled for October the next year. The 1936 Lumberjack Days fete was set back another month, to September. The three-day celebration included a grand parade, log rolling, hillbilly bands, window decorating and dress-up contests, a greased pole to climb, and exhibitions of boxing and football. By 1838, the emphasis shifted to the waterfront. A boat parade featured old river steamers, pleasure yachts, birch bark canoes, bateaus, and wannigans.

With the imminence of war in 1941, the celebration was discontinued. More than two decades later, a group of local citizens revived Lumberjack Days. In 1968, the traditional log rolling and beard growing were augmented by a kiddie parade, sidewalk sale, seaplane rides, and grand parade. For the 1990 celebration, events included kiddie parade, talent show, water ski exhibit, log rolling, wood carving, boat parade, softball, storytelling and theater productions, selection of Miss Stillwater, and the grand parade. A kickoff cruise on the paddlewheel boat Andiamo commemorated the arrival of the early lumbermen aboard steamboats.

(Anita Albrecht Buck--Stillwater, MN)

"CELEBRATE SCANDIA"

"Celebrate Scandia" was part of 1990's "Celebrate Minnesota," with all its small town festivals. The biggest event was in June on Midsummer's Day, and was held at "Gammelgarden" (old Swedish farm) in Scandia. Events included craft demonstrations, a smorgasbord dinner, and a program in the afternoon,

with music and Swedish folk dancers dancing around the Maypole.

In July another festival, called "Old Settlers' Day," took place about a mile down the road at the Hay Lake School, located on "Historical Corner." There is a monument there that marks the spot where Swedish settlers first came to Minnesota in 1850. Crafts were displayed and there was a program in the afternoon. There were many food booths and a special table with Swedish delicacies such as "ost-kaka," a porridge made from milk, eggs, and a special kind of yeast.
(Hazel Gronquist--Scandia, MN)

CHAUTAUQUA

This long ago and far away story regards the once-upon-a-time wonderful medium of entertainment called Chautauqua. A troupe of actors traveled throughout the country, particularly in the rural areas, to bring drama, comedy, and music to people in small towns and cities. For many, it was their only exposure to this cultural experience, and the rare opportunity to enjoy with family and friends an escape from the monotonous drudgery of hard work and long days.

Just a few miles from where my grandparents lived, in an almost natural amphitheater formed by the land along the James River (called Tacoma Park), the Chautauqua company would raise its large tent, set folding chairs and benches in place, and prepare for the huge numbers of people of all ages who would come to be entertained. On rare occasions, the director would invite local talent to perform. One of those people was my mother.

In 1918, World War I was devastating Europe. Mother had just graduated from high school and was attending Northern Normal, and also working a full-time shift as a master telegrapher at Western Union. She was a fine speaker, and had taken what was called in those days "elocution lessons." She had been the lead actress in many of the area home talent shows and plays. She was a big hit in her Chautauqua performance-- so big that she was asked to join the company on a permanent basis. She did not, however, preferring to continue her education and contribute to the war effort at Western Union and as a part-time depot agent. But to those who knew her, she was always a star!
(Dawn Blair Gullikson--SD--1918-19)

THEY CAME BY NIGHT

The anticipation began when the colorful posters, with their enticing pictures announcing the coming of "The World's Greatest Circus," appeared in some of the store windows of our small town.

The circus traveled by rail. It took a long string of box cars and flat cars to accommodate the many wagons, equipment, and animals. The performers rode in coaches. The arrival took place in the wee morning hours. The unloading and setting up at the fairgrounds was done with remarkable speed and precision by the so-called roustabouts, men who worked and traveled with the circus. By the time most of the townspeople were sitting down to breakfast, the "Big Top" was already in place, complete with bleachers, three rings, sawdust floor, and trapeze hanging from the top poles.

The parade, about midday, was no small part of the excitement. Not everyone could afford the admission charge to the tent--fifty cents for adults and ten cents for kids--but the parade had no price tag. Main Street was lined with people on both sides. Our waiting ears picked up the sound of the calliope before the string of ornate wagons came into view. Each was unique and was drawn by two or more teams of well-groomed horses. The contents of the wagons were as fascinating as their exteriors. Lions, tigers, and other animals paced restlessly in small confinements reinforced with iron bars.

We thrilled at the sight of several large elephants plodding single file, and laughed at the antics of the gay-costumed clowns with painted smiles and flappy oversize shoes. All too soon, this portion of the day's excitement was finished. The parade ended at the fairgrounds shortly before the afternoon show was to begin.

Before the tent was entirely vacant of evening spectators, various phases of packing and moving back to the rail cars had begun. Every person knew his job well, and the loading was done with the same speed and skill as the early morning unloading. Soon the wheels of the long train were rolling. Our visitors were gone. The fairgrounds were again quiet and dark. The early morning light would reveal only the trampled ground by man and beast.
(Ella Morse--Stevens Point, WI--1917-24)

THE VERY TALL CLOWN

When I was a small girl, my parents took me to see the Ringling Brothers Circus when it came to our county seat. We parked the car near the grounds and walked to the ticket office. I held my mother's hand and chattered about what we were going to see. When a man took my other hand, I assumed it was my father, but when I looked up to tell him something, I saw, instead, a very tall clown! I had never seen one before and I became hysterical with fright, to the embarrassment of my mother and the chagrin of the poor clown.
(Dorothea Thompson--Luverne, MN--1919)

NIKKI SELZER

When I hear the word circus, I always think of the time, back in 1935, when my husband, a friend, and I went to Mason City, Iowa, to see the Ringling Brothers Circus. Their main clown, Emmett Kelly, was putting on quite an act, and everyone was watching him. All of a sudden, he started to climb way up in the stands, and for some reason I had a queasy feeling. He pushed by everyone in our row, and then, bending over me, flashed a huge red neon heart. I've never quite recovered!
(Jo Cutler Allen--Mason City, IA--1935)

"COME TO THE FAIR"

"Come to the Fair!" As youngsters, we didn't need any encouragement. Every year, the county fair designated a day as "school day," which meant a holiday from school.

While we did not compete for the prize-winning red and blue ribbons, we did find so many appealing attractions. The setting was spectacular, with the large round barn for housing and displaying the farm animals; the sheds and stalls for jams, jellies, and other mouth-watering foods; the grandstand for viewing the sulky horse races; the merry-go-round; the ferris wheel; the games of chance; and, best of all, the high wires on which terrifying acts were performed by daring acrobats. With all these attractions, we looked forward to going to the county fair each year. A special invitation was not needed.
(Ole Schelsnes--WI--1920s-30s)

THE COUNTY FAIR

I looked forward with anticipation each summer to the county fair in August. 4-H was a big part of the fair, with everyone exhibiting the "fruits of their labors," whether it was their prized pig or cow; vegetables from their garden; an article of clothing they proudly modeled in the dress revue; or any number of other things.

Our church always had a food stand at the fair. Everyone brought food--chickens and pies galore! As a young girl, I worked in the food stand. This was my first "waitressing" experience, and I remember feeling quite important!

One year I exhibited chickens at the fair. Don't ask me why, for I never did like the "critters." Anyway, my chickens laid eggs during their stay, and the boys who were in charge of that building turned MY eggs in to the food stand and got paid for them (probably five cents). I was so mad!

When I was in junior high, my boyfriend won a big teddy bear at one of the carnival booths. I remember how proudly I carried that bear around the fairgrounds!
(Bonnie Hughes Falk--Blue Earth Co., MN--1950s-60s)

GROWING UP

BONNIE HUGHES FALK AND NORMA HUGHES SCHLICHTER

ESCAPADES

When I was in high school, we lived in St. Paul near the Capitol. We played in that area all the time, and we knew every nook and cranny around the whole building. In 1927, some friends and I crawled up to the bronze horses and carved our initials on one. Up until then we had thought they were gold. There was a stairway that wound around and around the dome. During the State Fair, people could climb up there and look out at the whole city.

In about 1929, I skipped school one day and went to watch Steve Holman, the stunt pilot they named Holman Field after, break the record by doing over 1400 loop-de-loops!
(Melvin Frerck--St. Paul, MN--1920s)

BUBBLE GUM

Although I lived just three houses away from Kircher's Corner Grocery Store in St. Paul's Midway area, I somehow never managed to be the first one in line for a precious "one" piece of bubble gum! Immediately following World War II, bubble gum was a rare find. Once the word hit the neighborhood kid "grapevine" that Mr. Kircher was getting his rare shipment, mass hysteria reigned, followed closely by a stampede home for the single penny to make the purchase.

The line moved quickly, but so did the carefully rationed-out gum. Some of the latecomers were left in line with a penny in their hand, tears in their eyes, and filled with the hope of being one of the lucky recipients next time.

That small, square, pink piece of "Fleer's Double Bubble," complete with a tiny, folded, comic inside, was our guarded treasure! By day, we chewed and blew bubbles until our jaws ached. Bedtime found us carefully stashing the single wad safely in its wrapper, only to start chewing again at daybreak!
(Caroleann L. Seidenkranz--St. Paul, MN--1940s)

SLOPOKE SUCKERS AND SUNFLOWER SEEDS

Slopoke suckers and sunflower seeds were a favorite during summer baseball games. Some people chewed up the whole sunflower seed, including the shell, and swallowed it. My friends and I didn't, because we were told if we did, it would get in our appendix and cause appendicitis!
(Vicki A. Johnson--Groton, SD--1950s)

As children, we had few toys--only a box full or so. Walkie-talkies were only in Dick Tracy's imagination, so we substituted oatmeal boxes, which were connected to carefully suspended taut strings that transmitted our voices quite well over some remarkable distances. Through this invention, we learned the theory of sound-wave transmission.

In the 1930s, as electricity came to our farm, we teenagers couldn't afford an electronic phonograph (rather new on the market), so we decided to try to make one. From an auto junk pile, we retrieved a horn motor. The speed was controlled by a rheostat made from an old aluminum pan and salt water. The magnetic phono tone arm was a counterbalanced, discarded, wall telephone receiver; to its diaphragm we connected a needle. The fidelity was horrible, but it worked!
(Ruben F. Schmidt--Shawano Co., WI--1920s-30s)

A ROLL OF ONE HUNDRED DOLLAR BILLS

My grandfather kept a roll of one hundred dollar bills on his dresser. I took a roll once, spent some of the money, and threw the rest over the neighbor's fence (to store it!). Then, I went there when I needed some money.

One day when Grandfather and the neighbor were talking over the fence, they spotted the money. The neighbor said it was his, but Grandfather suspected what had happened. A battle over the money ensued, and Grandfather ended up taking him to court. He told me to just tell the truth--to say that I had taken the money and put it there. However, when the judge asked if I had done it, I replied, "No." I got a wallop with his cane for that! In spite of my "testimony," Grandpa did eventually get his money back.
(James C. Zappa, Sr.--Cumberland, WI--1930s)

THE WINE TASTED A LITTLE WEAK

My grandfather kept a ten-gallon barrel of wine, which had a plug in it, in the basement. When I was about ten, I discovered that you could pull the plug out, put a straw in, and sample the wine. I would do this periodically, refilling it with water so you couldn't tell that any wine was missing.

When my grandfather's brother came from Italy to visit, they had some wine and immediately discovered that it tasted a little weak. Grandfather knew right away what had happened, and I got a good wallop on my legs with his cane for that, too.
(James C. Zappa, Sr.--Cumberland, WI--1930s)

When my cousins would come over to our farm for a little afternoon fun, we would go up on the platform in our barn, take the ropes that were used to pull up the hay, and swing way out over a plank driveway floor. One time when I was about ten years old, I happened to be the unlucky one who got the rope that didn't have a knot tied in it. When I swung out over the plank floor, I fell straight down (about twelve to fourteen feet)! I sat there dazed for awhile, and then everyone helped me into the house. Luckily, I didn't have any broken bones, but that quickly ended our afternoon fun.
(Elizabeth Juhl--Fenton, IA--early 1900s)

SUNDAY MORNING WATER TOWER CLIMB

On Sunday mornings, I had a newspaper route which I usually started around 5:30 or 6:00. When I had completed my route an hour or so later, I joined with my longtime childhood friend and partner in crime, who had also just finished his paper route. We then proceeded to climb the local water tower in the early morning hours when no one else was around to prevent us from doing such a foolish thing.

As one would expect, in the morning the tower and its girders were coated with dew, which made it extremely slippery. To complicate the climbing even more, there were no actual steps--just cross members in the beams, which you could sort of climb like a lopsided ladder. The best part came when you got to the top of the tank, which required an intricate maneuver to get from the tank of the tower to the roof. The roof protruded over the tank by about two or three feet, and although there was a ladder up the side of the tank and on the roof, you had to extend your body out to grab hold of the roof ladder, which then left your body dangling in midair while you pulled yourself up onto the roof. Then it was a few short steps to the light, where we would sit and gaze out on the scenery.

Our last act in this height-conquering ritual was to touch the light, which was the tallest part of the tower, and then take off our jackets and watch them slowly sail to the ground--like kites that had gone astray. I'll never know what possessed us to do this, other than the fact that it was a challenge, and in a small Midwest town, challenges became the thing to do.

Anyhow, one Sunday morning someone saw our jackets floating to the ground. We were caught red-handed! This activity came to a quick end when our fathers were told what we had been up to. However, this did not deter us in the least from seeking out other challenges, which were far more abundant in a small community than one would realize. It only meant that one had to be a little more inventive, and being young lads, fear was the farthest thing from our minds.

When I look back on this bit of foolishness, I'm just simply glad that I'm alive to tell it. You certainly couldn't get me to do the same thing today, even if I was paid!
(Mike Falk--Lake Crystal, MN--1950s)

SOYBEAN SWIMMING

On Saturday mornings, for an occasional diversion, my long-time friend (with whom I climbed the water tower) and I would go soybean swimming in the local grain elevator. We had discovered this unusual amusement simply by accident when we were looking for pigeons to capture at the top of the grain elevator. Although the grain elevator was closed Saturday mornings, we managed to find a small opening, which had obviously been left there to tempt young people to enter!

We would climb up to the top of the grain elevator and proceed to dive into the silo of soybeans, which acted like millions of tiny ball bearings on your body, giving almost the sensation of floating on water. We would then proceed to swim through the soybeans for awhile, until it either got boring or our clothes were so filled with the little ball bearings that we had to go down and empty them out.
(Mike Falk--Lake Crystal, MN--1950s)

NO EGGS TODAY

When I was a youngster, after I finished my chores, such as picking up cobs in the hog yard or sticks in the grove, I could go off exploring, climbing trees, etc. However, I was given specific instructions not to bother the bird nests in the trees. Mother had told me specifically not to touch any blue eggs, as they were special. I should leave them alone, as the birds that would hatch in the spring would be pretty and sing nice songs.

One particular day as I was climbing in a tree, I spotted a bird's nest. As I got close enough to reach into the nest, temptation got the best of me. "Oh boy, eggs, and three of them at that! Now, how am I going to get these three eggs down to the ground?" My intention was to use the eggs to make mud pies.

Since I had on my father's overalls, I had two pockets handy, but what was I to do with the third? Well, I decided to put it in my mouth! That was fine until I ran out of branches on my way down the tree and had to jump the rest of the way. CRACK!! You guessed it! The egg in my mouth cracked when I jumped, and when I spit it out, a little bird nearly ready to hatch emerged. I spit and spit until I thought I'd lost my tongue! It was terrible! I learned my lesson, and the other two eggs went back into the nest. To this day, I don't ever like to eat an egg!
(Marcile Hansen--Ringsted, IA--1920s)

An annual event in our small town was stealing apples late at night in the summer. One older gentleman protected his apples by hiding in a shed with a shotgun. Our gang was known to steal a few watermelons and pumpkins in the fall, too!

My uncle was the city policeman, so my gang was privy to inside information--where to stay away from, who had complained, etc. Having an uncle for a policeman had its disadvantages, too, like when he patrolled the favorite "parking" places!

Many of my friends tried smoking at one time or another. My most memorable smoke was when I went with my friend to her lake cottage. We would start a fire and then find driftwood to smoke. It had to be just right in order to draw air through. We became pretty good at telling what was good just by looking at it.

(Vicki A. Johnson--Groton, SD--1950s)

THE CLIMBER

My husband, Lance, has always been known for his climbing abilities. As a two-year-old, he could shinny up to the top of the kitchen cupboards. His mother told me that when he was a youngster, he cut limbs off their huge oak trees by climbing to the top. The whole neighborhood watched in horror as his mother stood below yelling at him to be careful.

While camping with friends in the late 1970s, Lance would always be in charge of firewood. He would climb trees and pull or cut off dead branches to burn.

In Hawaii one year, the group we were with was sent on a scavenger hunt. One of the items listed was a coconut. We weren't able to find any on the ground, but that wasn't a problem for Lance. He scooted right up the smooth trunk of the coconut tree and retrieved a fresh coconut!

In Jamaica, we toured a plantation with coconut trees. A man demonstrated how the natives could climb the trees; then he asked if anyone wanted to try. No one volunteered, but as the jitney was about to pull away, we noticed Lance hanging from the top of the tree! He just couldn't resist.

Every so often, I look for Lance and can't find him anywhere, even though I know he is home. I have often found him walking around on the little overhang outside of our house. He climbs out a window and walks on the ledge to fix something, get a better look at an animal across the road in the woods, or just to scare the kids by looking in their windows when they least expect it!

(Shirley Hughes Selzer--Spencer, IA--1950s-Present)

"THE CLIMBER"

Minneapolis Star and Tribune photo, Minnesota Historical Society

1959

ANDY FALK

KATHY BLAIR AND VICKI JOHNSON

GAMES WE PLAYED

Mable, Mable,
Set the table.
Don't forget the
Salt, vinegar, mustard,
PEPPER!!
(Turn the rope fast)

Teddy bear, teddy bear,
Turn around.
Teddy bear, teddy bear,
Touch the ground.
Teddy bear, teddy bear,
Tie your shoes.
Teddy bear, teddy bear,
Read the news.
Teddy bear, teddy bear,
Go upstairs.
Teddy bear, teddy bear,
Say your prayers.
Teddy bear, teddy bear,
Turn out the lights.
Teddy bear, teddy bear,
Say good night.
G-o-o-d-n-i-g-h-t

HOPSCOTCH TOURNAMENTS

Every winter in the country school I attended, we had hopscotch tournaments. We drew the hopscotch grids on the floor with chalk. There was only room, by squeezing, for two grids between the seats, so there was one for the big kids and one for the little ones. The competition was really heated. I wonder if any of my contemporaries, sitting tense before a TV during the "Super Bowl," can remember being just as excited watching to see whether their favorite player tossed his leather mitten in the right square, or willing him not to step on any lines.
(Mae F. Hardin--ND--1920s)

CLOTHESLINE JUMP ROPES

During recess time at school, we often jumped rope. The jump ropes were clotheslines, and some were very long. There was a girl at each end, and you had to be good to play with those older girls. Most of the time you did your jumping individually, but remember, not too much or the shoes might give out!
(Jerrie Steinwall-Ahrens--Dakota Co., MN--1930s)

PERFECTING MY "HULA" SKILLS

A couple of years ago, my daughter got a Hula-Hoop for her birthday. I'm not sure who was more excited about the gift, her or me! It brought back all kinds of memories of the hours I had spent trying to perfect my "hula" skills.

During recess at school, my friends and I would have competitions to see who could "Hula-Hoop" the most times in a row. It also was fun to see what new areas of the body you could come up with to gyrate the hoop from. When we became bored with those two ideas, we used the hoops as jump ropes.

I have found that I can still swing my hips enough to keep the hoop going, but I don't think I'll challenge anyone to a competition soon!
(Shirley Hughes Selzer--Lake Crystal, MN--1950s)

MUMBLETY-PEG

Mumblety-Peg was very definitely a boys' game. The girls never played it, but they were allowed to stand by and watch. We kept our distance, because it was played with a very small pocket knife. Some of those knives were fancier than others.

The boys drew a circle about two feet around, usually in a dirt area--not grass. They would sit or kneel around this circle and,

in a certain way, flip the knife blade toward the center--the target. Whoever came closest to the target was the winner. I know they had some sort of score and rules, but I'm not sure of the specifics. There was never any thought of danger or violence involved.
(Mary E. Strong--LeCenter/St. Paul, MN--early 1900s)

THE TEETER-TOTTER EPISODE

At morning recess one mid-April day, I made the mistake of getting on a teeter-totter with Ralph, a classmate who outweighed me by about twenty pounds. While not basically a mean kid, Ralph did get a big kick out of someone else's discomfort. Each time his end of the plank got near the ground, he threw his weight onto it extra hard, thus giving my end a whipping effect which nearly threw me off my perch. This went on for a couple minutes, and I kept imploring him to stop or I would get off. He ignored me, so on my next turn at the low end, I attempted to dismount. My feet had just touched the ground when Ralph repeated his bouncing tactic. The swiftly-rising plank caught me under the chin in a vicious uppercut blow. Unfortunately, I had my tongue between my teeth at the time. The force of the blow lifted me off my feet, and I dropped to the ground, bleeding profusely from the mouth, my tongue nearly severed.

Seeing that I was hurt, Ralph and another boy came immediately to my aid, half-carrying, half-dragging me into the school building. When the teacher and principal arrived on the scene, they decided that I should be sent home, which meant that I was expected to walk the half-mile under my own power. Since my knees were still pretty wobbly and I was becoming sick to my stomach from all the blood I had swallowed, the teacher decided to send one of the bigger, stronger boys to accompany me. She chose, of all people, Ralph! He accompanied me all the way home until I had set foot in my yard; then he turned tail and ran full speed in the direction from which he had come.
(Allan Degnan--West St. Paul, MN--1926)

MARBLES

Marbles at our school was a game more akin to bowling than it was to the conventional style of marble playing. For the most part, two types of marbles were used--"immies" and "crockeries." "Immies" were very pretty glass marbles, all different colors, made to simulate a natural agate. Depending on their size, they could cost as much as a nickel each. On the other hand, "crockeries" were ugly marbles, which came in two colors--a dull blue and a dismal brown. They could be bought at the corner store for as little as five for a penny.

66

Occasionally, someone would show up with an "aggie" or a "steelie." An "aggie" was a true natural agate, which through a complicated grinding process was ground into a perfect sphere. These were truly beautiful marbles, and, even in the impoverished days of the early 1920s, might cost up to fifty cents. On the other hand, a "steelie" was a steel ball which had originally been intended to be a ball bearing in some large piece of machinery, but which had never reached its intended use.

To start a marbles game required a minimum of two players, although as many as seven or eight could participate. A boy would place an "immie" on a sidewalk division line, then sit down about a foot behind it, with his legs outstretched and spread wide to form a "V." Then the game would commence.

The "overboard" rule was an interesting one. When a game was in progress, there were usually as many kids watching as playing. Any "crockeries" that were "bowled" and missed, or hopped out of the "V" of the boy's legs, were "overboards," and could be legally grabbed by any of the bystanders. Thus, a boy might come to school in the morning without any marbles, and by diligently grabbing "overboards," he could go home with a substantial haul.

(Allan Degnan--West St. Paul, MN--1920s)

Minnesota Historical Society

PLAYING MARBLES, ST. PAUL, ca.1925

EARNING SPENDING MONEY

TRAPPING GOPHERS

When we were growing up, we had to earn our own spending money. There wasn't ever any allowance like the kids get today. In the summer, we girls would go out trapping gophers. We would get a bounty of two cents for a stripped gopher, three cents for a gray gopher, and five cents for a pocket gopher. Then we would go with our dad in the double buggy and horses to town to spend our money. Of course, in those days we could get a lot for one cent. We all learned to earn and spend our money wisely.
(Ada Ronnei Pederson--Pope Co., MN--1910s)

CORN DETASSELING

Corn detasseling is a Midwest phenomenon that I guess would sound a little bit strange to people from other parts of the country. As it was explained to me, the process of pulling the tassel from a mature corn plant neutered its sex. This allowed for a hybrid to be developed through pollination from the tassels which were left intact after every six rows of detasseled corn.

Corn detasseling was one of my first real jobs, aside from a newspaper route and mowing lawns during the summer. This was certainly one job I'll never forget, as it was unique from all others. It was a very lonesome job--just you, the corn, and Mother Nature.

The job usually started early in the morning when it was still somewhat cool and the air damp with dew, which meant that all the cornstalks were wet. You'd go into the field with a light sweatshirt, which became drenched with dew after only about fifteen minutes. The rest of you also became somewhat wet. As the day progressed, the temperature would rise, and you'd get that nice clammy feeling like you were in a sauna bath. With cornstalks rising at least six feet, you could not see where you were going, nor was there any breeze to provide relief from the sweltering heat and muggy atmosphere.

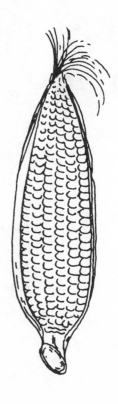

All tassels had to be pulled from each of the stalks, which seemed to number in the millions. Being less than six feet tall at the time, I had to do a considerable amount of reaching to get the job done. The inspectors who checked your work did not want you to bend the plants in order to pull the tassels, but then they weren't always around to see how the job got done! It was a very lonely occupation that caused one to feel somewhat humble in the midst of all this "sea of agriculture."
(Mike Falk--Lake Crystal, MN--1950s)

I worked as a carhop at the local drive-in for three summers. There weren't any stalls or drive-up windows in those days. We had to walk out to each car, take the customer's order, and then carry their order out on a big metal tray. The tray had a lever underneath which we had to "finagle" so it would fit on each car. The strategy varied, depending on the style of the car. This was a little tricky, especially when there were six heavy root beers on the tray at the time! Root beer was five cents for a small mug, ten cents for a large, and baby root beers were free.

Cars parked randomly in front of the little building. I can't remember how we kept track of all the orders--probably license plate numbers or the make of the car. It wasn't usually a problem, since we knew most of the customers in this small town. However, at the conclusion of band concerts or softball games, when everyone arrived at once, it was a little more difficult.

When people were through, they would blink their lights or honk their horn, and we would pick up their tray, hoping there might be a small tip. I still have my log book of those "all-important" tips. It was usually only a couple dollars a night, but important nonetheless.

One highlight of working at the drive-in was when the owner took all the employees to the Holiday House in St. Peter. When I was growing up, we never ate out, so this was an exciting experience. I remember being so impressed with the lavish decorations, huge menu, and wonderful hors d'oeuvre tray. I was overwhelmed!

(Bonnie Hughes Falk--Lake Crystal, MN--1960s)

FROM PAPER BOY TO PRINTER

When I was growing up, I had many diverse jobs.
--In the sixth through the ninth grade, I got up at 6:00 every morning to deliver the Minneapolis paper. My route was scattered all over town, so I rode my bike--my faithful dog, Mac, running alongside. The thing I hated most about this job was collecting, so I'd always put that off as long as possible.
--A couple summers I worked on a vegetable farm in the Minnesota River Valley, hoeing the weeds in the watermelon and raspberry patches. This was an extremely HOT job. I was paid a dollar an hour and could work as many hours as I wanted.
--One summer I worked at a pea viner. I remember later on when I graduated from college and was applying for jobs, a frequent question from the person interviewing me would be, "What is a pea viner?" It's really a rather simple operation. Peas grow on vines in fields; a machine cuts the vines and loads them onto trucks; then, they're hauled to the pea viner. The viner is a large circular drum that knocks the peas out of

the pods and into boxes. I logged the trucks as they came to the viner.

--The summer before my senior year in high school and the summer after I graduated, I worked at Yellowstone National Park as a cook at Old Faithful Inn. I was a breakfast cook one year and a dinner cook the next. I remember when Roy Rogers and Dale Evans came in to eat, everyone was quite excited. One source of entertainment was going to the West Yellowstone City Dump in the evening to watch the grizzly bears. In retrospect, this probably wasn't a real smart thing to do, especially in a convertible!

--In 1965, I worked at the Tony Downs Canning Factory for awhile. They canned turkey and chicken for army "C" rations. Little did I know that I would end up eating those "C" rations a couple years later when I was in Vietnam!

--While attending Mankato State University, I worked part-time at Carlson's Wedding Service, a company that employed many college students. I printed letterhead and wedding supplies, and even printed my own wedding invitations.
(Tom Falk--Lake Crystal, MN--1950s-60s)

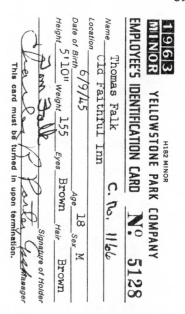

BOUNDARY WATERS BOY SCOUT CANOE BASE, 1958

LOOKING BACK

A WONDERFUL PLACE TO GROW UP

White Bear Lake was a wonderful place to grow up. There was a large meadow and hayfield near what is now Highway 96, where we would fly kites, pick wildflowers, etc. There were plants that had a lot of brown seeds on them that we called "Indian Tobacco." We tried to smoke it in a pipe, without much success. We also tried corn silk to make cigarettes, but didn't have much luck there, either. So we pulled lily pads out of the lake and dried the long stems in the sun. They turned black and hard, and were porous on the inside. We broke them in short lengths and had "organic" cigarettes which smoked pretty hot, so we had to give that up, too. Our folks went along with all these things, figuring we would learn the hard way. Some of the older kids had a pack of cigarette papers and a small sack of Bull Durham to roll their own, but no one really smoked very much.

The swamp west of the railroad tracks, with its large, dense, stand of tamarack trees, was another ideal place to have fun. We would set snares for rabbits, mink, and red squirrels, which we never had much luck catching. It was a good place for wildflowers, too, and you could be Daniel Boone without too much imagination. The kids also cut down smaller tamarack trees to make parts for homemade iceboats. The swamp drained into Lake Jarvis. In the spring the northern pike would migrate all the way up there looking for a place to spawn. We managed to get a few of them.

The island on Goose Lake was another fun place. The highway didn't cut through the lake then, so we had to have some sort of boat to get there. It was primitive, and we built underground shacks and log cabins (junior size, of course). Wild grapes, choke cherries, and lots of various flowers (blue and yellow violets, Dutchman's-breeches, etc.) grew on the island.

Even though there was no radio, TV, or many telephones, we were so busy swimming, fishing, skating, and sliding down hills with sleds, skis, and even pieces of sheet metal, that we always had lots to do. We made our own whistles out of willow branches, trapped muskrats, and speared frogs in the fall. Lots of times on a misty night, there would be so many crushed frogs on the highway that it would become slippery. We would go out with a flour sack, catch about half a sack full, and have frog legs for dinner the following day.

(Buster Johnson--White Bear Lake, MN--1918-24)

"BUCKTOWN"

I grew up in a Polish neighborhood on the northwest side of Chicago, called "Bucktown." Ours was a proud neighborhood.

Everyone went to the Polish church and the Polish school, and the good nuns kept us in line. Children were called home from play by their first name in Polish.

Easter was a big holiday in the Polish community. It marked the end of Lent and the season of Penance. At noon on Holy Saturday, children were dressed in their finest as they accompanied their parents to the local church to have their food baskets (containing ham, eggs, bread, cakes in the shape of lambs, etc.) blessed for the Easter dinner. In some cases, the priest came to the home to perform the blessing.

On Christmas Eve, a sacred tradition in the Polish home was the breaking of bread or wafer before the family ate the evening meal. The parents or elders always went first. As each individual took their piece, they made a fond wish to their partner.

As a youngster, I was raised by an older brother who took care of me while my dad was at work. My mother died when I was four. During those years, we went to a movie every Saturday. I can still remember the various serials: Buck Rogers, Tom Mix, Flash Gordon, etc. TV will never duplicate the daring feats of my heroes.

Chicago will always be home to me because of the memories I have of growing up there.
(Chris Twar--Chicago, IL--1930s)

LITTLE TOWN ON THE WIND-SWEPT PRAIRIE

Long ago and far away in the little town of Haynes, on the northwest border between South and North Dakota, a town so small you were almost out of it before you were in it, my father accepted a position as the chief mechanic for the state-owned lignite coal mine--a pretty good job in those very, very hard years. So, in the middle of summer, he moved my mother, my two younger brothers, and me to this desolate, god-forsaken place, where we lived in a house that sat right on the sidewalk and had a store front.

The most thrilling entertainment on a warm Saturday morning was climbing the low hills south of the highway and hoping you might be lucky enough to see a rattlesnake shed its skin; or listening in the night to the eerie, lonesome howling of the coyotes that lived around there in great numbers, and waiting for the answer from the half-tamed coyote (kept by the woman depot agent as her protector) to its wild brothers and sisters.

Much as I hated to move there and leave my friends and school, it turned out to be the most caring, friendly place I have ever lived. Everyone knew everyone else, and they wholeheartedly welcomed our family into the community.

One morning on the way to school, my younger brother and I ran like the dickens to see why so many people were gathered around the post office. When we got there, we found out that the rural mail carrier had whipped out his pistol and shot a

72

large snake on the sidewalk. They said it was a blue racer. I have never heard that name again, but, believe me, if the townspeople said it was a blue racer, it WAS a blue racer. Those folks knew about snakes! Instead of the usual warning when leaving your house, "Watch out for cars," of which there were few, it was, "Look out for snakes," of which there were many!

The year was 1930-31, when the veterans of World War I, my father among them, marched on the nation's capitol, demanding the bonus that had been promised them. When it was granted, my father took his bonus money and purchased a garage in a small South Dakota town about two-hundred miles away. How sad I was to leave this tiny town on the wind-swept prairie--the town and its people, with their welcoming arms and big, big hearts.

(Dawn Blair Gullikson--SD--1930s)

BOOKMOBILE MAGIC

In the 1930s, twice a month during the summer, the Ramsey County Bookmobile came to Lake Owasso and parked under the willow trees at the end of our lot. A tattoo on the horn summoned us like the Piper's call. Children from all along the lake shore trooped into the van, dark and cool against the bright oven of summer. Bare feet welcomed the chill of the brown metal floor. There we selected reading for the next two weeks, often wearing dripping bathing suits, which puddled on the floor and muddied the sand we tracked in. But no one scolded us. Instead, the librarians ignored the mess and directed each of us to books they knew we would enjoy.

There I first met Winnie the Pooh, Tom Sawyer, and Richard Halliburton, and discovered the excitement of *Gulliver's Travels* and the tragedy of *The Bridge of San Luis Rey*, on the shelves of the Bookmobile. At length, this battalion of children, armed with six or eight books apiece, left the van. That marked the end of swimming or canoeing for the day. Then, each of us found a shady spot, sometimes in community under the willows, sometimes alone in a separate haunt, and settled down to escape into written adventures.

In August the librarian said, "You may take books today, but they will have to be returned to the main library in St. Paul." What a shock! The last visit of the Bookmobile meant a return to the city, to shoes, to school, to scheduled meals and structured time.

Through fall, winter, and spring, we patronized our branch library. I formed the reading habit that has enriched my life. But never have I forgotten the special magic that existed on the shelves of the cool brown Bookmobile parked in the green shade of the willow trees.

(Anita Albrecht Buck--Lake Owasso, MN--1930s)

Growing up in rural America in the 1950s was probably somewhat different than it was in the city. When most of our parents bought their first TV in the mid-'50s, we caught up on the trends and styles by watching "American Bandstand" and other shows. Everyone had their record collection of 45's, and usually a cheap little phonograph to play them on. Later, it was a big deal when the long-play records came out.

We wore the fashions and colors of the day, went to ball games on Friday nights, and hung out at the local hamburger shop. Because everyone knew everyone in small towns, kids had to behave. Each kid had a reputation with the adults, whether it was good or bad. Also, local citizens wouldn't hesitate to discipline any child they thought wasn't behaving, or they would call his or her parents.

In the schools, there were always favorite teachers, and then those not-so-favorites. Rumors about teachers were rampant in small towns, mostly figments of someone's imagination. Class enrollments were usually very low. There were only forty-six in my graduating class. We were a close-knit group, and many of our activities included the whole class. Almost everyone showed up at the high school activities--ball games, plays, and music concerts.

Most of the kids "went steady," which was a big deal. Conversation included who was going with who. Occasionally, there were parties, but mostly you took your date out for a hamburger, malt, and fries, and then found a place to park. There was a lot of hugging and kissing, but most kids were virgins on graduation day.

Fifteen was "the age," because that's when you got your driver's license. Before that, you went to away ball games on the student bus. If you had a girlfriend, getting one of the back seats on the way home was very important! Once you had a license, then the task was to get the family car on Friday or Saturday night.

Living on a farm, I was always kept busy. Farm work and responsibilities started as soon as you were old enough to do the work. I resented not being a "town kid." They could hang out after supper every night, while I was lucky to get to town on the weekend.

During the summer, there were band concerts in town on Saturday nights. Everyone came to shop and to listen to the band. After each song, people would honk their car horns in appreciation. Each small town had a baseball team in those days. People really got excited about the games, and there were usually a couple of hot rivalries with neighboring towns. Another favorite summer activity was going to the drive-in theaters ("passion pits"). Movies about World War I impressed us boys. Going "in service" was a choice some of my friends made. Registering for the "draft" was a right of passage that some, I'm sure, approached with mixed feelings.

JOHN L. FELSCH

If we drank, it was usually a special occasion, like the last night of the class play or the end of a sports season. It usually didn't amount to much--maybe a few beers some older guy was convinced to buy for us. Also, some cigars or cigarettes were usually consumed at these occasions.

Everyone went to the prom, even if they didn't have a date. Most of us ended up at an all-night party. High school graduation was an important event. Our parents had an open house for friends, neighbors, and relatives. We kids stayed a respectable amount of time, and then went out to party.

We can't choose the time when we grow up, but, when I look back on it, the '50s was a nice decade in which to grow up.
(John L. Felsch--St. Charles, MN--1950s)

"SURVIVAL OF THE FITTEST"

When I think about that small nondescript South Dakota prairie town where I grew up, I first remember the streets. They were mostly gravel. The cottonwoods grew along the boulevards, arching to touch the trees on the far side. It was like traveling through a forest tunnel when I walked or rode my balloon-tire bike through there.

The homes were mostly white, each having a yard large enough to respectfully label it a yard. No postage stamp size swatches of green suburban grass surrounded by concrete; rather, "real" yards that had independence. These were lawns that weren't catered to. They weren't pampered with fertilizer, thatching, weed killers, or sprinklers. These were "survival of the fittest" lawns. Sure, the grass grew sporadically, looking as though it had its fill of home barbering, but you could play baseball or football, ride your bike, or construct a mini-road on these lawns. Neither they nor parents complained about abuse. They understood their role in nurturing children and families. Maybe the problems with the family unit in America today can be tied to over-coddled lawns. We ought to investigate that.
(Brian Blankenburg--SD--1950s)

SCHOOL DAYS

KATHERINE BOWEN, ELLSWORTH ESPENSON, ALICE ESPENSON

"WHISPERS"

When I was in the sixth grade in country school, my report card for the third and fourth month of 1924 had a 75 rating for conduct, and the notation "whispers."

We had double desks in the school, so two could sit at the desk, the top of which could be tipped down when not in use. Since school enrollment was low, I had a double desk to myself. My whispering was not with a seatmate, but with others nearby, and, evidently, loud enough to be noticed.

After receiving that low grade, I must have learned my lesson, as the conduct rating was in the low 90s thereafter.
(Ole Schelsnes--WI--1924)

"COCK-A-DOODLE-DOO"

The first time I remember going to school was as a guest of my older sister. It was not unusual to bring a younger brother or sister to school for a day. You shared their wood desk all day-- all those wonderful books, a tablet of lined paper, and the smell of the wooden cedar pencils. It was always a very special treat to borrow the teacher's pencil--unchewed, well-sharpened, and an eraser intact. It felt clean, too!

Being all of five years old, I noticed that the other students would get up and recite for the teacher. I heard a rooster crow off in the distance, so I stood up and did a very nice "cock-a-doodle-doo" for everyone, to their amusement and my sister's embarrassment. She never forgave me or took me along again!
(Jerrie Steinwall-Ahrens--Dakota Co., MN--1930s)

DOING HOMEWORK THE QUICK WAY

I attended first grade in a country school. There were three in my grade--two girls and me. When our teacher would be teaching some other grade, I would sneak out through the back entry room where coats and overshoes were kept, and come back in where the eighth graders were. I'd then have one of the boys do all my homework real quick, and sneak back to my seat and goof around! I don't think the teacher ever caught on how my homework got done so fast. I even got a better grade on it than Peggy and Janet did, both of whom were real smart! All three of us went on to be teachers.
(Gary Schlichter--Fairchild, WI--1943)

There was no hot lunch program when I went to school. We carried our lunches from home, wrapped in newspaper and tied with string. The lunch might consist of something like this: homemade bread, leftover roast beef or egg salad, cheese on Fridays, a home-canned pickle, an orange, banana, or apple, and once in a while, a powdered sugar doughnut. Those doughnuts made good "trading" material!

In colder weather the older girls helped the teacher make hot chocolate for lunch time. Sometimes I helped pass out the crockery--white farmer coffee cups. Oh, the smell of that chocolate still sweetens the memory!
(Jerrie Steinwall-Ahrens--Dakota Co., MN--1930s)

A LONG, LONELY WEEK

My brothers and I boarded at a country school five miles from home. We left on Monday morning and came home Friday after school. It was a long, lonely week.

As a boarder, one job was to pump fresh cold water from a well some distance from the school. We would use this water to fill the wash basins and glasses in our dorm rooms. Sometimes in the winter the old coal stove wouldn't heat up to the second and third floors where our dorms were, and the water would freeze in the basin. At times, there were up to twenty boarders at the dorm.

We had no telephone, and we would get lonely. We really looked forward to Fridays when we could go home. Some rides home were quite memorable, with a tractor pulling us in a wagon. I remember one bad winter in the early 1950s when we had to stay at school for three weeks!
(JoAnn Wanner Prom--Hebron, ND--1950s)

WALKING TO SCHOOL

We got to school by walking a mile or so. The road was a typical gravel road--hot, dusty, muddy, or icy. We would sometimes lay an old purse, with a long string attached, on the road--carefully covering the string with gravel. We'd then take the end of the string and hide in the tall grass until a car came along. When the car stopped, my brother would yank the string hard; then we'd all laugh and run like the dickens!
(Jerrie Steinwall-Ahrens--Dakota Co., MN--1930s)

We went by horse and buggy to the one-room school I attended. I do not remember much about the first year, except that the Hoyers and Henry Danielson were the only Swedes in the school. The other thirty-five students were Danes, and we really were not at all welcome. It was not safe for me to go out on the playground during recess periods, or even to the toilet, and my brother Henry could not hitch up our horse to go home until the others had left the school ground. That was my first experience with racial/cultural discrimination.

Henry Danielson had been raised in a Swedish home where English was not spoken, so he knew practically no English. The teacher knew no Swedish, so I, as the only other first grader, learned from the teacher and then taught him, since I knew both languages. If I had trouble, I had two older sisters and an older brother to help me.

Swedish/Danish relationships were really not much better my second year of school, but they were "tolerable." After my second year in the Rockfield School, Dad petitioned to have our quarter-section of land transferred to the Marshalltown School District, since that building was half a mile closer to our home. Probably the main reason was that most of the children in that school were Swedes rather than Danes. The petition was denied. However, it really wasn't too bad, for now my brother Henry was one of the "big boys." Furthermore, another family had moved to the farm next to ours and they had four children in school. Arthur, one of their sons, was also one of the "big boys." Thus, the Swedish/Danish balance was now nine to thirty-three, which was a little better. Also, a French family had moved into the district, and with three French children to pick on as the "minority," the Swedes were spared!
(H. Conrad Hoyer—Clay Co., SD—1913-15)

DO YOU STILL DO THIS KIND OF WORK?

In our conservative German farm community during the early 1930s, most parents viewed education beyond the eighth grade as appropriate only for the more elite. However, for my parents, education for us meant at least attending high school, even though the school was fifteen miles away. I believe I was the first boy from the Hohn Country School to attend high school. During the week I stayed in town, only coming home on weekends and in the summer.

In the summer of 1937, the year I graduated from Shawano High School, a farm neighbor called on my father and found me busily shoveling manure from the gutter behind the dairy cattle. He stopped in surprise and remarked, "Do you still do this kind of work?" I don't remember what I answered, but that question jabbed at my inner core; I was challenged to show him and the community what I could still do! It was time to instruct the community what "education" does and does not do for a lad!

The annual school district meeting would soon be held, with all the taxpayers attending. Aha! A perfect setting for me to make my point! Maintenance and cleaning were always on the meeting's agenda; and, as in prior years, the cleaning of the boys' and girls' outhouses would go to the lowest bidder. My father happened to be the chairman, and I startled him, and everyone else, as I bid the job down to $1.40! So, a few days later, I hitched Dad's horses to the manure spreader and, really rather easily, fulfilled my contract. I showed them what an "educated" lad was still able to do! Besides, Dad received some free fertilizer for the farm!
(Ruben F. Schmidt--Shawano Co., WI--1930s)

TRANSITION

The transition of graduating from a country school, where there were eight or nine students, and going to a high school of about 200, was a traumatic event for most farm kids. I was lucky that I had some city cousins whom I visited in the summer, so I at least knew some kids and a little about how to act. Still, most of us were very shy.
(Wayne Feller--SD--1950s)

ROYAL SCHOOL #1, 1929

THIS CERTIFIES THAT

Russell Hughes

has passed the State Board Examination in SPELLING

having written the same in the Public Schools of BLUE EARTH County

and attained a grade of Passed. PLUS

Date Apr. 30, 1927

County Superintendent of Schools.

RINGING OF THE BELL

At 8:15 each morning, Mr. Wilford rang the big school bell. It was tolled eight or ten times and was loud enough to be heard for several miles. This was "first bell." At 8:20 "second bell" was tolled; anyone still some distance from the school had better start to hurry, because they were in danger of being tardy--a "cardinal sin." At 8:25 the "third bell" was tolled. At this point, anyone still outside the school went in, put his hat and coat in the cloakroom, and sat at his desk. At exactly 8:30 a loud electric bell, known as the "tardy bell," was rung. This signaled the start of the morning session. The electric bell was also used to announce the beginning and end of each recess period, as well as the end of each school session.

All bells were rung by Mr. Wilford, our janitor, who although being low man on the totem pole, really "ran" Sibley School! Mr. Wilford timed the bells on his nickel-plated Ingersoll watch, which was kept in the breast pocket of his bib overalls. It was kept secure by means of a heavy black shoelace, doubled, and looped first through the clasp on the stem of the watch and then through a buttonhole in the overalls.
(Allan Degnan--West St. Paul, MN--1920s)

MEMORIZING POETRY

In poetry we read and enjoyed the works of Longfellow. Especially interesting were: *The Village Blacksmith*, *The Wreck of the Hesperus*, and *The Children's Hour*. These three were memorized verbatim by most of the class. Also memorized were some of the poems of Whittier, among them the very nostalgic *In School Days* and certain selected stanzas of Whittier's extremely lengthy work, *Snowbound*. *The Landing of the Pilgrim Fathers* was learned and recited during the Thanksgiving season. As the Christmas season approached, we learned Edgar Allan Poe's, *The Bells*, and another poem, entitled *The Bells of Christmas*. These latter two were often recited in unison before dismissal on the final days before Christmas vacation.
(Allan Degnan--West St. Paul, MN--1920s)

SPELLING BEES

My sister was very good at spelling bees. One time she won a little statue of a man and woman all dressed up in pretty clothes, probably doing the minuet. I still have it. It might

have cost a nickel or a dime back then, but it is priceless to me now, for my sister is no longer living.
(Jerrie Steinwall-Ahrens--Dakota Co., MN--1930s)

HE PASSED WITH FLYING COLORS!

When I was in the fourth grade, we learned the multiplication tables, how to multiply compound numbers, and long division. It was just about this time that my dad, who was a brakeman for the old Chicago and Great Western Railroad, came home from work one day feeling very dejected. The company was going to give examinations the next week to senior brakemen in order to find qualified men to be promoted to the rank of conductor. He knew his chances of passing were very slim because of his lack of knowledge in arithmetic. (Dad had left school before completing the third grade back in the 1890s). Addition, subtraction, and simple multiplication he understood, but long division he knew absolutely nothing about.

The following day I brought my arithmetic book home from school. For a couple of hours that evening, and again the following evening, we drilled in the rudiments of long division. Dad was a good pupil. With the book for a guide and with me to explain, he learned very quickly. On the third evening, I set up a few fairly difficult problems, which he worked smoothly and accurately. He was ready!

On the day of the examination, Dad went down to the office, oozing confidence. When he returned a few hours later, his confidence was undimmed. When the results came in, Dad was elated. He had passed with flying colors!
(Allan Degnan--West St. Paul, MN--1920s)

PUSH-PULLS AND OVALS

It is unlikely that anyone under sixty-five or seventy will know what the Palmer Method was, let alone being taught to use it. In our school, at a certain time each morning, we were ordered to clear the tops of our desks, get out pencil and paper, sit up straight, and be ready to start writing "push-pulls" and "ovals" when the old Victor Phonograph began to play "The National Emblem March."

After what seemed to be an endless session of wasting one of our precious sheets of tablet paper with those tiresome and ugly little scratchings, the music was stopped and we resettled into a straight-backed position, placed our arm flat on the desk, palm down, and wrote a number of words or sentences using a circular movement of the entire arm. The results were generally big, sprawly, and undecipherable. The teacher demonstrated the method on the blackboard, which was easy for her with all that

space to write on, but when that half hour was over, the majority of us reverted to our own little method of tight-fisted scribbling!
(Ida Posteher Fabyanske--Ramsey Co., MN--1920s)

LONG LIVE *THE GOLDEN BOOK OF SONGS*

Putting up the flag and reciting the flag salute were the first orders of the day back in the 1920s and 1930s in the good old country schools. But just as important was the singing period. Lucky was the school that had the luxury of a pump organ and a teacher who could play it, but all the equipment that was really needed was a supply of *The Golden Book of Songs*. It contained such a great variety--enough to satisfy everyone's choices. They included: "Battle Hymn of the Republic," "America," "America the Beautiful," "Dear Little Robin," "Old Black Joe," "Darling Nellie Gray," "Home on the Range," "Carry Me Back to Old Virginny"--to name a few.

I know they offer the basics of music and have lots of nice songs today, but the heritage is missing. Very few children know the songs found in *The Golden Book of Songs*. I think this is sad.

A few years ago when I tried to order a copy, I was told that it was no longer being published, but just lately I saw a new copy and was told that it is again in production. LONG LIVE *The Golden Book of Songs*!
(Mabel Winter--Wheaton, MN--1925)

EDUCATION WAS A NATURAL BY-PRODUCT
OF OUR FAMILY'S WAY OF LIFE

Before I was old enough to go to school, I was at home with either my father or my mother at my side throughout the day. When I got older, they were present before and after school. I received a great deal of my education outside of the country school's walls. My parents were busy with the unending work on a Wisconsin dairy farm, but I had an ever-present opportunity and expectation to "work" with them. So I learned, rather passively, to have a vision for accomplishment, and I learned first hand to work toward goals. Rather subtly, I learned the concept of motivation.

During non-school days, I was at home with my parents. My mother and I would page through the Gurney Seed Catalog, ordering "penny packets," small envelopes of seed packaged especially for children. Later, I planted these seeds, watched the seedlings grow, weeded them, and harvested the summer and fall crop. My mother was there to see that I understood the entire process. Also, I was shown maps and learned where I was in relation to the Gurney Company and Yankton, South Dakota.

My father had only a seventh-grade education, but his presence and interest in my learning made him an educator as well. Before I was able to help appreciably with the farm chores, while my father was milking cows by hand, he would pose problems for me, such as: "There are three calves in this pen and six sheep in that pen; how many calves and sheep are there altogether?" This learning gradually evolved into some real brain-teaser challenges! He made it a game, and I was always ready with "Give me another!" Education was just a natural by-product of our family's way of life.
(Ruben F. Schmidt--Shawano Co., WI--1920s)

"MARCH, LEFT, RIGHT, LEFT, RIGHT"

In the fall of 1923, the teachers got together and decided that the school needed a phonograph. Some excellent phonographs were being produced especially for school use, and they featured a large, laminated, wood "Morning Glory" type of amplifying horn. The power that turned the turntable was of the spring-wound type, so it had to be wound with a hand crank before each record was played.

Some of the records that came with the phonograph were marches by John Phillip Sousa. Favorites were "The Stars and Stripes Forever" and "Under the Double Eagle," which were played for our daily recessional out of the building.

Thirty seconds before the dismissal bell, the phonograph was started and the sound of march music filled the building. At this point we were given the order "Mark Time, Left, Right, Left, Right." When the bell sounded, we were ordered to "March, Left, Right, Left, Right!" We marched out of the classroom, through the hall, and out the front door, not breaking step until we were on the sidewalk.
(Allan Degnan--West St. Paul--1920s)

HOW I LOVED SCHOOL!

How I loved school! I attended a Catholic school in a small rural community in northwest Iowa during the Depression years. Since I grew up on the farm and was the oldest in the family, I found school to be a challenge and an escape from the drudgery of farm work. Therefore, as a student, I was studious and always tried to do my best.

To reward the students for good papers and good work, the nuns would pass out "holy cards," small picture-like cards of Christ or the saints. How excited I would be to receive a "holy card," and to bring it home to show my parents. To this day, I still have my collection of "holy cards," packed among my box of school memories.
(Darlene Lonneman Philiph--Ashton, IA--1934-41)

84 END OF THE YEAR PICNIC

I remember the school picnic at the end of the year, with all those wonderful games of baseball, tug-of-war, gunny sack races, wheelbarrow races (one unlucky kid got to be the wheelbarrow), relay races, and--prizes! And, of course, food--lots and lots of home cooking. Ladies would pile it high on the tables. We had such a good time! Now, it was time to take our shoes off for the summer.
(Jerrie Steinwall-Ahrens--Dakota Co., MN--1930s)

HE WAS THE "HIT" OF HIS CLASS REUNION

My husband and I were short on time as we hurriedly packed one hot summer day to drive to his small hometown high school class reunion in a neighboring state. We arrived at his dad's place just in time to change and leave for the pre-dinner gathering at 4:30. My husband rushed from the bedroom looking well-dressed, but there was panic on his face. He had forgotten his shoes!

Thinking his scruffy old tennis shoes wouldn't do, he decided to quickly drive to the one small general store in town to see if they had any shoes. They did--two pair--both men's dress shoes. One pair was much too small, but the other pair was just the right size. What luck! As he tried them on, however, his joy turned to bewilderment. One shoe fit fine, but the other felt very "different." It turned out one was a size 9 1/2 and the other a size 12! The clerk, seeing his dilemma, said, "Take the shoes--there's no charge!"

So my husband, after making me promise not to say a word to anyone at the gathering, spent the evening in one size 9 1/2 shoe and one size 12 shoe. I held out admirably until the dancing began. None of my urging would keep him off the dance floor, for he loved to dance! That's when I broke down. After stumbling across the dance floor, tripping over the size 12 shoe and laughing uncontrollably, I told! Everyone derived much enjoyment from his situation, and he was the hit of his class reunion!
(Norma Hughes Schlichter--Fairchild, WI--1980s)

CLASS OF 1935, LAKE CRYSTAL, MN (11 ABSENT DUE TO MUMPS)

GROTON, SD, 1920s

RECORD OF PROGRESS

Subject	1	2	3	4	Final
	B	B	B	B	B
Reading				A	A
Spelling					
Arithmetic					
Language					
Social					
Penm					
Art					
M					
P					

Letter Award

Lake Crystal High School

Lake Crystal, Minnesota

This Certifies That

Bonita Kathryn Hughes

Has satisfactorily completed a Course of Study prescribed for Graduation from this School and is therefore awarded this

Diploma

Given this twenty-ninth day of May, ninet

Superintendent of Schools

LAKE CRYSTAL H.S.

YEA! TEAM

EXTRA-CURRICULAR ACTIVITIES

LEADING THE BAND

Being head majorette of my school's band for three years was probably the highlight of my high school years. At least it rates pretty high up there with the junior and senior proms and dating.

Baton twirling isn't something that I had always dreamed of doing. I did take a few lessons, along with dance lessons, when I was around seven or eight, but most of my upper elementary and junior high days were preoccupied with wanting to be a cheerleader. My big sister was a cheerleader at that time, and she would teach me cheers to show my friends. Somehow, I never quite made it on a squad. Instead, on a whim, I signed up for a marching clinic. While parading around the gym mimicking the instructor, I was told I had real potential! That was the beginning.

After many hours of practice, I was chosen to twirl in front of, and lead, the band. I never knew there could be so much power in one little whistle! I could make that band turn circles if I wanted to. I, along with two other majorettes, took lessons from the Mankato State University twirler. She had performed at the Indianapolis 500, and could twirl with fire. We were definitely in awe! We learned so much from her, and we performed at ball games and tournaments. It was all very nerve-wracking, but a great experience. On days when we would march in 90 degree temperatures and my feet would bleed from popped blisters, I wondered why I had gotten into this!
(Shirley Hughes Selzer--Lake Crystal, MN--1960s)

CHEERLEADING DRESS CODE

As a "B" squad cheerleader, we wore circular skirts with no length designated, but they were well below the knees. The skirts were heavily starched and a real challenge to iron. Underneath, we wore gold sateen bloomer pants. This was to insure proper coverage of underwear when we twirled!

The year I "made" the "A" cheerleading squad, a new dress code was instituted. The skirt's hemline had to touch the floor when we were in a kneeling position. Yes, they were checked!
(Vicki A. Johnson--Groton, SD--1950s)

REAL FUR COATS

Our five queen contestants (all seventeen years old) went to the closest town that had a fur store and checked out, "on approval," REAL FUR COATS (mine was mink). No parent signature was required. We kept the coats for three days, wearing

SHIRLEY HUGHES SELZER

Coach, center, forward, guard.
All together, hit 'em hard.
Hit 'em high, Hit 'em low,
Yea team, Let's go!

Two bits, four bits,
Six bits, a dollar.
All for Groton
Stand up and holler.
Rah, rah, rah, rah, rah,
Rah, rah, rah, rah, rah,
Rah, rah, rah, rah, rah.
GROTON!

We got the pep (clap twice)
We got the steam   "   "
We got the coach   "   "
We got the team   "   "
We got the
Pep, steam, coach, team,
Let's give fifteen.
Rah, rah, rah, rah, rah,
Rah, rah, rah, rah, rah,
Rah, rah, rah, rah, rah,
Team!

Victory Victory is our cry,
VICTORY
Are we in it?
Well I guess,
Victory Victory,
Yes, Yes, Yes!

88

*Choose not a friend
From outward show.
Feathers fly high,
But pearls lie low.*

2 young
2 go
4 boys

*When you get married
And have twins,
Don't come to me
For safety pins.*

Yours till the buffalo
runs off the nickel

*Roses are red,
Violets are blue.
Rain on the rooftop
Reminds me of you.
Drip.
Drip.
Drip.*

My ♥  4 U

*Forget me not,
Forget me never,
Till all your teeth
Fall out together.*

them to all the homecoming events, including the bonfire. We had such a roaring fire that we were afraid the coats might get singed, so we had the guys stand in front of us to shield us from the heat.

When I think back, I marvel that we were allowed to get the coats in the first place, wear them everywhere, and then return them. People must have been more trusting then.
(Betty Johnson Rabe--Ellendale, MN--1950s)

AUTOGRAPH ALBUMS

Rummaging through my trunk, I came across a little pink book--my autograph album from junior high. The cover, which has a girl with a ponytail on it, is a dead giveaway as to the time period! Memories of sock hops, slumber parties, bus rides to football games, and BOYS (all those girlhood crushes), flashed before me as I read through the verses written by schoolmates, relatives, and teachers, and I thought about the significance each had in my life. Whether our relationships have flourished or faded, rereading the verses brought back a rush of sentiments as true as ever.

Autograph albums made the rounds at parties, in school, at family gatherings, and at camp. The verses, a hodgepodge of the sentimental and the mocking, contain compliments, advice, best wishes, and insults. Many of the verses relate to love and marriage, and there was always a flattering little verse or two by some smart aleck. Verses of a more thoughtful nature, however, balanced out those sarcastic entries. The overriding theme of the autograph verses is friendship, whether expressed in a sentimental, cynical, or humorous way. In addition to the verses, sayings and symbols are scrawled in the corners, along the sides of the pages, or even upside down.

I became intrigued with autograph albums and the verses written in them, and began researching these little books, which are often gathering dust in attics. Some albums from the turn of the century were unveiled. What gems they are! The covers are often made of velvet, and some of the pages--written in Spencerian script--are lavished with floral decorations and original works of art. The verses of that time period often reflect a high moral code and speak of death and meeting in heaven.

Teens of today have gotten away from the tradition of writing in autograph albums. They will not have these quaint little books of verse to remind them of the friendships they have formed through the years. But they will have their own memorabilia to look back on, perhaps notes written in yearbooks. Whatever the medium, there will always be some means of expressing friendship.
(Bonnie Hughes Falk--Lake Crystal, MN--1950s)

My autograph book, packed in a box and stuck in a closet, had not been looked at for many, many years. It brought back memories, both happy and sad. The happy ones were of school pals, tennis games, pow wows, and swimming and hiking with many of the people who had signed the book. I must admit that some were forgotten. The sad memories are of relatives and friends who have passed away. In reading the autograph book, it also brought to mind a dear friend whose wedding I stood up for and who I hadn't seen or talked to for a long, long time. I called her and after reading to her the date and what she had written in 1934, we talked for quite some time about families, relatives, and friends.
(Helen K. Giannini Zappa--St. Paul, MN--1930s)

MEANINGFUL AUTOGRAPHS

I was a Camp Fire Girl when I had my autograph album. The book was ordered from a Camp Fire catalog. Many of the autographs are from classmates, but others are from Camp Fire girls I went to camp with that summer. It was fun finding my album and looking at all the old autographs, but most meaningful were the autographs of my grandmothers and my dad, all of whom are no longer living. I didn't remember that my mom had written in it, either. It was fun to see my sons' reactions to "Mother's autograph book."
(Vicki A. Johnson--Groton, SD--1950s)

Let not our friendship
Like the roses, wither,
But like the evergreen
May it last forever.

Yours till Roy Rogers
rides the kitchen range

Kind hearts are the gardens,
Kind thoughts are the seeds,
Kind words are the blossoms,
The fruits are kind deeds.

Don't B ♯
Don't B ♭
Just B ♮

GROTON, SD, 1920s

Art Fleming Photo

LAKE CRYSTAL, MN, 1958

GROTON, SD, 1950s

Art Fleming Photo

LAKE CRYSTAL, MN, 1968

FASHION AND FUN

Minnesota Historical Society

ca. 1955

WHAT WE WORE

As you read the following fashion stories, think back to some of the outfits you have worn through the years. I bet some of them bring a smile to your face; or maybe a frown, as you wonder how you ever went out in public wearing that! (BHF)

PLAYING DRESS-UP

VERNELLE SUEKER FALK

Playing dress-up! What fun that was! It was during the 1920s that I was at the age of "dressing up" in my mother's--or sometimes a cousin's--old clothes. My friend and I would parade around the house, sharing tea with our dolls, and pretending all sorts of grown-up activities.

We would put our dolls in my big sister's wicker doll buggy, don dresses that would trail in the dust if we didn't tie a sash around our waist and blouse them up a little, put on high heels, and, if we were lucky, maybe a big hat to set off the costume. I don't remember being such a "brat," but Mother says if I couldn't have the brown shoes to match the brown dress I wore, I wouldn't play. They had to match! Sometimes I wonder what made me that way. Certainly not because we had many choices of clothes. There were no pretty red, blue, or even navy shoes in those days--just black or brown. To this day, it goes "against the grain" for me to be "uncoordinated" in either my clothes or my house.
(Marian Quam Stoneback--Lansing, MN--1920s)

MY SINGER SEWING MACHINE

My energies were often directed to the sewing machine. In the early years of my marriage, I practiced making school dresses or sun togs for my girls out of feed sacks, which then had pretty prints with flowers, stripes, etc. Ready-made dresses were few and far between. Midnight often found me whipping up something special for someone for a special party or Easter or Christmas.

The first thing I ever bought without my husband with me was an electric Singer Sewing Machine. It was also the first thing I ever bought and paid for on the installment plan! It lasted a good many years, and sewed everything from sheer wedding dresses to upholstered furniture. Having a yen for pretty clothes can get to be too much of a good thing, but it did make me learn a lot about the value of a dollar and how to make the "most" out of the "least."
(Marian Quam Stoneback--Lansing, MN--1920s-30s)

In the summer we wore very light, no sleeve, short-legged underwear called BVDs, but in the winter we had "REAL" underwear--long legs, long sleeves, button-up-the-front style. In the earliest years of the 1920s, the rear ends were of the four-button, drop-seat type, which were, at best, inconvenient.

One almost forgotten feature of long underwear was the itching. When a suit was new, the lining was soft, fleecy, downy, and lush. Then, after two or three launderings, all this downy softness underwent a gradual change. The lush fleece began to gather into mean little balls and pips. With each ensuing washing, these pips drastically increased in number and itch potential. The first few days of each long underwear season were pure agony.
(Allan Degnan--West St. Paul, MN--1920s)

BULGES AROUND THE ANKLES

Long before the blue jean, slack, snowsuit era, cold weather meant wearing long underwear to keep warm. We were willing enough when it was cold, but when the days began to warm up a little in the spring, we would try to get out of wearing it; however, Mother insisted one shouldn't make the change too suddenly or we would surely take our "death of cold." But as soon as we got out of her sight, we would pull down our stockings, pull up the underwear to above our knees, and go our merry way. However, getting that stretched out long underwear back down to our ankles and tucked smoothly into our stockings before we got home from school was another story.

We didn't fool Mother one bit. She knew the minute she saw those big bulges around our ankles that we had been cheating. What a day it was when she finally gave up and put the long underwear away for the summer!
(Marian Quam Stoneback--Lansing, MN--1920s)

HER BLOOMERS WERE BRIGHT PURPLE

Anyone who ever wore bloomers will never forget them! They were made at home from any fabric that was readily available, inexpensive, or left over from something else. If fabric was purchased especially for bloomers, it was usually cotton sateen. I'll never understand why so many of them were made in black, bright green, or bright purple. The black gym bloomers we wore were equally "attractive!"

The teacher's desk in our school did not have a back panel; in other words, it was a knee-hole desk, which always gave us a good view of the teacher's bloomer-covered knees. Her bloomers were usually bright purple and were held firmly below her knees with three rows of elastic. The hem of her crisp

VICKI A. JOHNSON

94

linen dress would curl up in the back from sitting such a long time, so when she stood and turned her back, we always got a rear view of the elastic bottoms of the purple bloomers!
(Ida Posteher Fabyanske--Ramsey Co., MN--1920s)

CLEVER USES FOR FEED AND FLOUR SACKS

Feed and flour sacks were a precious commodity during the Depression. When empty, they were turned inside-out, and we soon learned which end of the string to grasp in order to remove the stitching in record time. After that, they were washed, bleached again and again, and hung out in the sun. This process was repeated until they became snowy white. From then on, they became dish towels, luncheon cloths, underwear, aprons, pillowcases, and many other household items.

We dreaded the thought of using them for dresses, skirts, or blouses (not so now), although during those years it was often necessary. For a time, the 4-H clubs offered a "Thrift Project," and making garments from flour sacks took away a little of the embarrassment. Prizes were given at the county fair for the most clever and original uses of the sacks.
(Ida Posteher Fabyanske--Ramsey Co., MN--1920s)

TWO SIZES TOO LARGE

Mid-October was the time for the purchase of a new pair of shoes. These were leather shoes of the most durable type available--ankle height and not dressy. They were always bought about two sizes too large to allow for normal growth of the feet. However, by a mysterious process, the shoes wore out at exactly the same time they began to fit properly!
Allan Degnan--West St. Paul--1920s)

MY "OTHER" PANTS

I always had two pair of pants--my everyday (school) pants, and my "other" pants. My "other" pants were worn only on Sundays or other "dress-up" occasions. For example, my mother would announce, "Mrs. Nelson is giving a birthday party for Helen this afternoon, so be sure to wear your "other" pants.

"Other" pants became everyday pants through the natural process of attrition. The changeover invariably occurred coincidentally with the opening of school each September. At that time, my last year's school pants would be tried on and carefully examined. Almost always, they would be either too worn out or outgrown to the point that they must be retired to "after-school-knocking-around" clothes. At that point, a new pair of

pants would be purchased. These, then, became my "other" pants, and last year's "other" pants became my school pants.
(Allan Degnan--West St. Paul, MN--1920s)

"WHEET WHEET"

I always enjoyed getting a new pair of corduroy pants. These came in two basic colors--dark brown or navy blue. However, it was not the color, but rather the sound of corduroy pants that made them attractive. To wear a new pair of corduroy pants on a cold winter day made one "think spring." The pleasant "wheet wheet" whistling sound they emitted with each swing of your legs was very similar to the spring mating call of the Bob White. As the ribs of the corduroy gradually wore away, the whistling lessened, both in volume and in tone quality, until, as they approached retirement, they scarcely whispered.
(Allan Degnan--West St. Paul, MN--1920s)

THE "MULTIPLE" DRESS

My mother was a beautiful seamstress. My confirmation dress was a sheer organdy--white, of course. Very simple, with a sash and five rows of faggoting around the skirt, at the neckline, and on the edge of the sleeves. It was lovely!

We didn't have many dresses then. I became quite expert with "Rit" and the color remover. That dress became multiple--once pink, then blue, orchid, and pale green.

We always "dressed up" for church, Ladies Aid, and birthday parties--our main social activities. The female part of our congregation always sat on one side of the church, and, with much amusement and anticipation, looked forward each Sunday to my beautiful "new" dress.
(Ferne R. Warren--Lewisville, MN--1920s)

THE SNOOD

I used to wear a snood (small netlike cap) to keep my hair in place. They came in all colors and were worn for both sport and dress. Ann Sheridan, the movie actress, often wore one and made them popular.
(Elayne DeZelar--Red Wing, MN--1940s)

NOW GET YOUR APRON ON!

"Now get your apron on!" I can still hear my grandmother's words of advice to any of her kin--daughters, granddaughters, nieces--when we were about to begin any project that involved work around the kitchen. My grandmother learned to be very creative in her apron making. Her pride was that everything could have some use; nothing was ever thrown away in her household. Colorful feed sacks were often used, along with backs of worn out men's shirts. She could always find a bit of bias tape or lace to make them look pretty.

There were many kinds of aprons for various uses and occasions. The big cover-all kind of apron was useful for carrying things--eggs from the barn if you found a stolen nest; little baby chicks in the spring; or fruit jars from the cellar. They usually had a generous-sized pocket. I remember Grandma usually had something good in that pocket, like a piece of store licorice if I was in need of comfort.

There were the Sunday or "company" aprons, which were tied in the back of the waist with a neat, very precise bow. Then, of course, there were the wedding aprons. All the young girls serving for a bride's wedding would have matching little aprons made in the bride's colors.

Apron fashion has changed through the years, but they are still around. Today, a trendy gift shop might offer an elaborate, expensive apron for the man of the house to wear as he barbecues the Sunday night burgers. Also, you may find the cutesy "his and hers" aprons made especially for combined culinary efforts or "togetherness" in the kitchen. My dear grandmother would have been puzzled by this. In her day, the only aproned men she knew were behind the counter in the butcher shop.
(Joy Liberda--Dakota prairie--1930s)

WHERE DID ALL THE APRONS GO?

Once upon a time, every good housewife had a drawer at least partly filled with stiffly-starched and crisply-ironed aprons. Aprons, really catchalls, were as varied as the weather. They ranged in style from the large Hoovers and Mother Hubbards, to small dainty tea aprons for "best." Dark prints were used for the everyday aprons, as they didn't show the dirt.

A Sunday apron was usually white with, perhaps, trim of wide, hand-crocheted lace--made during any spare moment there was. Company coming? Mother would quickly hang her everyday apron behind the pantry door and don a freshly-ironed apron--now ready to receive the guest. Little girls had their pretty, but practical, cover-ups, the pinafore, or as they were commonly called, the "pinny," which made a school dress go for days.

Exchanging apron patterns was an enjoyment at "teas" or Aid. To be asked for your apron pattern was quite an honor. The beautiful, but impractical, tea apron pattern had to be borrowed or ordered from "The Farmer" or another magazine. My limited sewing skill was sorely tried when I borrowed a semi-circle apron to copy the pattern.

How many uses for aprons? Let us count the ways! Handy as they were around the kitchen, they had other uses, too, like drying a toddler's tears or wiping that little drippy nose! And how convenient the apron was if one walked out to the barn or hen house. An apron could hold corncobs for starting tomorrow's fire or a few wood chips garnered from near the woodpile. Perhaps one found a few eggs to be cherished for a cake or cookies.

Now, tell me, where have all the aprons gone? Does a new pattern possibly lie in the bottom of a drawer or box in your house?
(Margaret Seeger Hedlund--Pope Co., MN--1930s-40s)

SIMPLE CLOTHES

The clothes we wore were simple. My brothers wore sweaters and knee pants--never, never jeans or overalls; that was for work in the fields. Poor as we were, that was a strict rule. My sister and I always wore dresses. We might have had two each, one for school and one for Sundays. The bloomers most always matched the dress, and there was a pocket on the front of the bloomers to carry a pretty hankie. Our stockings were heavy lisle, many times mended by spring, and, in cold weather, the long underwear--yes, with the trap door! You were lucky if you had short sleeves on the underwear. Otherwise, you spent a lot of time tucking it up under your dress sleeve, pretending it didn't exist. I don't know why we were so concerned, because everyone wore it.

Shoes were practical brown oxfords--hand-me-downs--and worn until there were lovely holes in the leather soles. Then you could add a piece of cardboard for an inner lining, and, when Daddy had time, he'd get his shoe-fixing tools out and repair the shoes himself.
(Jerrie Steinwall-Ahrens--Dakota Co., MN--1930s)

DOG COLLAR

The 1950s was an era filled with many fashion fad memories. One seldom-mentioned fad that I will never forget was the "dog collar." No, not the one that our four-footed, furry, tail-wagging pet wore around his neck! Rather, the one that we girls wore around our ankle, atop the multi-rolled, white bobby sock.

There was a definite purpose as to how and why we wore these colored, plastic collars. Wearing the collar on your right ankle indicated to the world that you had a "steady" boyfriend. Obviously, if the collar adorned your left ankle, you were "available and looking." I know why I especially remember this fad; my ugly, green collar never moved to my "right" ankle! Instead, it found a permanent home around the neck of another popular 1950's fad, my autograph hound dog.
(Caroleann L. Seidenkranz--Anyplace, U.S.A.--1950s)

There were many memorable styles of head scarfs in the 1950s, but whether your choice was a red or navy blue bandana square, a long, plaid wool, or a tiny, colorful, chiffon square that barely covered your flowing ponytail, you ALWAYS wore the knot of that scarf "on" or "above" your chin! The higher you could manage to wear it, the better. There were few, if any, advantages to this fashion fad. On windy days, the scarf ends often wound up in your mouth. In Minnesota's frigid winters, you were assured a frozen neck!
(Caroleann L. Seidenkranz--Anyplace, U.S.A.--1950s)

MY MEAGER WARDROBE

In 1954 I went to school in town. A cousin in my class told me I needed to enlarge my meager wardrobe, so I sewed several cotton and corduroy skirts, using three yards of material each. The cotton skirts were 100% cotton and wrinkled easily. Later, I added the stiff, sugar-starched crinolines. We used about a cup of sugar to two cups of water, and then hung them dripping outside on the clothesline to dry. In winter, the flared felt skirt with bulky knit sweater and snap down snow boots were in style. Our feet got quite warm with the fleece-lined boots we'd wear all day in school.

We wore small scarfs, with tiny little pleats, around the neck. Sometimes we'd have some jewelry hanging from the scarf and tie it behind the neck. Pop beads and earrings with various colored snap-on buttons also were popular.
(JoAnn Wanner Prom--Hebron, ND--1950s)

PONYTAILS AND BERMUDA SHORTS

--Ponytails--I usually wore a bow in mine. For awhile though, I wrapped a strand of hair around the rubber binder to hide it. On special occasions I always wore flowers around my ponytail; one time in the spring, I wore flowers from a spirea bush. For the prom and sweetheart ball, I ordered a ring of sweetheart roses to match my corsage.
--Clip earrings (with changeable decorations); ankle chains; ID bracelets; proper pearls; long gloves (at least to the elbow for prom); white shoe polish on white fabric tennis shoes (cheerleaders' shoes had to be "sparkling" white); clear nail polish; strapless formals; saddle shoes (black and white with plaid shoelaces); white bucks (red soles) with a white powder bag always available to touch up smudges; two pair of bobby socks (one white and one colored); sweaters with white starched and ironed collars; artificial flowers at the neckline.
--Bermuda shorts--The first pair in Groton created quite a stir. Most kids said they wouldn't be caught dead in them, especially

VICKI A. JOHNSON

guys. Up until then, the only time guys exposed their legs was on the basketball court!
--Garter belts and panty girdles--I used a garter belt to hold up my nylons. I was told proper young ladies wore panty girdles so their bottoms didn't jiggle in skirts and slacks, and the crack didn't show!
(Vicki A. Johnson--Groton, SD--1950s)

THE "SHIFT"

One night I went shopping with my parents at Montgomery Ward. While there, I saw a dress that was really different. It had no waistband, but went straight down. We asked the clerk what it was. She said it was a new style called the "shift." It cost nine dollars, which was quite expensive for that time. Therefore, I was surprised when my dad, who was usually quite conservative, bought it for me. I wore it to school the next day. Because it was new and different, everyone noticed and commented on it, and it soon became a popular fashion trend.
(Cindy Salberg Lerfald--White Bear Lake, MN--1963)

CRINOLINES--THE STIFFER THE BETTER

All the girls wore crinolines in the 1950s. The more and the stiffer, the better. I loved hearing my crinolines rustle as I walked. I often wore several, so they would stick out farther. Mother starched them, so they would be stiffer.

One day, a classmate told me about a sugar and water solution that would make the crinolines stiffer than starch could. Mother agreed to try it. When I got home from school, she said this was her first and last sugar solution. She had hung the crinoline on the line to dry, and the bees descended on it!
(Merideth Allen Chelberg--Charles City, IA--1950s)

A STACK OF CRINOLINES

Raising two daughters during the crinoline years was quite an experience. There was a storeroom upstairs by their bedroom where they stacked the crinolines one over the other. One prom or other school affair, they had two girlfriends (and their crinolines) stay over. At that time I thought, "What do women do who have four daughters!"

I imagine that crinolines will surface again some day. I sure don't envy the mothers!
(Lucille Blair Johnson--Groton, SD--1958-60)

Prom time--dressed to the hilt--the necessary four can-cans under my formal to make sure it stuck out (pinned, of course, with safety pins). Sudden movement of the jitterbug--four can-cans on the floor around my ankles. Complete mortification!!
(Susan M. Grace--Groton, SD--1950s)

I HAD TRULY ARRIVED!

Remember all the young women's fragrances? I'll never forget Evening in Paris, which came in the little blue bottle with silver print, and which was available at the local drugstore cosmetic counter. As I became more sophisticated, Tweed was what I used. Tigress by Faberge, and Cotillion and Nearness by Avon were also popular.

One of my fondest memories is of a boy I met at the lake one summer. He was from Chicago (which is a long way from Groton, South Dakota!). For Valentine's Day, he sent me a bottle of REAL perfume, My Sin by Lanvin. I had truly arrived! This was used only on special occasions, like prom night.
(Vicki A. Johnson--Groton, SD--1950s)

MIKE JUHL

Minnesota Historical Society

MISS MINNEAPOLIS AND MISS ST. PAUL, 1925

WHAT WE DID FOR FUN

ROLLER SKATING

I used to roller skate on the sidewalk and two or three times a week at the local roller rink. I always rented skates at the rink; they fit over my shoes. Some of the more lucky ones had shoe skates; the girls' skates were usually white. The rink was very large and had records playing different types of music.
(Elayne DeZelar--Red Wing, MN--1940s)

ICE SKATING

Ice skating was very popular when I was growing up. The skating season started about Thanksgiving and continued to about Christmas, or until the first snow came. It was nothing to see a hundred or more people skating as soon as the ice was safe. Of course, we kids always rushed the season and got wet a few times--no casualties that I remember.

The part that sticks in my mind is the number of older people who skated. I remember one man in particular who had figure skates and usually dressed in a black suit and hat. He would make figure eights, jump turns, etc., and he was in his seventies! But we couldn't understand why anyone would want such short skates. You couldn't go too fast, and they sure as heck weren't suitable for skating completely around the lake as soon as there was ice around the edges. We got tired enough as it was with our regular skates, which clamped on our shoes, and came off periodically. Shoe skates, as we called them, came later. After circumnavigating the lake, we would go to bed, and the muscles in our legs would still be jumping most of the night.
(Buster Johnson--White Bear Lake, MN--1930s)

THE "WE" CLUB

When I was in high school, there were four of us girls who were close friends and did fun things together. When the weather was nice, we would sometimes pool our meager supply of coins (probably twenty-five cents each), and buy a few wieners, buns, and marshmallows. Then we'd walk a few miles from town and have a wiener roast in a grove of trees belonging to one of the girl's uncles. This was in the late 1930s, so wieners weren't expensive then. We called ourselves "The WE Club." (WE stood for wiener-eaters!). It didn't take a lot of money to have a good time in those days.
(Mary Simonson Thompson--Groton, SD--1930s)

SLUMBER PARTY

My last slumber party was on my birthday in 1951, but I had many before that. I really don't know how my folks put up with it, now when I look back. Usually Mother would fix supper for us, and we'd play some games and make popcorn and fudge. Then we'd all have to pin curl our hair for school the next day. One or two in our group would usually go to sleep early, but the rest of us would lay in bed talking and giggling half the night.
(Janice Meredith Fredericksen--Lake Crystal, MN--1947-51)

CAMP FIRE GIRLS

I began Camp Fire Girls in third grade and continued through until I was a sophomore in high school. Dating and extra-curricular activities then broke up our group. In junior high, Camp Fire Girls became very important to our social life. If we needed a party, we could always do it under the auspices of Camp Fire Girls!

I can remember our first campout. There were no sleeping bags then--we all had army blanket bedrolls. We hiked to Krueger's Grove, a mile out of town. Our breakfast consisted of an egg fried on a rock that had been in the fire all night!
(Vicki A. Johnson--Groton, SD--1950s)

WILDFLOWERS

There was a stream near our school, and in the spring we would pick flowers or clover and make wreaths and crowns for each other, or hold dandelions under each other's chin to see if you liked butter. If there's a yellow reflection on the underside of your chin, you do like butter.

I remember there was a rock along the road that looked like an altar. We girls would stop and put wildflowers and pretty berries on it and say our prayers. We were ever so holy!
(Jerrie Steinwall-Ahrens--Dakota Co., MN--1930s)

SATURDAY NIGHT MOVIES

As a teenager, Saturday night meant free movies on the vacant lot uptown. Our small town of about 100 nearly doubled as farmers from the surrounding area drove in for the movie, to do some trading at the general store, and to have popcorn from the popcorn stand. As I remember, the movies were paid for by the local businessmen, who ran a rather crudely printed or typed ad on the screen before the movie and during the changing of the reels halfway through the film.

Many a romance began at those Saturday night movies, as boys and girls met and sat together on a blanket, sharing a Tom Mix or Roy Rogers adventure, or occasionally something a bit more sophisticated.
(Marian Quam Stoneback--Lansing, MN--1930s)

OH, WHAT FUN WE HAD AS TEENAGERS!

Oh, what fun we had as teenagers in the 1930s! How we looked forward to Saturday nights. We danced the polka, fox trot, and waltz--never missing a dance all night long. The dances were in the town hall on a regular basis; otherwise, we went to ballrooms, of which there were many.

There were tag dances, where the guys were tapped on the shoulder and you then changed partners. There were also mixers, with the gals on one end of the hall and the guys on the other end. We danced across and then rushed to someone we would like to dance with.

We went to movies on Wednesday, Friday, or Sunday nights. My memorabilia consists of a list of all the movies I went to. I also have diaries, scrapbooks, letters, etc., of all those wonderful events. How I treasure those precious memories!
(Mae Hanson Hughes Kjos--Lake Crystal, MN--1930s)

THE "SILENT SCREEN"

I remember going to a movie almost every Sunday afternoon. The movie was five cents and candy was one cent. I imagine the parents felt it was a cheap way to get some peace and quiet on a Sunday! There was always a lady playing the piano, following the various actions on the "silent screen"--sad--glad--excitement--etc. Her "hoof beats" in the westerns were really quite stimulating!
(Mary E. Strong--LeCenter, MN--1923)

SATURDAY AT THE MOVIES

The line-up to get in to the ten-cent movies in the late 1940s is nearly as memorable for me as are the "flicks" that I eventually viewed! The line for the Hamline Theater, located on University Avenue, wrapped right around the corner onto Asbury Street each and every Saturday afternoon. There was always the "heads or tails" given in line by the early arrivers, which naturally led to many arguments! Once at the ticket booth, ten cents, plus an additional two cents entertainment tax, was collected.

Next stop was the candy counter, where, with my lone five cents, I would very carefully choose the best and longest-lasting deal for the entire afternoon. Good choices were the boxed,

chewy candies--Dots, Snaps, and Nibbs--but the Holloway sucker was by far the best!

Where to sit was another big decision, keeping in mind Mom's last words, "Don't sit too close to the front. You'll ruin your eyes!" At long last, the lights went out and a pretty predictable line-up followed, featuring one of the favorite western heroes--Hopalong Cassidy, The Lone Ranger, Roy Rogers, or Gene Autry. Sky King joined us on the screen frequently, as did Tarzan. Laughs were a million, with the *Looney Tunes* characters. Lots of commercial ads were intermingled, along with a full-length feature. There was a weekly "serial" that had kept us guessing all week, and was sure to entice us back in line the next Saturday!
(Caroleann L. Seidenkranz--St. Paul, MN--1940s)

SATURDAY NIGHT DANCE

No young people of today ever had more fun than we had at old Marston Moore on a Saturday night. In my much older, wiser mind today, I can see it as it was--a stark, shabby, old community hall on a railroad siding by a grain elevator on the Dakota prairie. But, oh, the happy times--the expectations of a young teenage farm girl, waiting with excitement for Saturday night to come. We worked hard on the farm all week, so any fun was greatly relished.

Come Saturday evening, the chores were hurried so we could get the whole family ready to go. When I say the whole family, that is exactly what it was--from babies to older grandparents. No one in our community had any thought of baby sitters.

The early arrivers would light the gas lanterns and start the coffee water boiling on the big gas stove. The mothers felt this to be their responsibility. Then, somebody would get up on the stage and start "tuning" up the fiddle. Several men in the community could do that. My dad and grandpa were both fiddlers. Usually two or three would take turns playing the tunes for the dancing during the evening. Sometimes there was a piano player, too; someone who would chord on the old piano and keep on key with the fiddle.

Boys and men gravitated to one side of the room and girls and women to the other side. Men always asked ladies to dance, never vice versa (well, hardly ever). If there weren't enough men to go around or they were too bashful, two girls would dance together, with much giggling and flushing of faces.

No alcoholic beverages ever appeared at these parties. Back in the '30s, no one could afford that anyway. Most of the boys wore new bib overalls and light shirts. Girls were pretty in bright-colored cotton skirts and blouses. Everyone scrubbed up very clean.

My favorite dance was the square dance and my favorite caller was my dad. I can still hear him--"All join hands and circle to the left, swing that gal that looks so neat, now the one with the great big feet."

As the evening wore on, a stag line would form at the back of the room, young men jostling each other about in good humored laughter. Some of the bolder girls might join in, but I was much too shy for that. As the little children and babies grew tired, they were put down on benches to sleep peacefully, covered with a coat or blanket.

Midnight came all too soon, and it was time for lunch--hearty sandwiches, homemade cake, and hot coffee in tin cups. Everyone would be hungry after so much vigorous exercise.

All good things must end, and all too quickly we needed to clean up the hall, wash the dishes, and put things away for next time. Then we piled in the old Model A Ford and headed down the road for home. I sat in the back seat with my sleepy, younger brother. As the car bumped along the dusty road, I looked out at the wide, dark, Dakota sky, and thought about that snappy, dashing, red-faced young farmer from across the township line whom I had danced with...TWICE!
(Joy Liberda--Dakota Prairie--1930s)

FUN IN THE FIFTIES

Our entertainment consisted of swimming at the pool or in the water hole, going to movies almost every Saturday afternoon, and roller skating. Other activities included Girl Scouts, slumber parties, and sewing club. Also, I spent several summers at camp.

We would meet at the local armory to skate. I remember doing the "bunny hop," a popular dance then, on roller skates. Some weekends were reserved for dancing. On the weekends that Whoppee John played old time, we would pull big garbage cans from the alley over to the armory window, and climb up on them to listen to the music and talk to the band members.

In school, we loved exchanging billfold-size photos. We could hardly wait to get our yearbooks, as we wanted everyone to sign their names or write something in it. It's fun to look through them now and read what was written.

My favorite singer was Frankie Avalon, and his song, "Why." He had several other songs I liked, too, such as "Venus," "Gingerbread," and "Bobby Socks to Stockings." Of course, Elvis Presley was a favorite singer. "Gone With the Wind" and "Peyton Place" were two movies I remember well. I read a lot of horse stories, and mysteries were my favorite.
(Elaine Lee--Benson, MN--1950s)

"AMERICAN BANDSTAND"

"American Bandstand"--what memories! I remember walking home from Harding High School in 1957 and 1958, singing

106

TEEN AGE SPECIAL
SUNDAY, JUNE 28 — 7:30 - 10:30
KATO BALLROOM
Vacation Dance Party
IN PERSON   IN PERSON
Gary STITES "LONELY FOR YOU"
Freddy CANNON "TALLAHASSEE LASSIE"
Frankie FORD "SEA CRUISE"
JOHNNY AND THE HURRICANES "CROSSFIRE" Orchestra
The MYSTICS "HUSH-A-BYE"
Barbara EVANS "SOUVENIRS"
Carl DOBKINS JR. "MY HEART'S AN OPEN BOOK"
ALL IN PERSON   ALL IN PERSON
Adm. $1.55 Per Person — Parents No Charge

TEEN-AGE ATTRACTION
KATO BALLROOM
7:30 - 11:00
SUNDAY, JANUARY 25
IN PERSON
WINTER DANCE PARTY
THESE TOP RECORDING STARS IN PERSON
BUDDY HOLLY AND THE CRICKETS "PEGGY SUE"
THESE TOP RECORDING STARS IN PERSON
BIG BOPPER "CHANTILLY LACE"
THE TOP RECORDING STARS IN PERSON
RITCHIE VALENS "DONNA" "COME ON, LET'S GO"
DION AND The BELMONTS "I WONDER WHY"
Extra Attraction FRANKIE SARDO
Admission $1.50 (Parents No Charge). Dress Right To Feel Right)

ANOTHER WONDERFUL TEEN-AGE
SHOW AND DANCE
SUNDAY, AUGUST 30, 7:30 TO 11:00
KATO BALLROOM
ALL IN PERSON
Record Stars Dance Party
GARY STITES "A GIRL LIKE YOU"
JIMMY CLANTON "MY OWN TRUE LOVE"
THE TEMPOS "SEE YOU IN SEPTEMBER"
THE BELL NOTES "THAT'S RIGHT"
and ORCH
SANTO & JOHNNY "SLEEP WALK"
DICK CARUSO "I'LL TELL YOU IN THE END"
ALL IN PERSON
Adm. $1.50 Per Person; Parents Invited (No Charge)

all the latest hits with my friends, Karen, Barb, and Carol. The minute I got home, I would drop my books, say "Hi" to Mom, and run next door to my very best friend Karen's house to watch "American Bandstand."

While we pigged out on cheese and onion sandwiches and homemade french fries, we could hardly wait to see if Justine and Bob would still be together on the show, and which song would be number one. We would sing, dance, and giggle through the whole show, and then wait for tomorrow and another "American Bandstand." This show taught most of my generation how to dance and what clothes were neat.
(Joanne Strong DiIoia--St. Paul, MN--1950s)

THE KATO BALLROOM

When I was in junior high school, my girlfriends and I often went to dances at the Kato Ballroom in Mankato, Minnesota. Since we weren't old enough to drive, our parents took turns taking us. We always looked forward to these special events, and it was so exciting to see our rock and roll idols in person.

I still have most of the advertisements that appeared in the newspaper, as well as many of the stars' autographs. Many times five or six groups would appear at the same dance, and there would be an M.C. I particularly remember Bill Diehl, who was at WDGY at that time. Some of the "big names" I remember seeing include: Bobby Rydell, Jimmy Clanton, Duane Eddy, Carl Dobkins, Jr., Johnny Cash, Freddy Cannon, Santo & Johnny, The Mystics, The Tempos, and many more.

On January 25, 1959, I stood right up front, totally enthralled by Buddy Holly and the Crickets, Dion and the Belmonts, the Big Bopper, and Ritchie Valens. A little more than a week later, Buddy Holly, the Big Bopper, and Ritchie Valens were killed in a plane crash in Iowa. We were devastated.
(Bonnie Hughes Falk--Mankato, MN--1950s)

Minnesota Historical Society

BUNNY HOP, ST. PAUL, 1956

HOLIDAYS

MIKE, TERRY, AND TOM FALK

NEW YEAR'S DAY

TERRY FALK

HAPPY NEW YEAR! That exclamation is heard around the world at midnight on December 31 each year. Out with the old; in with the new! A time for New Year's Resolutions—going on a diet; balancing the checkbook; cleaning out the cellar/attic/ garage; starting a diary or journal; the list goes on and on. It is a Norwegian custom to have rice pudding with an almond in it on New Year's Eve. Whoever gets the almond will be lucky all the next year! (BHF)

STARTING THE NEW YEAR

I always started the new year by going to my father's house New Year's morning. We would have coffee together, and Dad would put a shot or two of whiskey in the coffee. No matter how late I was out the night before, I was expected--and always was--at Dad's house bright and early. He was always waiting to begin the new year with me.
(James C. Zappa, Sr.--St. Paul, MN--1920s-60s)

NEW YEAR'S RESOLUTIONS

1. *forget ?? (boyfriend)*
2. *don't swear*
3. *control temper*
4. *study harder*
5. *go to catechism*
6. *keep room clean*
7. *be more thoughtful*
8. *don't gossip*
9. *take care of clothes*
10. *record in diary--*
a. kisses; b. rides; c. cars;
d. dates; e. shows; f. boy-
friends, g. important
songs; h. temperature;
i. kind of day
(Vicki A. Johnson--
Groton, SD--1958--
16 years old)

VALENTINE'S DAY

HOMEMADE OR THE PENNY VARIETY

About a week prior to February 14, we always prepared a cardboard box for our valentines. We decorated it with red and white crepe paper, and cut a slot in the top. Then, during the ensuing week, everyone brought their valentines to school and deposited them in the box.

Most of the valentines were of the homemade variety, some of which were ingeniously and cleverly cut out with scissors and colored with crayons. Many more were of the penny variety, bought at one of the corner grocery stores. Occasionally, some boy might be so enamored with one of the girls that he would get carried away to the extent of spending a WHOLE nickel on just one valentine!

On the afternoon of February 14, we distributed the valentines. Two boys, appointed by the teacher to serve as "mailmen," went up and down the aisles delivering the valentines. Everyone received a satisfactory "pile" of them. There was lots of giggling, a great deal of blushing, and everyone had lots of fun!

(Allan Degnan--West St. Paul, MN--1920s)

EASTER

THE HOUSE SHONE AND SO DID WE

Easter was the most important holiday in our home; it over-shadowed Christmas. Easter was preceded by six weeks of Lent, which meant extra fasting, extra church services which we must attend, and a thorough housecleaning. Our local paper-hanger was also a confirmed alcoholic, but he made a true effort to abstain from alcohol during Lent. Therefore, Easton's housewives tried hard to book him during that six weeks. Despite his "taking the pledge" during Lent, it was a little extra insurance not to pay him until the job was entirely done!

My mother was an accomplished seamstress, and by Holy Saturday all of us were newly outfitted for Easter; the house shone and so did we. The church bells on Easter Sunday pealed gloriously. The day started with Mass, of course. Everyone in the church was dressed in new clothes, and the Communion lines were like style shows!
(Loretta C. Lehman--Easton, MN--1930s)

GETTING OUTFITTED FOR EASTER

I remember all the preparation my mom went through to get her four girls ready for church on Easter morning. It started weeks before Easter, when my parents would take each of us separately to buy our dress, hat, shoes, gloves, and purse--all matching, of course. I chose my outfit very carefully; to me it was a very important decision. When I got everything home, I would hang the dress on the outside of the closet door, put the shoes on the floor, and hang the hat on the hanger with the purse. I then stood and admired the complete outfit. I couldn't wait to wear it!

When Saturday came, we had to start our weekly bath a little earlier than usual. Mom had to rip an old sheet apart so she could make "new" curlers for our hair. After our hair was all rolled up and a few bobby pins for spit curls were put in place, we started shining our new patent leather shoes with Vaseline. We had to make sure they were really shiny! After we went to bed, Mother washed all the ribbons for our hair. To dry the ribbons, she wrapped them around a glass so they wouldn't have to be ironed. In the morning, it was fun to see how the ribbons had fallen off the glass and looked so smooth.

I'm sure my mom was tired by the time we all sat down in church on Easter morning. She probably looked at the four of us and thought we turned out "okay." I think in those days, the parents had a certain pressure to try to outdo--or at least com-pete--in having the most presentable family on Easter morning.
(Cindy Salberg Lerfald--White Bear Lake, MN--1950s)

CINDY SALBERG LERFALD

As a child, we had a tradition of making Easter baskets and dying eggs the Saturday night before. We would design and cut our own baskets out of Clorox jugs, and decorate them with crayons, pictures, etc. Today, my two kids still dye eggs the night before Easter, but they don't make their baskets; they have boughten ones.
(Terri Ball Snider--Woonsocket, SD--1960s)

NIKKI SELZER

THE NEW DEAL

At Easter time we took eggs--large and small; white and brown; duck, goose, and chicken--to the New Deal, and traded them for a free soft-serve ice cream cone. Prizes were given for the biggest egg, smallest egg, etc.

They served beer in the New Deal (it was a bar), and my best friend was cautioned not to go in any farther than the ice cream machine. My Grandpa Jack played "Euchre" there, so I went all the way in. Also, you could buy cheap magazines at the New Deal. For a nickel, you could get paperbacks, comics, and any type of magazine that was a month old; the only "catch" was that the cover had been torn off!
(Vicki A. Johnson--Groton, SD--1950s)

BEAUTIFUL EASTER EGGS

My maternal grandmother, who came from Czechoslovakia, used to make beautiful Easter eggs. I remember sitting at her kitchen table watching her do them--my nose always too close!

First, she boiled the eggs. After they were cool, she etched designs on them with a special needle dipped in hot wax. These designs were flowers, leaves, and marks of all kinds. The eggs were then set aside to dry, before going into the "color bowl." Colored cloth or boiled onion skins were used to get the colors--red, purple, or blue. They were so pretty, we hated to eat them!
(Mary E. Strong--Lonsdale, MN--1915-23)

THE ANNUAL EASTER EGG FIGHT

Easter marks the annual Easter egg fight in our family. Everyone takes their hard-boiled egg and tries to crack the tip of the other person's egg without cracking their own. The more point on the tip of the egg, the better. Grandpa Giannini always picked out his egg the day before, and you better be careful not to crack his egg before Easter! He really took this egg fight seriously! The winner is the only one left with an uncracked egg.
(Helen Giannini Zappa--St. Paul, MN--1920s-Present)

FOURTH OF JULY

SCOTT FALK
MISSY RICHIE
ERIC FELSCH

I remember my dad telling me about the grand celebrations that were held on the Fourth of July in Cambria, Minnesota, the community where he was born and raised. Although Cambria is now somewhat of a "ghost town" compared to what it was in its heyday, this small Welsh community in the Minnesota River Valley continues to show its love for its country by celebrating this patriotic holiday each year. (BHF)

OLD-TIME SETTLERS CELEBRATE

Cambria held its first Fourth of July celebration in 1871, in a ravine back of John Shield's house near the bank of a creek. Seats were cut into the hillside, shaded by trees and covered with hay. It was said that those were the first cushioned seats in Minnesota! The stage was made from a hayrack on a wagon, and there was a little stream of water running between the seats and the stage.

On that memorable morning, a great crowd of old-time settlers converged to that one place, going in lumber wagons drawn by horses, mules, or oxen. Many were there before the sun was up. The program consisted of competitions in composing original poems, impromptu speeches, and essays. There were more than a thousand people present at this celebration. (Excerpt from *Our Roots of the Cambria Presbyterian Church, 1855-1980*)

A GRAND OCCASION

Celebrating the Fourth of July in the Cambria, Minnesota, area was a grand occasion. Many of those who had moved from the area or had relatives there would come to Wagner's Grove for the day.

The day before the celebration, a few farmers would go to the grove to destroy any evidence that it was a cow pasture! There were always one or two stands where we could buy ice cream cones, pop, and firecrackers, with the money we kids had been saving for weeks.

There was target shooting and horseshoe pitching for the men, and a baseball game in the morning. At noon, the families would all eat together. Shortly after dinner, we enjoyed a few numbers by the band and singing by a male quartet or choir. This was followed by a talk by some well-known person, usually someone from Minneapolis or St. Paul who had a connection with one of the locals.

(David Wendell Hughes--Cambria, MN--early 1900s)

When I was growing up in South Dakota, the Fourth of July was always celebrated by going to Tacoma Park for a picnic. My mother would make a new dress for me and my five sisters for the big event. There were no picnic tables in those days, so each group found a shady spot under the trees and spread a blanket and tablecloth wherever there was room.

There were so many people that it was hard to find a place to park. Sometimes, there were a few carnival attractions--merry-go-round, etc., but we loved walking on the footbridge over the James River, where we would watch the people swimming or boating. There were numerous summer cottages at Tacoma Park, and many people from Aberdeen spent their summer vacations there.

One time, en route to Tacoma Park, our family stopped in Groton at the home of my uncle and aunt, where I went to the backyard outhouse. While I was gone, my family loaded up the car and left for the park! Because there were eight children, plus my parents, nobody missed me. When I arrived at the park with my uncle and aunt, I still hadn't been missed! What a blow to my ego!
(Mary Simonson Thompson--Groton, SD--1920s-30s)

Minnesota Historical Society

ca. 1935

HALLOWEEN

HARNESSED COWS

We never heard of "trick or treat" when I was growing up, and even if we had, everyone lived too far apart for children to go from door to door. Halloween was more of a teenage holiday, and the favorite trick was tipping over outdoor toilets! Also, sometimes when farmers would do their morning chores, they would find that someone had harnessed all their cows, or perhaps dismantled a piece of machinery or a buggy, and then reassembled it on the machine shed roof!
(Mae F. Hardin--ND--1920s)

GHOSTS

I am now eighty-seven years old, but I well remember one Halloween night of long ago. I lived on a farm and went to high school in Wheaton, Minnesota. During my freshman year, I invited several friends from town to spend the night with me to go out "Halloweening."

It was a beautiful moonlight night. The little country school was on our land, hidden in a grove of trees in the middle of a field. We decided to go to the schoolhouse and play a few "innocent" pranks. We were loitering along, almost at our destination, when out of the grove came two ghosts, running and hollering. We didn't bother to go back to the road, but took the shortest path toward home--the ghosts in fast pursuit!

All of a sudden, we encountered a barbed wire fence. Somehow, we managed to roll under the fence with only a few rips in our clothing. The fence was a bigger barrier to the ghosts, however, with their flying white garb, so we gained a bit of ground there. The distance was about one-half mile, and I'm sure we broke a speed record! Just before we got home, the ghosts gave up, but we didn't slow down until we "hit" the house. (I wish I had some of that endurance today!)

Now, we had time to assess what had happened. Before going on our adventure, we had called some friends in town to tell them what we were going to do. This was in the days of party lines, and it so happened that our neighbors were "rubbernecking." Two of the older boys quickly got some sheets, and went to the schoolhouse before we did. This was one time a prank backfired!
(Mabel Winter--Wheaton, MN--1918)

One year, two friends and I spotted a junk pile. As a prank, we thought we would haul all the lumber, planks, etc., into the middle of the street. This was hard work, and it took us a long time to get all the heavy boards moved. Just as we were finishing, a cop stepped out of the dark and said, "You can put it all back now, girls!" He had been watching us the whole time, but had waited until we were all done before stopping us. That way, he thought he would teach us a lesson--and he did!
(Mary B. Twar--Two Harbors, MN--1930s)

HALLOWEEN NIGHT FOOTBALL

"The Green Bay Gools vs. the Houston Hags. This is Howard Ghostsell live from Gool Stadium. We are ready for the kick-off; Houston is kicking off. Green Bay gets to the 15-yard line. Joe Ug is the quarterback. First and ten on the 15. He is in the shotgun; he puts the ball in a shotgun and pulls the trigger. Frank Poof caught it and scored. Score 7-0. It is half time; stay tuned for more."

"This time Green Bay kicks off. Houston gets it to the 40-yard line. Henry Hag is quarterback. My how times flies; it is already the fourth quarter and it is fourth down. Houston is going for a field goal. They make it as time runs out. Green Bay wins. This is Howard Ghostsell signing off."
(Scott Falk--White Bear Lake, MN--1980--age 9)

THE "REAL" BATMAN

When my son Andy was three years old, I took him to a nursery school Halloween party. He was dressed as Batman, and was mighty proud of his costume. When we got out of the car, he saw another boy dressed as Batman. He stopped "dead in his tracks," paused a moment, and with strong conviction said, "But I am the REAL Batman!"
(Bonnie Hughes Falk--White Bear Lake, MN--1978)

ANDY FALK

THANKSGIVING

Each year for the past forty-five years, my family has gathered in Alden, Minnesota, to celebrate Thanksgiving Day. This family tradition has become very important to all of us. Therefore, this section will be dedicated to my family's celebration of this special holiday. I asked my Aunt Selma, at whose house we celebrate each year, to share some of her feelings about Thanksgiving, and a little about what is involved in preparing for the big day. (BHF)

FORTY-FIVE YEAR TRADITION

Since the mid-1940s, our families have gathered at our home in Alden for Thanksgiving. Five generations have been a part of this tradition. Some of those who were the little children when we began are now grandparents. Out of the first two generations, only two members are still with us. The others live in our memories and conversations as we celebrate each Thanksgiving Day. A special joy has been welcoming new members to our family circle--sometimes a new bride or groom--sometimes a new baby. Over these forty-five years, our gathering has grown from about fifteen to forty.

PREPARATION FOR THE BIG DAY

Preparation for Thanksgiving always begins with my fall house cleaning. In my large, hundred-year-old house, I have twenty large windows which must be washed inside and out. The drapes are all hung out on the clothesline to air, and the curtains are all washed and pressed. Some years have found last minute pressure put on workers laying carpeting, or some other special project.

A couple days before Thanksgiving, we move a lot of furniture around and get the living room all set up with big chairs, so the men can watch the football games on TV. In the dining room and den, we extend our two big tables, each seating twelve people, put the tablecloths on, and place the chairs around the tables.

SHOPPING

A couple weeks before the big day, I start shopping. I reserve two turkeys, one close to twenty-four pounds and the other about fourteen pounds. I start bringing home loaves of bread for dressing, which I dry on a cookie sheet in the oven. I crush the toasted slices with my hands, filling a big tupperware container. I don't like the crumbs to be too fine. If I buy some croutons, seasoned or plain, I smash them a little. I like to use a couple packages of Pepperidge Farm seasoned stuffing mix to add flavor.

My shopping list includes several kinds of breakfast cereals to be used in snack and bar recipes, for afternoon and evening munching. I also buy a couple gallons of apple cider and a supply of pop. Many years ago, we acquired a little Coke machine, which the little folks enjoy. A small bottle of Coke fits inside, and by pushing a lever, the bottle gets raised and fills the little glasses held by little hands.

Perhaps the shopping I am most "fussy" about is finding beautiful fresh fruit for my two table centerpieces. One of the fruit arrangements is put on a beautiful, tall, glass pedestal cake plate--a family heirloom.

Over the years, more and more of the traditional menu comes from the guests. Now, besides all the pies and salads, come the candied sweet potatoes, assorted raw vegetables, dips, pickles, olives, and bars. My part includes the turkeys, dressing, potatoes, gravy, rolls, and home-frozen corn. One year after a bountiful dinner, there was discussion on the topic "too much food--what can we leave out?" After much input, there was a consensus that we could leave out the peas!

THE DAY BEFORE

By Wednesday, the bars, snacks, caramel corn, cranberry relish, etc., have all been made. The rolls are baked and delivered by a friend. The house has been decorated with Pilgrims, turkeys, Indian corn, gourds, and pretty leaves.

This is the day we set the tables and get out all the serving dishes. When my son and daughter arrive, they are ready to lend a helping hand setting the tables, peeling potatoes, washing the turkeys, and whatever else needs to be done.

The last job of the day is making the dressing. To the prepared dried bread crumbs, I add lots of onion, celery, and sage leaves. Then I am ready to add the moisture. To the broth, which has been made from boiling the turkey necks and tails, I add a couple each of onions, carrots, and celery stalks, plus salt and pepper. To the turkey broth, I add several cans of chicken broth and a pound of butter. I stir and add broth until the dressing seems the right consistency. The prepared turkeys are placed in the roasters and filled with dressing. I always put a little dressing around in the roasters wherever there is room. This gets a little crusty and provides favorite samples for many of our gang as they check out the kitchen when they arrive.

To prepare the turkeys for the oven, I rub them with melted margarine. The smaller turkey is baked in the electric roaster. Over the big turkey, which goes in the oven, I place a very thin cloth or cheesecloth which has been marinated in a mixture of margarine and broth. At about 1:30 a.m., I put the turkeys in the ovens and go to bed.

The leaves, which I have saved and waxed, have usually come from very special places. Last fall, we vacationed in Salem, Massachusetts, when the leaves were carpeting the ground and tempting me to pick up a few "perfect" ones to bring home. The year before, our colorful leaves and acorn decorations came from New Salem, Illinois, where we visited the Land of Lincoln. Then, there is my Plymouth Rock. I like to feel that our Thanksgiving is a little akin to the Pilgrims and Plymouth Rock, as I look around to select a special place to exhibit the souvenir stone I picked up at the base of the big Plymouth Rock in Massachusetts.

THANKSGIVING DAY

We awaken on Thanksgiving morning to the good smell of roasting turkeys, sage, and onion. I am always anxious to check the turkeys and do some basting. If the turkeys look good and the weather looks beautiful, we are off to a happy start on this special day.

One of the jobs left for this morning is arranging the centerpieces, using the pretty fresh fruit that has been washed and polished. It is perfectly "legal" to eat grapes and whatever else appeals to our guests. By evening, the centerpieces look like they have really been enjoyed.

The real excitement begins shortly after 11:00 a.m. when the folks begin arriving--some at the back door and some at the front. They bring lots of hugs, greetings, and presents, as well as all the elegant food. After the long ride, everyone is always interesting in checking on progress in the kitchen. This is the time for sampling pieces of the crusty dressing or bits of liver or gizzard. The guys get settled in the living room to watch the football games on TV, and the women pitch in on the many jobs involved in getting the dinner on the table. The candied sweet potatoes are put in the oven, the relish trays are filled, and the pies are cut. In our family, there have been generations of "olive samplers." Discretion must be used to decide when it is "safe" to set the olives on the table!

"Oohs" and "aahs" fill the air as we view all the beautiful salads and pies that have arrived. Many of them are favorites which have become part of our traditional Thanksgiving menu. But we are always introduced to some new ones, too.

It is nearly 1:00 p.m. when we are ready to serve. Before we sit down, everyone joins hands for our special Thanksgiving Day prayer, which we all sing to the tune of "Edelweis." It is especially beautiful as we sing it through the second time, after a little practice!

After everyone is seated, some of the women become very efficient waitresses, and make sure everyone gets well-fed. After the meal, the delicious pies are served. Usually there are at least six choices--pumpkin, pecan, apple, sour cream raisin, lemon meringue, whipped cream, grasshopper, macadamia nut--to name a few. Sometimes, we sample a little of each! Everyone wishes they had saved more room.

When the first shift--mostly men and children--is finished eating, the tables are cleared and reset for the women. We have a great bunch of men who wait on us while we enjoy our meal. In the meantime, they wash up the dishes from the first setting.

In the afternoon, folks relax and enjoy visiting, watch the football games, play a card game or a new board game, or put a large jigsaw puzzle together. The children play with toys--paper dolls, puzzles, Fort Apache, etc. If the weather permits, many go for a walk around the lake. Mid-afternoon, we bring out a variety of snacks, apple cider, and pop. Our supper is served buffet style, and is made up mostly of leftovers. To top off the meal, everyone is given the opportunity to make an ice cream sundae to enjoy with bars and cookies.

THE DAY COMES TO AN END

As we come to the end of another wonderful Thanksgiving Day together with our special family, I am always so thankful and happy, as everyone leaves me feeling truly convinced that they really treasure our Thanksgiving tradition in Alden. We share many precious memories from all these years.

The children have always been special. They have made me feel so good as they bring me pictures they have made, stories they have written, and other presents. I am so pleased that each generation seems to inspire their children to look forward to going to Aunt Selma's for Thanksgiving.

A special year for me was 1987 when Bonnie had a project quietly going on during the afternoon. At the end of the day, she presented me a set of beautifully expressed comments from everyone present that day. They wrote about what coming to Alden for our traditional Thanksgiving celebration has meant to them. Even the youngest children who could not write had a page with a drawing on it. The expressions are beautiful, and I treasure them deeply.
(Selma Anderson Hughes--Alden, MN--1940s-Present)

Following are a few comments from family members:

Mother--The first Thanksgivings I can remember were when we lived above the bank. I would sit in the front window, looking around the lake, trying to catch the first glimpse of cars as they approached. In the afternoon, we kids would play, the women would sit around the table looking at catalogs, and the men would play cards (this was before television). Thanksgiving now is the only time our entire family gets together, except for weddings and funerals; that is why it is so important. Love, Tom.

HOW TO COOK A TURKEY

1. *Biy a 70 pund turkey.*
2. *Bring houm.*
3. *Unrap turkey.*
4. *Mix 1/2 loaf of bread.*
5. *3/4 can sage.*
6. *Little bit of pepper.*
7. *3 eggs.*
8. *Haf galin milk.*
9. *Litl bit of salt. Salt is not good for you.*
10. *Throw out gilets.*
11. *Put together seasonings.*
12. *Cook turkey at 100 for 1 hour.*
13. *Eat turkey.*
(Nikki Selzer--Spencer, IA--age 7)

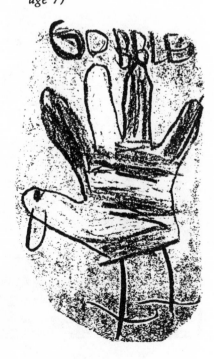

120

Aunt Selma--For as long as I can remember, Thanksgiving has always meant another very special trip to Aunt Selma's. The building excitement as we prepare to leave; the contest to see who would see the water tower first; the ride home with Grandma and Grandpa; singing carols and seeing the Christmas lights turned on for the first time. I remember snitching olives and chunks of crusty dressing before dinner, then snacking all afternoon. Thanksgiving is a day full of wonderful rituals and family love. It is more than a holiday; it is an annual trip into the past, a day when the entire family, even those no longer with us, are together and laughing again. I only hope my children get to share these memories.
(Mark Fredericksen)

CHRISTMAS

THE WONDERS OF CHRISTMAS

The windows of the sometimes steamy farm kitchen generally displayed intricate and curious designs etched by Jack Frost, to which I added my own carefully colored paper sketches of Santa Claus, sleds, decorated trees, and the like. I often spread out my projects on the bottom side of an inverted cardboard box, while I sat on a homemade couch padded with a rustling corn husk mattress. We called it the lounge. From this vantage point I could survey the whole room and the cold north windows.
(Ruben F. Schmidt--Shawano Co., WI--1920s)

THE CHRISTMAS EVE STREETCAR RIDE

Christmas Eve in the 1940s was special to my family. Since we didn't have a car, we would set out, all bundled up and loaded with gifts and excitement, to catch the streetcar several blocks from our home. We were on our way to spend Christmas Eve with my grandparents, aunts, uncles, and cousins. There were usually only a few people on the streetcar at that time, so we had it nearly to ourselves for this one-half hour trip.

After a Bohemian Catholic meal, singing, and visiting, we would once again catch the streetcar for the trip home--it always seemed to be snowing. On our way home, no one would be on the streetcar except my family and the driver. My sister and I would start singing Christmas songs, and soon our parents and the driver would join in. I was sometimes allowed to pull the bell string at our stop.

The sound, smell, feel, and motion of the streetcar is still in my mind and heart. I think of it every Christmas. We never missed having a car, and Christmas Eve was never the same once we got one.
(Joanne Strong DiIoia--St. Paul, MN--1943-51)

THE CHRISTMAS DOLL

When I was a little girl, it was a treat to go to our small town with my parents. One day while in town, I saw the most beautiful doll in the drugstore window. How I longed to have that doll! However, I knew it was impossible, as it cost $5.00.

We never had a Christmas tree, but my dad (Santa) would decorate with whatever he could find at home. Much to my surprise on Christmas morning, there among the Christmas arrangements was the doll. My grandma had bought it for me.
(Thelma Guenther--Alden, MN--1920s)

One year, I got a pair of second-hand roller skates under the Christmas tree. I quickly put on the skates and went down to the basement, which had a cement floor, in my Aunt Laura's house. I skated around and around this small area, having the time of my life! It didn't take much to please a child in those days.
(Marian Quam Stoneback--Lansing, MN--1920s)

THE BLACKBOARD DESK

Santa seldom brought his goodies in person, but came and went silently while we slept. I have forgotten about many of the gifts, but in our attic there is a large musical top that still plays, and a spring-wound metal "Model T Ford" that I drove up to a cardboard filling station. It was easily assembled and came complete with metal gas pumps operated by a crank.

The present I appreciated the most was a blackboard desk that I received when I was about four or five years old. I was fascinated with the fifty or sixty panels, each about five by eighteen inches in size, that I rolled into view for gleaning information. They stimulated my curiosity in such new activities as arithmetic, history, geography, grammar, and drawing. That desk was later used by our children. I still have it, but I need to repair and salvage some of those precious panels after so many years of wear and tear.
(Ruben F. Schmidt--Shawano Co., WI--1920s)

CHRISTMAS COOKIES AT BEDTIME

Every year, in the month or so before Christmas, I baked lots of cookies and stored them in our freezer downstairs. One of our sons had a bedroom downstairs, also. The year he was about twelve years old, I went into his room one night about 8:00, and discovered four nice cookies all set out to thaw on the bookshelves next to his bed.

I found out that each night he would take a few cookies out to thaw, so that they would be ready to pop in his mouth when he went to bed! I was glad I made this discovery before Christmas Eve, or I would have been surprised to find no cookies in our freezer!
(Norma Hughes Schlichter--Northfield, MN--1976)

Mom used to make white and dark fruitcake. After the fruit-cakes were baked, she would wrap them with a cloth soaked in Dad's homemade wild grape wine, and put them in a Red Wing crock to age two months before Christmas. They contained dried citrus fruit and lots of nuts and dates. They were terrific! Usually the fruitcakes were for our family. However, once in a while, Mom would give them as a gift to someone special.
(Elayne DeZelar--Red Wing, MN--1930-40s)

GIFT EXCHANGE

On the fifteenth of December, we would always have our school Christmas name exchange. Each child wrote his or her name on a small slip of paper, folded it, and put it in a box. Then, each student picked out a slip to see who they would buy a gift for. Then, on the last day before Christmas vacation, we would have our gift exchange. The monetary expenditure for these gifts was limited to ten or fifteen cents. A variety of small trinkets or toys in this price range could be purchased at any of the corner grocery stores in the area, or, if one managed to get downtown, there was a very large selection at either Woolworth's or Kresge's.
(Allan F. Degnan--West St. Paul, MN--1920s)

SANTA HAS A RING JUST LIKE OTHO'S!

When I taught in a rural school before my marriage, I asked Otho, one of the older boys, to dress up as Santa, and distribute the presents and candy after the Christmas program. His little sister was in the first grade that year, and while Santa was giving out the presents, she came up to me and said, "Miss Simonson, Santa has a ring just like Otho's!" I don't believe she ever realized that Santa really WAS Otho!
(Mary Simonson Thompson--Groton, SD--1940s)

A LITTLE TRICK OF MAGIC

One Christmas, my mother asked my brother and me if we had seen any reindeer tracks around the yard. We dashed outside, and sure enough, there they were, right up to our front gate! As it turned out, my dad and two uncles had pulled the cutter for nearly a quarter of a mile, and then had led a cow up one track and back the other. We were too young to notice that the tracks on the right side were backwards, where they had led the cow back to the barn. Their little trick of magic had worked!
(David Wendell Hughes--Cambria, MN--1900)

December 14, 1950
Dear Santa Claus,
Please bring me an electric train and a pair of skis and a sled and two Hopalong Cassidy guns and holsters and cowboy hat. Thank you for the toys last year.
Dennis Herman
P.S. I live right north of the funeral home on Lincoln Street. Thank you. Goodbye.

December 20, 1951
Dear Santa,
Please bring me a farm set, two guns and holsters, saddle, scout knife, wristwatch, BB gun, a big grader, field glasses, and a fire truck. I help my dad feed the pigs and I help my mom do the dishes and I make my bed every day. I hope you are safe. And I hope you bring me a lot of toys. Is Rudolph okay and all the other deer, too?
Your friend,
Dickie Hanson

December 25, 1952
Dear Santa Claus,
Last year I got an electric train. This year could you get me some more cars for it because all I got is five cars?
Could you get me some skate straps to brace my ankles and a Roy Rogers outfit and gun? Could you get me a pair of skis and a Tommy-gun? I would like it.
Paul M. Smith, Jr.

We always had a Christmas party at school, complete with a tree with candles, cotton snow, and tinsel. There was also always a Santa with a cotton beard. When I was in the third grade, I remember Santa reaching under the tree for a present, and catching his beard on fire from a lit candle! He was so afraid that we would find out who he really was, that he didn't pull the beard off until AFTER he had run outside.
(Melvin Frerck--Barronette, WI--1917))

December 20, 1951
Dear Santa,
    Are you coming to Lake Crystal this year? I'd like to have a bicycle or farm set, cash register, and ferris wheel. Why don't you ring the bell this year so I can see you?
                Love,
                Forrest Walters

December 25, 1952
Dear Santa Claus,
  Merry Christmas. I do not think I want much. I would like a little chef stove and some storybook dolls, ice skates, and some big books. Goodbye, Santa. I have been good most of the time. If I do not get any toys, it would be okay.
            Your friend,
            Donnis Ann Cramblit
P.S. My brother wants an electric train. My other brother wants a tractor and other things a three-year-old would want. That is all now.

December 24, 1953
Dear Santa Claus,
    I have been a good girl. Will you please bring me a Cinderella wristwatch, a doll and dollhouse, a trumpet, and some fancy things.
            Love,
            Roberta Johnson
P.S. And fill my stocking full.

SHERRY & VICKI JOHNSON

SCOTT FALK

For our very first Christmas together in my hometown in Wisconsin, my wife and I went out and bought the first tree as it was being unloaded. My wife was a very homesick girl from Denver, and we felt the tree might help. We hurried home to decorate it. I guess we should have suspected that the tree was dry, since needles were falling to the floor as we decorated it, but we were much too excited with thoughts of our first Christmas together in our own home.

Each day, we would sweep up a large pile of needles, until finally one day before Christmas, all the rest of the needles fell off. Not one needle remained on our "stick tree"! All we had was pretty bulbs, lights, and tinsel. My wife took all the decorations off the tree, while I went out to buy another one. Then, we decorated our second tree for that holiday season.
(Jerry Sutliff--Boyceville, WI--1959)

THE SCHOOL CHRISTMAS TREE

A few days prior to Christmas vacation, the Christmas trees were always put up and decorated at our school. The decorating was done by the children of each class. Although there were a few manufactured ornaments, most of the decorations were homemade by the kids. Strings of popcorn, laboriously sewn one kernel at a time and draped around the tree, looked very festive. The same was done with strings of cranberries. Many-colored paper chains also festooned the branches, along with tinfoil tinsel. There were no lights on the trees, as strings of colored lights were just becoming available in the stores.
(Allan Degnan--West St. Paul, MN--1920s)

SPELLBOUND

We never saw our Christmas tree until Christmas morning. We believed Santa trimmed it while we slept. My dad has a terrible fear of fire, and of course, we had real candles on the tree. Each evening after supper, he would place a bucket of water by the tree, light the candles for a few minutes, and we would sit there--spellbound! Too soon, the candles were put out. Fortunately, the emergency pail of water was never used.
(Mary E. Strong--LeCenter, MN--1911-23)

All my life, the Christmas tree was a big deal in our family. When I was young, we would leave early in the day to pick out a tree. My mother was extremely "picky," and we would stop at every lot in St. Paul. Finally, she would find "just the right one."

The tree would be put up a week before Christmas. We kids were only allowed to put on a few ornaments, which she would rearrange when we were gone! Each ornament was different and had a special meaning and story. Even the tinsel was put on piece by piece with loving care. Our tree was always perfect and loved by all.

To this day, my mom comes to our home and helps put up the tree. She still goes down during the night when we are asleep and moves everything around!

(Joanne Strong DiIoia--St. Paul, MN--1945-Present)

ADVENTURES
ON WHEELS

WE CONQUERED THE WORLD IN ONE DAY

The time was the summer of 1935. My friend Dick and I dreamed about taking a trip to Winona on our bikes, something that was unheard of at that time. The distance from our farm, which was in the city limits of Rushford, Minnesota, to Winona, was twenty miles. In the early '30s, Minnesota Highway 34 was rebuilt, which made it a super highway for its day-- all nice, smooth blacktop.

The bikes at that time were single speed. My friend's bike was a balloon-tire job. Mine was a Wards "Hawthorne," with small circumference tires, which I purchased in 1932 for about thirty dollars. I took the money out of my savings account just before the banks closed for good, but that's another story.

To get out of Rushford, you had to go up a long hill. The road was cut out of limestone bluffs about 400 feet high. To ride a bike up a hill like that was impossible, as we later found out. We had absolutely no idea how long a trip like this would take, but we decided to do it, come what may.

The day of the trip finally came. We got up early, ate a good breakfast, and the two of us, ages thirteen and fourteen, set out on the greatest adventure so far in our young lives. Departure time was 5:00 a.m. We got to the big hill I spoke of earlier, and when we got about one-half mile up, we had to walk, pushing our bikes the rest of the way--another mile or so. Then, on to Winona across the southern Minnesota prairie. What a beautiful morning it was!

About four miles from Winona, we went down a hill into the valley. The hill was similar in height to the one we had walked up fifteen miles earlier. What a thrill to go down this long hill without pedaling! We broke all speed limits! However, we knew as we went down, that later in the day we would have to go up again, but no use worrying about that now. We just enjoyed the moment.

Soon we were at my sister's house in the east end of Winona. The time was 7:00 a.m. We had made the trip in two hours. Unbelievable! We rode around town, taking in all the sights. We ate at a fancy restaurant (for us) and went to a movie--a very big thrill for two small town boys. As I remember, we headed for home--twenty more miles--about 4:00 p.m. I don't recall our arrival time, as it was old stuff by now. We had just about conquered the world in ONE day!
(Al Kjos--Rushford, MN--1930s)

AUTOMOBILES

"TIN LIZZIE"

Ah, yes--the old Model T Ford, or "Tin Lizzie," as everybody called it. Old Henry Ford called his first car a Model A, and he went through nineteen models before reaching the letter "T," which finally turned out to be a winner. It could actually be taken apart and put back together with nothing but a monkey wrench and a pair of gas pliers. There was no worry about the oil pressure, because lubrication was by something amiably known as the "splash system." When the little four-cylinder engine ran out of oil, it simply seized up and quit, at which time you poured in another quart and went merrily on your way, none the worse for wear.

There were some inconveniences. When climbing a steep hill, of which there were many in those days, all the oil went to the back of the pan and the front bearings ran dry. Therefore, it was wise to go about halfway up the hill and then turn the vehicle around and back up the rest of the way, so that both the front and rear bearings got enough oil!

My very first car was a Model T, when at the tender age of eighteen, I began courting my wife-to-be. Gasoline was ten cents a gallon, and patching inner tubes was simply a way of life. Now, fifty-six years later, we are still riding around in a Ford, except now it's called an Escort, and gasoline is more than one dollar a gallon.
(R. Kuehn--St. Paul, MN--1930s)

MODEL A

In the spring of the year, the creek that ran between our farm and the schoolhouse always went over its banks and made a new path. When it appeared to be a bit hazardous, my brother went that far with me in the morning and drove the car across. But one afternoon the water got higher and higher and was flowing much more swiftly. He called the neighbors to catch me and tell me to go another way (several miles farther), but because of a snowstorm that afternoon, the neighbors didn't see me coming.

I approached the watery roadway with caution, but decided to try it anyway. Well, the whole front end of the Model A fell into the washout on the road. I had to crawl out in ice water up to my hips! Luckily, there were neighbors just a few yards away, and an old German lady found me some dry clothes. Then we called my folks, and my dad and brother came after me. However, the car had to stay there overnight. The next day it was completely frozen in. It didn't hurt the motor, but it

Of my old Ford
Everybody makes fun.
They say it was born
In 1901.
Well, maybe it was,
But I'll bet
She's good for many
A mile yet.

The windshield's gone;
The radiator leaks.
The fan belt slips;
The horsepower squeaks.
She shakes the screws
And burrs all loose,
But I get 40 miles
On a gallon of juice.

And when I can't get gas,
I burn kerosene.
And I have driven home
On some paraffin.
With high priced cars
They give you tools,
Some extra parts
And a book of rules.

But all I've carried
For fifteen years,
Is some barbed wire
And a pair of shears.
And if old Hank Ford
Still stays in the game,
I'll buy another
By the same darn name.
(Author Unknown)

was not an easy task getting it out and running again. It is a miracle my brother let me keep on driving his car after that episode!
(Mary Simonson Thompson--Groton, SD--1940s)

IT WAS A COLD RIDE

We procured our first touring car, a Model T Ford, in the early twenties. Without any heater, and with the wind penetrating around the sides of the flapping isinglass curtains, it was a cold ride during the wintertime. It had no starter, so you cranked it, with the spark lever set just right. Hopefully, it would start rather than break your forearm if it backfired!
(Ruben F. Schmidt--Shawano Co., WI--1920s-30s)

1931 CHEVROLET

My dad surprised me with my first car--a 1931 Chevrolet. We went to town one day, and when we were ready to go home, he showed the car to me and said I could drive it home. I wished he would have told me before we were ready to leave so I could have driven around town, showing it off to everyone! The car was a two-door, with wire wheels. I sure had lots of adventures in that car.

One winter when I was dating Evelyn, my wife-to-be, we went sliding on a big hill near her place. When we were ready to leave, I tied the sled behind the car and was sitting on it. I guess she didn't realize I was on it, because she took off--lickety-split! I was hanging on for dear life and thought for sure I was going to fly right off!
(Raymond Hanson--Lake Crystal, MN--1930s)

THE SHINY, BLACK 1937 CHEVY

The first car I learned to drive was the family car, a shiny, black 1937 Chevy. My parents taught me how to drive by driving down the long, narrow farm lanes and on the back country roads.

When I was a freshman in high school in 1941, I obtained a school permit to drive the family car to school. This was a high point in my life. I was overwhelmed, because this offered me the opportunity to participate in extra-curricular activities after school hours.

Reminiscing on one occasion, I can remember "cruising" Main Street with my friends after a softball game. After driving up and down the street a few times, the town policeman approached me and sternly said, "Darlene, I think it's about time you park the car now." This driving experience happened dur-

ing World War II when there was gas rationing, and it communicated a powerful message to me that there was to be no unnecessary driving. It also illustrates how the whole nation was tuned in to the war effort, which was, "Get the boys home again."
(Darlene Lonneman Philiph--Ashton, IA--1940s)

UP ON BLOCKS

On the first of October every year, our cars went up on blocks. Even if we had Indian summer, it didn't matter. When October 1 came, the cars went up and didn't come down again until May 1. You just didn't drive during that period.

When we took the car off the blocks in the spring, we'd go shopping in Duluth. Our idea of shopping was to buy the clothes we had to have, and then go to the ice cream store for a treat--an ice cream sundae. We thought that was great! It didn't take much to make us happy then. I can still see those marble-topped round tables.
(Mary B. Twar--Two Harbors, MN--1930-40s)

"YOU'RE A FARM GIRL, AREN'T YOU?"

After completing the behind-the-wheel portion of my driver's license test in the early 1950s, the policeman said to me, "You're a farm girl, aren't you?" My immediate reaction was to look at my shoes to see if there were telltale signs of my having been out in the chicken yard just before going to town for the test! When I saw, gratefully, that was not the case, I answered that, yes, I was a farm girl and asked how he knew. He replied that it was because I was a good driver and that farm kids were usually the best drivers, at least at that age, because they had been driving farm vehicles for probably two or three years before reaching legal driving age. I'll never forget how happy I was to find out THAT was the reason he knew I was a farm girl!
(Lois Eugster--Oregon, WI--1950s)

BLUE AND WHITE CADILLAC

A 1951 blue and white Cadillac was the outstanding car of the 1950s for me. This 1951 Cadillac was quite "awesome." It was driven by the guy I had my first big crush on. He was a farm boy; I was a town girl. He came from country school to town as a freshman to begin his high school years. I can also remember the excitement when the first Thunderbird came to town.
(Vicki A. Johnson--Groton, SD--1950s)

Some guys in our town had their own cars and they often "customized" them. If an argument arose about whose car had the best drag speed, it was settled south of town late at night on what we called our "drag strip."

As far as my dad was concerned, it was out of the question for me to have my own car. If I needed a car, I could use his. It was a Nash, which definitely WASN'T considered a "cool" car. I took a ribbing about the reclining seats it had. Whether they were used or not shall remain my secret!
(John Felsch--St. Charles, MN--1950s)

THE DAY OUR "SUPER BEETLE" BECAME A PLAIN OLD "BUG"

One of our family's favorite cars was the bright yellow Volkswagon our son had when he was in college. It was a "Super Beetle" (with a special engine), and was the first car he had that was basically just for his use.

One fateful summer day (our son was home that summer), the "Super Beetle" became a plain old "bug." This is how it happened. I was driving blissfully down a quiet street, when the driver of a passing car motioned frantically at the back of my Volkswagon. I pulled over and found a stream of black smoke pouring out the back of the car. The engine was on fire! A resident of a nearby house came running out with a fire extinguisher to put out the fire, but we ended up needing a new engine. There went the "Super" part of our "Super Beetle!"

The yellow "bug" survived that and a few other traumas before it went to its grave. We all mourned a little when it died, but our yellow "bug" gave us a few good miles and many good stories.
(Gary Schlichter--Northfield, MN--1984)

THE "SUPER BEETLE"

THE "BUG"

For our son's graduation, my husband and I decided to get him a car--nothing expensive--just something for him to get around in during the summer. One day when he came home from school, he and I decided to visit a few used car lots, just to look at what was available in our price range--about $500.

Tucked away in one corner of the first lot we visited, sat a 1978 Camaro. Now, you have to understand that MY eyes and HIS eyes saw two different cars! I saw a beat up, rusted out, re-painted, junker of a car, while he saw a "mint" Camaro. I tried to divert his attention to some other cars, but, unfortunately, he was "hooked." So, for the rest of the summer, this "mint" Camaro graced the street in front of our house.

There were a few "minor" things wrong with this car. After all, you don't get a whole lot for $500! In our rush to buy this "gem" before anyone else got it, we had failed to look in the trunk. When we got it home, we discovered it had no spare tire or jack! Among other things--the doors opened with difficulty; it leaked when it rained; it used oil; the screw that held the air filter fell into the carburetor; and the shift lever wasn't connected. However, all of these "minor" problems were overlooked, and he loved his new Camaro.

It did get him through the summer (just barely) and we were able to sell it (at a slight loss). I'm sure the neighbors were glad to see it go, as it made quite a "roar" when he took off each morning.

In retrospect, I don't regret the purchase. The hug he gave me when we got the car home more than made up for all the "minor" inconveniences.

(Bonnie Hughes Falk--White Bear Lake, MN--1989)

THE "MINT" CAMARO

TRAINS

AH, THE THRILL OF IT ALL!

I am still very thrilled by trains--the sound of the whistle when it signals a crossing or warning, and the ride over the different routes--country, small towns, big stations. I love them all!

We lived across the road from the train tracks when I was very young. The depot was down the road a ways, and a lot of town people would go to watch the trains come in and leave. It was a special thrill if someone came to visit in our town. Small thrills like those can never be replaced or duplicated today.

I married a man who worked for a railroad--in the office. We took many wonderful trips together. I still like to travel by train. I find it very relaxing to sit back and listen to the clackety-clack of the wheels, and to watch the changing scenery. Ah, the thrill of it all!
(Mary E. Strong--LeCenter, MN--1911-Present)

RIDING THE TRAIN WITH MY GRANDPARENTS

Flying was unusual in the 1950s. If you didn't drive, you took the bus or train. My grandparents didn't drive, but they often took my sister and me with them on trips. We were willing to go by bus, but we preferred the train. You could walk around on the train. When we got bored, my grandpa would parade us through the cars, and we would stare at the other passengers as we walked by. Our favorite destination was the dining car. We had to stand in line at mealtime, but when we finally got to sit, it was at tables with white tablecloths. My grandparents would complain about the prices, especially having to pay fifty cents for coffee (but it did include a pot)!

After dinner, the train attendants made up our berths; we usually slept in the top berth and my grandparents in the bottom. Then we'd traipse down to the end of the car to the rest room to wash up, brush our teeth, and change into pajamas and robes. We especially enjoyed watching the toilets flush! Occasionally, we stayed in "roomettes," and then we had our own small bathroom. This was more luxurious, but it wasn't quite as exciting as having to walk through the train in our robes. Also, we felt more cut off from the other passengers.
(Meridith Allen Chelberg--Charles City, IA--1950s)

LIVING IN A RAILROAD DEPOT

I had a rather transient childhood; moving from place to place because my dad was a railroad agent. He ran the stations in many small towns in Minnesota and North Dakota. During the Depression, many stations were being closed. As they closed, the agents could choose another depot, based on seniority. If a station opened, per chance, the agents could bid on the job. Consequently, some moved by choice, while others were bumped from their jobs.

The depot was the home of the agent and his family. I lived in several depots while I was growing up. The depot would have an office and waiting room at one end, with the living quarters (which consisted of several bedrooms, a kitchen, and living room), and a warehouse on the other end. The depot I remember best was in Honeyford, North Dakota, a town with a population of thirty-two. We lived there the longest, about four years.

After hours, the waiting room became part of our home. There was a big stove in the center of the room and we took our Saturday night baths beside it. There was no water supply in town; people had to go to a well in the country. However, the railroad agent had his own water supply because the railroad had an ice house next to the depot.

A lot of times we used to play on the platform. As I recall, it really wasn't very wide. I learned a respect for trains; my mother instilled that in us kids. It used to bother me when my dad had to give orders to the train men. Often the trains wouldn't stop--the passenger ones would, but not the freights-- unless they had freight to drop off or pick up. But sometimes orders would come over the telegraph and my dad would have to write up the order and give it to the engineer. My dad would stand on the platform holding a long stick with a hoop on it. Then as the train came through, the engineer would put his arm through the hoop and pick up the orders.

We would play in the warehouse if it was raining. It was a great place to ride a bike in a big circle. In the stockyard, which was empty a good share of the time, we could do lots of climbing. We would see who was the bravest, who could balance best, etc. It was great fun!

Sometimes when we'd have relatives stay overnight, they'd ask, "How could you sleep through that noise?" But we got used to the noise of the trains and didn't even hear them at night.

(Pat McClure Hanson--Honeyford, ND--1930s)

THE RAILROAD OWNED THE TOWN

The railroad owned my hometown of Two Harbors. They owned the light company, grocery store, hospital; they owned US--lock, stock, body, and soul! They would furnish everything for various festivities--entertainment on the Fourth of July; treats at the Halloween bonfire, and prizes for best costumes; and bags of nuts, candy, and oranges at Christmas time. I remember that during the Depression all the men were cut from six days to three days, so that everyone could keep working.

Once a year we would take a trip on the milk train from Two Harbors to the Twin Cities. We would leave at 11:00 p.m. and get there at 6:00 a.m.--a seven-hour trip for that short distance!
(Mary B. Twar--Two Harbors, MN--1930s)

TAKING THE TRAIN TO TOWN

My father worked for the Northern Pacific Railway all of his life. Railway employees were given passes, allowing their family members to ride free. When I was very young, my mother and I would take the 10:00 a.m. train from White Bear Lake to St. Paul. We would shop for an hour or so, and then meet my father for lunch. To return home, we had to make decisions. Do we take the 2:00, 4:00, or 5:00 p.m. train? The 5:00 train, which my father took every day, stopped at the White Bear Depot and also a mile north, allowing my dad and other passengers who lived north of town to detrain closer to home.

Back then, we had four choices of transportation to go from White Bear Lake to St. Paul--the streetcar, the train, the bus, or our own car. Each method of transportation took about twenty minutes. The train, streetcar, and bus cost twenty-five cents. How does that compare with today?
(Guy Fisher--White Bear Lake, MN--1930s)

WHERE DO THEY PLUG THE TRAINS IN?

When I was very little--maybe four or five--my dad was driving the car, with me standing up in the back seat right behind him. Daddy worked for the Great Northern Railroad, and was telling us about the electric trains that were running out West. I asked, "Where do they plug them in?" There was quite a lot of laughter from the family, so, being a ham, I asked it again and again. I was finally told to be quiet. I never did find out how the trains ran!
(Jerrie Steinwall-Ahrens--Dakota Co., MN--1930s)

Minnesota Historical Society

THREE TYPES OF GREAT NORTHERN LOCOMOTIVES, ca. 1915

STREETCARS

EVERYONE RODE THE STREETCAR

There was a time when everyone rode the streetcar. No matter where you wanted to go in the city, a streetcar could take you there within a few blocks. In the summertime, you could lower the windows and bask in the breezes. Smokers rode standing up on the rear platform, swaying back and forth as the trolley careened down the street and around curves. In the wintertime, you warmed by the heat from a little coal fire somewhere in the nether regions of the vehicle. One rarely saw the motorman, because he sat in the very front of the car in his own little curtained-off compartment. There usually was a sign there saying, "Unlawful to engage the motorman in conversation," so presumably his was a lonesome job, unlike that of the conductor, who greeted everybody with a cheerful smile as they entered and dropped their dime in his little glass box.

In the wintertime after heavy snowfalls, there were often deep, icy ruts where the streetcars followed their rails. Woe to the motorist whose car fell into one of these slippery ruts! Many autos carried deep, flattened indentations on their hoods where they had slid under a streetcar when unable to stop.

In time of war, there was a little streetcar called "The Dummy Line," which ran from the city limits at West 7th Street, through the Fort Snelling area, for the benefit of the armed forces temporarily stationed there. The ride was free, and the little streetcar was only about half as big as the normal trolley. There was a set of controls at each end of the car, and when it came to the end of the line, the motorman simply lifted off his little handle from the control box, walked to the other end, and proceeded in the other direction.
(R. Kuehn--St. Paul, MN--1930s)

Minnesota Historical Society

STREETCAR TO WILDWOOD PARK

When I was about sixteen years old, we gals used to take the streetcar out to Wildwood Park in the White Bear Lake/Mahtomedi area. It was a nice park for all ages, but we especially liked going to the dances on Saturday night. Believe me, many a romance began there!
(Mary E. Strong--St. Paul, MN--1927)

CAMARADERIE ON THE STREETCAR

When we use the word "streetcar," it is often accompanied by a groan, and we know it dates us. But to me, it is also accompanied by many memories. Several characters who rode on my line come to mind. One lady wore all white, with a mask over

WILDWOOD PARK

her face to protect her from "germs." Another was an older lady who always wore long, glamorous gowns. She was a mystery to us, until we read in the paper that she had promised her artist husband on his death bed that she would always wear a long dress, as she had when she posed for him.

During World War I, I sometimes sat with a Japanese fellow worker and received "dirty looks" from other passengers because we were at war with Japan. When I rode alone, I often heard some sad commentaries from people sitting behind me. The streetcar, at other times, could become a thing of joy when we got a bunch of friends together just to ride for the fun of it. We could ride across the whole city for less than a dime, singing songs and laughing at each other's antics.

The buses may be more comfortable, but the streetcars brought more camaraderie, especially when it lurched and a "straphanger" would inadvertently land in someone's lap! People got acquainted riding with the same people all the time. You could judge a man's manners by watching to see if he would give up his seat for a lady. Motormen were considerate and would sometimes wait for me if they saw me coming. Chivalry was alive and well in those days, and I miss that.
(Hazel Gronquist--Minneapolis, MN--1940s)

FLOYD HUGHES

MY FATHER DROVE A STREETCAR

Early in the Depression, my father left the family farm in Blue Earth County to move to Minneapolis. He drove a streetcar to earn money while taking business classes. When I was a child, he planned a special day for our family. On a trip to Minneapolis for a performance of the Ice Follies, we stopped a distance from the auditorium so my brother and I could experience a streetcar ride the rest of the way. What a fun day!
(Alice C. Hughes--Minneapolis, MN--1950s)

Minneapolis Star-Journal photo, Minnesota Historical Society

AIRPLANES

AIRPLANE RIDES FOR FIFTY CENTS

Horses and buggies were common in my childhood, but we rarely saw an airplane. However, when I was eight or nine, a pilot landed in a nearby field--this was called "barnstorming"--and offered rides at fifty cents a person. My dad made two trips to that field so that my siblings and I could have an airplane ride in an open cockpit plane. Now THAT was exciting!
(Loretta C. Lehman--Willmar, MN--1930-31)

A FLYING HERO AND HEROINE

When I was a child, flying was also young. I remember well the summer day when the headlines were full of the awe and excitement of "Lucky Lindy" landing in Paris after a solo Atlantic flight. Disbelief and wonder! He was everyone's hero.

Flying grew fast. It was only a few years later that we were all anxiously awaiting news of Wiley Post and Will Rogers, who were on an around-the-world flight. They crashed and never made it home. The public mourned our well-loved humorist.

Amelia Earhart--the name still makes me sad. I can still see her tousled hair and shy smile. She was my heroine! There was no one like her. When she disappeared over the Pacific on an around-the-world flight, I went into shock. I must not be alone, because there are people still trying to discover what happened to her.
(Mae F. Hardin--ND--1920s-30s)

MY GRANDFATHER--AN AVIATION PIONEER

Around 1910, there was a lot of news about flying airplanes. My grandfather decided to be the pioneer of White Bear Lake aviation. He used lightweight wood to make the framework for his airplane. He didn't have money for a motor, so he decided it would be a glider, pulled into the air by a motorboat. He built a platform on the back end of a motorboat, and there was a winch to let out the rope to pull the plane like a kite.

The motorboat roared out across the lake. The shore was lined with spectators to watch this "crazy fool." The plane lifted off the deck, with my grandfather at the controls. When all the rope was played out, the plane started to jerk back and forth. Then the rope broke, and the plane gained altitude for a minute or so before setting down in the water. He sat there enjoying the successful flight, as the plane sank. Finally, when the water was up to his chin, he swam out to get picked up by a boat.
(John W. Johnson--White Bear Lake, MN--1910)

KEITH SUEKER

MADELIA SENIORS, 1930

DAVID WENDELL HUGHES AND FRIEND

ANIMAL TALES

RUSSELL HUGHES

ANIMAL TALES

THE RUNAWAY TEAM

The following incident happened when I was nine years old. We had moved to a new location, where my dad put up all the buildings. He had quite innovative ideas and wanted to put in a water system. Of course, there was no electricity or motors, so he devised a gravity system. The idea was to put a big tank up in the hay barn and lead underground pipes to the various buildings. A windmill supplied the water.

Dad ordered a big, galvanized, cylindrical tank, about ten feet high and six feet in diameter, and it came to the depot in White Rock, South Dakota. We lived about four miles out of town. Dad had made a flatbed out of a hayrack, and the men securely fastened the tank to the rack with ropes, etc. All was ready. Dad got into the tank, the open end toward the horses. Rob and Dewey were a very spirited team of horses, and they had never carried a load like this before. Not only were they frightened by this monstrosity, but when they started out, there was a terrible rumble and roar from the tank. Dad knew he was in for a challenge!

Dad held onto the reins with all his might, but he couldn't control the pace of the horses. It was a mad race for four miles. The sound and sight attracted quite a few spectators along the way. There were no corners to turn along the road, but Dad wondered what would happen when they got to our driveway. Well, the horses were still going at breakneck speed, but "miracle of miracles," they made the corner, with the tank and Dad still intact! Rob and Dewey stopped when they got to the barn. (Mabel Winter--Wheaton, MN--1912)

THE IMPORTANCE OF HORSES

We had a huge barn. Pilots flying between Devil's Lake and Winnipeg used it as a landmark when they flew their little planes "by the seat of their pants." It had to be large, for it housed about twenty head of cattle, at least ten big Belgian horses, plus our purebred Belgian stallion. Also, my mother had her own matched pair of black Morgans to pull the buggy.

The horses did all the work on the farm. Farmers took good care of their horses because they depended on them from planting to harvest, as well as dozens of smaller jobs in between--like hauling the grain to the elevator in town and hauling coal home. At threshing time there were so many teams hauling bundles to the separator and hauling grain to the granary, that there wasn't room for them all in the barn. Fortunately, it was warm enough to feed them outside and turn them out into the corral.
(Mae F. Hardin--ND--1920s)

My father had a team of horses named Barney Google and Mickey Mouse. They were large old plow horses. We children had to stay far away from them, as they were often mean. My mother would bake each of them a cake on their birthday and take it out to the barn for them to eat.
(Gail Bishop--Cloverton, MN--1940s)

THE TEAM OF OXEN

When my dad bought our farm in Wisconsin in 1915, a friend of his, a hog salesman in South St. Paul, had a chance to get a team of oxen cheap. He sent them to my dad, and we used them a year or two to break new ground. They were a good team. My brother Elmer used them to haul cordwood to a creamery in Barronette.

There was a little hill the oxen had to go up on the way to town. One winter, the sun melted the snow on the road; when the oxen hit the gravel, they stopped dead. Elmer got down and threw off half the load, and the team pulled the wagon up the hill. The next day the same thing happened, but he only threw off one piece of wood. The dumb oxen pulled the whole load up the hill! From then on, we always had to throw something off the wagon to get the oxen to pull it up the hill.
(Melvin Frerck--Barronette, WI--1915)

THE BULL THAT VISITED SCHOOL

It was in the fall of the year. The corn was picked and the fields were bare, except for the gleaning. The farmer who owned the fields across the road from the schoolhouse let his herd of cows out in the field. Since these fields were not fenced, the cows were allowed to roam free, which was a customary practice. In the afternoon, when the herd had eaten their fill, they wandered up on the school premises and bedded down. But not the bull. He was curious and decided to "explore."

The schoolhouse had double doors in the front and a low stoop in front of that. The double doors stood open because it was a warm day, but we had closed the inner doors that led to the classroom. Pretty soon we heard a noise, as though someone were pushing the dinner pails around on the shelf in the entry. It sounded like some were even being pushed completely off the shelf. I asked one of the boys to go and see what was happening. He opened the door and quickly closed it, exclaiming, "There's a bull in the schoolhouse!" I lost no time getting the children into a coal room that was built on the back of the building. There also was a back door, through which I dispatched two of the boys to go get help from a neighbor who lived close by.

Well, they had quite a time getting that bull out. The cloakroom was narrow, and the bull couldn't turn around. He had to back out, and in doing so, he slipped on the smooth floor. He became a bit vicious before they succeeded in getting him out. Fortunately, there was a window at one end that they finally pried open so they could "shoo" the bull out. By that time, school was almost ready to be dismissed, and parents were on hand to get their children. Their favorite and only topic was, "The Bull That Visited School."
(Amy Frederickson Meyer--Brown Co., MN--1931)

TIME TO GET THE COWS IN

Rounding up the cows was a full afternoon job. I'd saddle my spirited horse and away I'd go. The pasture was big, as it surrounded the total 194-acre farm. The territory was comprised of bluffs, hills, and thick woods.

Thoughts come to mind about times when it had turned dark and foggy and the cows hadn't come home to be milked. I'd set out to find them, not knowing which direction to start. The frightening and thrilling part would be when I'd pass too close to a tree, and a limb would brush my cap off, or a low-hanging limb would switch me in the face, sometimes knocking me off my horse. One night I particularly remember. At the exact moment a branch was striking me in the face, a screech owl screamed out at me! I nearly died with fright.
(Al Kjos--Rushford, MN--1930s)

COW PATROL

Cows were an important part of my childhood. Since there was no dairy in town, Dad kept two cows. We had quite a bit of land, so he built a small barn for the cows, and a chicken house, so we had plenty of eggs and milk and a good supply of chickens to eat. It seemed that almost everyone in town "kept" chickens.

During the summer, Dad rented some pasture land two blocks from home. When I was nine or ten, it was my brother's responsibility to take the cows to and from the pasture twice a day. This was during the worst Depression years. To get to the field, we had to cross the railroad tracks and enter the driveway to the field, which was also the driveway to our local flour mill.

Easton's flour and pancake mix were considered good products in those years. The miller was a mild-mannered and kind old gentleman. He, his wife, and their grown daughters lived in a nice house on the adjoining property. They had two goldfish ponds on their land, so their lawn had a certain park-like ambience.

Next to the field where we delivered the cows to graze after their morning milking, was the hobo "jungle." In those days, the jungle was usually inhabited. Thus, taking the cows back to the pasture was always the beginning of fun for Billy and me. We often checked on the goldfish (unique things in our life then, and great fun to watch). Often the miller, kind Pete Weaver, would boost us up into the mill, which was a fascinating place to play. I don't remember that Mr. Weaver ever spoke a word to us, but Billy and I could give one another rides on the little two-wheeled cart that the miller used to move sacks of flour around. It was always fun to be there.

The third thing we could do was sit on the fence and visit with the hoboes. Hoboes, in those times, were men down on their luck who hoped to find a few days' work on nearby farms, often having left a wife and children at home. These men were good storytellers. During the two years I was on "cow patrol," not one of those men ever touched us, nor did they use any bad language when we were around. Our parents knew that we visited with them, and we were never warned away from them.

(Loretta C. Lehman--Easton, MN--1932-33)

THE CALF WITH THE BROKEN LEG

One night, one of our cows had a little calf. Somehow that calf got away from the mother and got in between two horses. (The horses and cows were all in the same building.) The horse stepped on the little calf's leg and broke it. I felt so terrible. My husband said that there was nothing we could do; we would have to kill the poor little thing. I said, "No. Let me try something." Well, I got a pair of my husband's old overalls and a peach crate. Then I put little wooden pieces on the calf's leg and wrapped and wrapped with strips torn from the overalls. The little calf got along fine and the leg healed. Now, that really meant something to me.

(Elizabeth Juhl--Lake Crystal, MN--1940s)

THE MEAN ROOSTER

Growing up on the farm, my younger sister and I rode the school bus every day. One spring was especially harrowing for us walking to meet the bus, for a mean old rooster would come running at us the minute we stepped out the door and peck at our legs and feet. It only took a few times for me to figure out that if I sent my sister out FIRST as a diversion, I could make it to the bus untouched!

(Norma Hughes Schlichter--Lake Crystal, MN--1950s)

August 24, 1953
Dear Miss Johnson,
   Enclosed is my check in the amount of $65.92 for the hog I purchased at the 4-H sale on Saturday, August 22. I personally want to thank you for this dandy pig and for caring for it after the sale. Without a doubt, it will be the best pork my family has ever had.
   Best wishes to you and the 4-H.
                                        Sincerely,
                                        Donald M. Christenson, Sheriff
(Betty Johnson Rabe--Ellendale, MN--1953)

THE FISH POND

   I always liked fish, so when we built our new house, the carpenter said he would cement a hole in the backyard for an outdoor fish pond. I thought that would be great.
   When my husband was gone threshing, I took the tractor, hooked a wagon on, and went out in the field to get some dirt to build up the area behind the pond. Then I went to various pastures, looking for nice stones. I ended up making a very nice big rock garden, and I even had a bridge across the pond. It was filled with fish and there were lily pads on the surface; the frogs loved sitting on those. One time we counted twenty-two frogs! The kids who visited really enjoyed that fish pond.
   In the fall before it froze, I took the fish out of the pond and put them in an old washing machine in the basement, keeping them there all winter. I had an air pump to keep the water moving. One spring when I returned them to the outside pond, there were ninety fish!
(Elizabeth Juhl--Lake Crystal, MN--1951)

A TRAGIC DEATH

   We had many dogs and cats, but the most amusing pets we had in our early marriage were parakeets. The first three or four (one at a time) were very tame and would fly out of the cage and sit on our shoulders. One even tried to say a few words. Our last one met a tragic death.
   We had a cage on a tall pole in the dining room. One day a neighbor came by, and I was holding the screen door open while we visited. Suddenly, I heard a thump inside. A cat had sneaked in through the open door, and seeing the bird, had jumped on its cage. Well, the cage fell on the floor and the parakeet came out. The cat came running out with the bird between its teeth. Unfortunately, that was the last of our parakeet!
(Ada Ronnei Pederson--Pope Co., MN--1950)

We had sheep on our ranch in eastern Oregon. In the fall, the stockmen would rent railroad cars to take the lambs to market. You could get about ninety to one hundred head in each car. The little train would come about three times a week, and we would take the lambs to the railroad.

We had a ewe named Judy that would lead the lambs into the railroad cars. They would put a ramp down and Judy would go up, with all the lambs following her. Then she would go around and down the ramp, and they would shut the door. She would go to the next car and repeat the process. Someone asked Uncle Jack one day why the ewe's name was Judy. Uncle Jack replied, "Haven't you ever heard of Judas Iscariot?"
(Eileene Barry McKee--Lake County, OR--1920s)

BABY CHICKS

I loved getting our baby chicks in the spring. We would order a hundred or so and also hatch some of our own. We would set about fifteen eggs under the "clucks"--the hens that would refuse to leave the nest after laying an egg. Then we would time the delivery of the new baby chicks to coincide with the hatching of our own, so that the hens would take them all.
(JoAnn Wanner Prom--Hebron, ND--1950s)

SKUNKS UNDER THE SCHOOL

Years ago, schoolhouses had little in the way of foundations. They sat right on the ground, and the space under the floor made a great home for animals. Some skunks moved under the school where I was teaching, and an "eager beaver" school board member set traps to catch them. Well, he caught one, and the animal made its unhappiness known! It didn't help matters when the board member dragged the trap out. We closed school until the building could be aired out.
(Dorothea Thompson--Rock Co., MN--1950s)

A BABY'S BEST FRIEND

My oldest sister was born in 1890 near Selden, Kansas, in a sod shanty with a dirt floor. When she was old enough, she was playing outside one time, when suddenly my mother heard the dog barking frantically. When she ran to see what was wrong, she found him between the baby and a rattlesnake. Mother killed the snake, rescued the baby, and cried over the dog, who was a hero!
(Dorothea Thompson--Selden, KS--1890s)

Shortly before I got married, I moved into a big, old rooming house located near "Old Main," the building where I worked on the Mankato State University campus. It was a hot August day when I moved in, and I was exhausted from carrying my belongings up the long stairway. That first evening I collapsed into the big, soft bed, preparing for a good night's rest, only to be awakened a short time later by a "swoosh" and a "thump." I quickly turned on the light and was startled to see several bats swoop past. I can't give a detailed account, since I was under the covers in the "flick of an eye," and didn't peek out again until morning!

The next day I told several colleagues about my plight. One of them suggested that if I left a light on, that might keep them away. I tried that the next evening, which only helped me SEE them better, especially the one landing on the nightstand right next to me! After an hour or so, I mustered up enough courage to awaken the little old lady who owned the house. She picked up her broom (which was located in one corner of her bedroom, presumably for the purpose of "extinguishing" bats), but by now the sneaky little critters had retreated to their hiding places.

Since I was completely exhausted from my second sleepless night, I called a taxi and went to a friend's house. The next day, after deciding that I just wasn't cut out to room with bats, I went back and removed my belongings.
(Bonnie Hughes Falk--Mankato, MN--1966)

MICKEY MOUSE AND TIPPY

One of the things I loved most about the farm where I grew up in North Dakota was the animals. Our black cat, Mickey Mouse, and our rat terrier dog, Tippy, who was black with a white tail, were great buddies. They would sleep together in a box in the basement. They raced each other to bed at night, but Mickey Mouse always won, since she'd take a short cut and jump off the side of the steps, while Tippy would have to run all the way to the bottom.

One winter evening we were playing cards in our kitchen, when we heard someone opening our adjoining basement door. We froze with fright! Then we saw Tippy and Mickey Mouse come to join us. While Mickey Mouse had stood on her hind legs and turned the knob, Tippy had pushed the door open!
(JoAnn Wanner Prom--Hebron, ND--1950s)

JOANN WANNER PROM

Looking through old photographs, I came across one that included our dog, Old Nig. It reminded me of the following story.

Roy was four when John, Stella, Mabel, Roy, Glen, and baby Myrtle drove off in the surrey to the Dewitt County Fair. Old Nig was supposed to stay home, but he insisted on following behind all the way to the fairgrounds.

The family stayed all day in that exciting place--bright tents, noisy hawkers, all kinds of livestock, and horse races. After a picnic lunch, came the preparation for the drive home. It was then that the family realized Old Nig had not been seen lately. John called for him, without response. The whole family called. They searched everywhere, but no Old Nig. A man said he had seen a dead dog down near the barns. He was a black dog, evidently kicked by a horse or hit by one of those new-fangled "otter-mo-biles."

It was Old Nig. John picked him up, carried his lifeless limp body to the carriage, put him under the front seat, and said, "We'll have a funeral for him when we get home." We climbed in, with strained faces and hearts, and drove quietly back over the dusty road. Roy, sitting in the front seat with his father and Glen, stared straight ahead. Then, looking down and breaking the silence, he said, "I see his tail." And then he said, "I'm gonna cry when I get home." But he could hold back no longer. "I'm gonna cry right now!" And he did.
(Roy B. Moore--Dewitt Co., IL--1912)

MIKE FALK

DOGS

I've had a lot of dogs, from purebreds to mutts;
I must admit at times, I thought they'd drive me nuts.
Penny, Cookie, Heidi, Fluffy; Rocky, Kirby, and Fritz;
No matter what their name was, I loved them to bits.

Jumpers, lickers, piddlers, biters; I've had a few of each;
Some followed instructions; others were impossible to teach.
I've taken them to the groomers, and also to the vets;
Each was one of my children, although they were just my pets.
(Bonnie Hughes Falk)

NORMA HUGHES SCHLICHTER

Dakota County Shorthorns, Minnesota State Fair, 1919

TOM AND TERRY FALK

AL KJOS

NORMA HUGHES SCHLICHTER

TERRY AND MIKE FALK

FAVORITE FOODS

CORN EATING CONTEST, 1950

FROM HOMEMADE ICE CREAM
TO SPAM

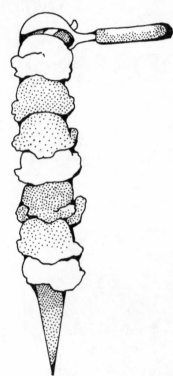

DIRECT FROM HEAVEN

One of my favorite childhood memories is from the 1940s. Times were hard on farms, so many Friday and Saturday evenings we would go to my grandparents' home to play a card game called "500." Later in the evening, my aunts would mix up a batch of homemade ice cream. They used real cream; in fact, all of the ingredients were "real"--none of the "imitation" stuff we use now.

My uncles would take turns turning the crank. When the crank got hard to turn, they would put a blanket on top, and one of us kids would sit on it to hold down the mixer. The result was vanilla ice cream that tasted like it was sent to us direct from heaven! I would eat so much that it felt as if I might burst!

(Jerry Sutliff--Glenwood City, WI--1940s)

MY GOLLY, IT WAS GOOD!!

I remember homemade ice cream so well. We had a wooden-type bucket with a churn handle and space around the churn for ice and salt. We had to churn for hours, it seemed, with each one taking a turn, because it was hard work. NEVER, and I mean NEVER, has anything tasted so good! It was creamy and rich.

Nowadays, they have electric freezers, but they don't compare to the old type. We used all pure cream and fresh eggs. My golly, it was good!!

(Mary E. Strong--LeCenter/St. Paul, MN--1916-Present)

GRANDMA'S HOMEMADE CHOCOLATE "GOOP"

When I was young, I can remember going to Grandma and Grandpa Ball's house on Sundays and holidays for dinner. My dad had eight brothers and sisters, and most of them would be there with their families, so it was a big get-together.

Sometimes we would make homemade ice cream. It was a family activity. We would all take turns cranking the ice cream, counting while the others took their turns. When it was finished, we always ate it immediately, and ALWAYS with Grandma's homemade chocolate "goop," which caramelized when poured over the ice cream.

Today, my family carries on this tradition, but we have an electric ice cream maker instead of the old crank kind. However, my two children still insist on having it with the homemade chocolate "goop."
(Terri Ball Snider--Woodsocket, SD--1960s-Present)

CORN ON THE COB

When I was a girl growing up on the farm, I can remember we loved corn on the cob. It wasn't sweet corn as we have today; it was field corn, picked at just the right stage. It was really a special treat.
(Selma Anderson Hughes--Watonwan Co., MN--1920s)

THEY LOVED THOSE SAUSAGES!

In the spring, Dad would always butcher a beef and three pigs. Some of the meat would be cut, trimmed, and fried down into pork chops, etc. Some was put in a meat brine. The ham and bacon were put in a brine and cured. After about three weeks in that brine, they were hung out in the smokehouse--a little building with poles across it. The beef and pork trimming would be ground into sausage. Then we made links and hung them on the poles in the smokehouse. What a treat it was when we cooked that sausage!

My brothers' friends would come over to play ball on Sunday afternoons. When they were through playing, they would come to the house and eat with us. How they loved those sausages!
(Elizabeth Juhl--Fenton, IA--early 1900s)

CARROT PIE

My parents always made an effort to make mealtime pleasant. There was always joking and laughter. We usually had a hired man--a young man from our neighborhood. One particular noon when the buttered carrots were passed to him, he jokingly said that he wouldn't eat them; they were rabbit's food! That afternoon I saw my mother looking through the cookbook. She seemed to be "bubbling over" about something, but I didn't ask her what she was so happy about.

The next day, we had pie for dessert. After the first bite, the hired man said, "This pie is delicious." When my mother could control her laughing, she said, "You have now eaten carrots and liked them. This is carrot pie!" He was a good sport about it and said he didn't care if there were carrots in it; it was delicious anyway!
(David Wendell Hughes--Cambria, MN--1910s)

I remember the first homemade pizza we had at our house. We had heard that pizza was supposed to be good. My mom, a "meat and potatoes" cook, decided to try it. It was a Chef Boy-Ar-Dee Pizza Mix. It looked okay when she put it in the oven, but as it began to cook, it started to smell. The smell was unfamiliar (parmesan cheese) and became stronger. It got so bad that we decided to throw it out--without even tasting it! Pizza did not become a "taste sensation" in our household for quite some time.
(Vicki A. Johnson--Groton, SD--1950s)

WATERMELON WAS HIS FAVORITE

Our last visits with a dear, faithful friend were in a nursing home. The conversations were easier when we talked about the "old days." I asked, "What do you remember about the Fourth of July when you were a girl?" She had lived on a farm in Iowa in the early 1900s. The question triggered a memory. "We always tried to have our first watermelon of the season on the Fourth of July. That was my dad's birthday and watermelon was his favorite.
(Alice C. Hughes--IA--early 1900s)

Minnesota Historical Society

ca. 1915

My mother had a large garden. She canned everything she could poke in a jar to feed her large family over the winter. She had that old wood cook stove going day and night in the hot summertime. I remember many nights she never got to bed until after 1:00 a.m., because that was the time the canner came off the stove. It was up again early in the morning to help in the barn and fields; then more canning after supper that evening.

My mother, at eighty-five years old, still has a garden and does a lot of canning. She loves to have the shelves in the basement full.
(Gail Bishop--Cloverton, MN--1940s)

PARSLEY

SAUERKRAUT

We grew a large quantity of cabbage in our garden, and we always made a lot of sauerkraut. We would cut the cabbage and put it in a large fifty-gallon barrel. Then we would stomp it with a stomper my dad had made from a tree. He would drill a hole in the top and make a handle for it. We would stomp and stomp the cabbage until it drew water. Then we would cover it with hardwood boards and put a stone on top to weight it down so the liquid would come over the cabbage. It then was put in the basement until it "worked." We'd cook the sauerkraut with pork chops and dumplings. It was delicious!
(Elizabeth Juhl--Fenton, IA--early 1900s)

SAGE

BUCKWHEAT CAKES

The favorite pancake in our home was buckwheat cakes. Mom would start making them when the first snowflake fell. Every day she saved a cup of mixture to make batter with the next day. We ate them until someone broke out with hives! Then that person was excluded for awhile, until, as the saying goes, "The poison was out of their system!" The pancakes were delicious and the cook was super!
(Lucille Blair Johnson--Groton, SD--1920s-40s)

ROSEMARY

PANCAKES COME IN ALL SHAPES

As a child, waffles and pancakes were among my favorite breakfast foods. Pancakes, however, were the most fun to eat, thanks to the creativity of my mother. Instead of making the traditional circle-shaped pancakes, she would make them into various objects, to the delight of my brother and I. I can still remember eating pancakes in the shapes of cars, happy faces,

THYME

animals, and letters that spelled out my name. It has stuck with me, too.

While on a retreat, I was in charge of making breakfast. As you might have guessed, the pancakes came out anything but normal! I made them in the shapes of the United States.
(Timothy A. H. Drake--White Bear Lake, MN--1970s)

THE BEST PART OF THE FAIR IS THE FOOD

If you're looking for a new and novel way to enjoy the Minnesota State Fair--the greatest state fair in the world--here is something you might try. In recommending this, keep in mind that it has been tried and found very successful!

Why not have a contest to see who can eat the most of their favorite fair food. If no one wants to compete against you, compete against your own record from the previous year(s). As a Pronto Pup lover, I have a contest with myself to see how many I can eat in one day. (Here the point is not to get sick, but how many you can COMFORTABLY eat!)

Plan your movement throughout the fairgrounds over the course of a day according to where you find particular food stands. Let me get you started.

Enter the main gate. After admission, head for the nearest Pronto Pup stand. If you stay on the main street, that Pronto Pup will last until you reach the footlong hot dogs. Order one smothered in mustard and grilled onions. Savor it as you near the grandstand and the RC Cola booth. Your pop will last as you cut across to the Dairy Building. Here you get a malt, which is heaven-on-earth! After you get your malt, stop at the french fries stand for a thirty-two ounce Barrel of Fries. Next, head for the Horticulture Building for sesame and honey candy. (Save it to suck on later.) Finally, wrap up your day enjoying the late show at the Grandstand. Before you go in, however, stop and buy a pound of saltwater taffy. You'll need this to tide you over through the show. After the spectacular fireworks, stop as you exit the Grandstand for a Pronto Pup. This will last until you get to the RC Cola stand. Get some pop and ANOTHER Pronto Pup at the stand next door. Just before you exit the fairgrounds, stop for the LAST Pronto Pup (and, hopefully, a new personal record).

The fair is over, but don't get yourself down. Remember that saltwater taffy you bought? Play the famous between-fairs contest to see how many pieces you still have left when the state fair comes around next year!

The moral of the story is, the best part of the Minnesota State Fair is the food!
(Karen Kuehn--White Bear Lake, MN--1980s)

CHOCOLATE SAUCE

When I was growing up, many Sundays when we got home from church, we would have fried chicken. For supper, we would have cold chicken sandwiches and vanilla ice cream with chocolate sauce, while we all watched "The Jack Benny Show." Now, every time I hear Dennis Day sing, I get hungry for that delicious chocolate sauce. The recipe is as follows:

1 cup sugar
1/4 cup corn syrup
1/2 cup milk
1 square chocolate

Boil all ingredients for "exactly" seven minutes. Add a dab of butter and serve hot over ice cream.
(Tom Falk--Lake Crystal, MN--1950s)

A SLICE OF FAT

When Grandma made a pork roast, she would cut off the white, hard fat and put it in a dish in the refrigerator. Every morning for breakfast, Grandpa would have a glass of hot water and a slice of that fat on bread. Believe it or not, he lived to be in his late 80s! Another thing they would do was put milk in a bowl and set it in the pantry to get thick. Then they would sprinkle it with brown sugar. It tasted like sour milk to me! They also ate meat pies, called "pasties." Soup was very important; they had it seven days a week, not as the entree, but before the meal.
(Mary B. Twar--Two Harbors, MN--1930s)

I ATE THE "WHOLE" THING!

One night Grandma had SPAM for dinner. It was such a treat! Since there were five of us, I didn't get enough of that SPAM, so the next day I went to the store and bought a can. I charged it and didn't tell anyone. When I got home I took that can of SPAM, along with a knife, up to my room and ate the WHOLE thing! I got so sick! Can you imagine how much cholesterol was in that can of SPAM? Needless to say, I didn't eat any more SPAM for quite awhile.
(Mary B. Twar--Two Harbors, MN--1930s)

SPAM SAVES THE DAY

While serving with the 2nd Infantry Division in Korea, I hitched a ride with three other GIs in the open back-end of a 3/4-ton weapons carrier. After riding most of the day without anything to eat, we flagged down an army supply truck to see if there was any food on board. All we could come up with was a

five-pound, olive-drab can of SPAM. I opened the can and used my bayonet to slice the meat! I've not eaten SPAM many times since, but when I do, this memory still comes floating back.
(Al Swanson--White Bear Lake, MN--1951-52)

"ALFREDS"

For over thirty years, "Alfreds" have been served as our favorite SPAM recipe. My Uncle Ted christened the tasty open-faced sandwiches, and the name stuck. My husband and four daughters have delighted in eating "Alfreds." Now my two married daughters have added this simple recipe to their collection, and my two-year-old grandson is a fourth-generation "Alfred" lover. The recipe includes:
1 large Velveeta cheese, about 1/2 pound
1 can SPAM
1 small onion
Grind or grate the ingredients together; stir to mix. Spread mixture on the cut side of hamburger buns to make open-face sandwiches. Place under the broiler a few minutes until browned.
(Caroleann L. Seidenkranz--St. Paul, MN--1950s-Present)

EVERYTHING'S COMING UP SPAM

The SPAM craze began on our confirmation summer trip in 1982. In a casual conversation, I told several people of a SPAM skit I had seen on "Monty Python's Flying Circus." I have no idea why, but the craze spread to become part of an annual SPAM Christmas party that lasted for three years.

To come to the party, a guest had to bring a gift made of SPAM. Gifts included a pair of microwaved SPAM boots, SPAM lips, SPAM earrings, a necklace made of SPAM balls, and a SPAMmie Patch Doll, which I created. Door prizes included banks, posters, T-shirts, stick-up clocks, patches, stickers, hats, and tote bags that had the word SPAM printed on them--all compliments of Hormel in Austin, Minnesota.

I currently teach Social Studies in Waconia, Minnesota, but I still recall those strange days at St. Andrew's Lutheran Church in Mahtomedi.
(Timothy A. H. Drake--White Bear Lake, MN--1982)

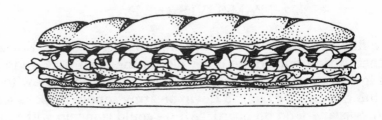

"LITTLE PILLOWS"

My favorite family Christmas tradition is spelled RAVIOLI. I remember Grandma Bacigalupo making hundreds of small, spinach-stuffed pillows each Christmas in the 1940s. What a true labor of love this was--in her small kitchen on Edmund Avenue!

I can clearly picture Grandma in her apron, bending over that "floured," wood kitchen table, rolling out the almost "elastic" dough to a perfect thickness. Oh, so carefully the spinach filling would be dropped by the teaspoonful onto that dough, in neat, even rows. It was then cut by the "magic" wheel into uniform-sized "pillows." Lacking kitchen counter space, the completed ravioli were then transferred to a bedroom and placed tenderly on a sheet-covered bed, waiting to be counted. The aroma of the spicy Italian sauce simmering on the old stove must have provided the incentive to continue this tedious task. What a gang Grandma fed each Christmas!

My Italian grandma was a great teacher and my German mom was an excellent pupil. Rolling the dough is still a labor of Mom's love, but modern kitchens have helped make things a little easier. While Mom is a wonderful teacher, I'm still a struggling student trying to perfect this tasty tradition! Hopefully, I will accomplish this lesson and be able to teach my own four daughters.
(Caroleann L. Seidenkranz--St. Paul, MN--1940s-Present)

RICE PUDDING

Following is a favorite recipe for rice pudding which is served at Old Settlers' Day in Scandia, Minnesota, each summer:

1/2 cup rice, uncooked	2 eggs
4 cups whole milk	2/3 cup sugar
1/2 teaspoon salt	vanilla to taste

Cook rice in milk, with salt, in a double boiler until the rice is very tender and has absorbed most of the milk. Mix eggs and sugar with the vanilla. Add a little of the hot mixture to the egg mixture to avoid curdling; then combine all ingredients in double boiler, cooking only until thick. The pudding can be served warm or chilled, with a berry sauce. Serves 6.
(Hazel Gronquist--Scandia, MN)

RICE FRITTERS

March 19, St. Joseph's Day, marks the return of the swallows to Capistrano. This is the only day of the year that we have rice fritters.

160

Rice fritters are similar to a thick pancake (with rice). They are fried and then coated with sugar. We usually gather at someone's home in the evening and enjoy visiting with family, along with eating. Following is the recipe for rice fritters:

1 cup flour	1 beaten egg
1 1/2 teaspoon baking powder	1/3 cup milk
1/4 cup sugar	1 tablespoon oil
1 1/2 teaspoon salt	1 cup raw rice

Cook rice in water. Mix all ingredients together and add cooked rice. Fry in small amount of grease. Coat both sides lightly with sugar while the fritters are still warm.
(Helen Giannini Zappa--St. Paul, MN--1920s-Present)

GERMAN FAVORITES

At holiday time, food was never forgotten. Mother always made the usual "Kuchen" (cakes), "Pfeffernuesse" (peppernuts), and coffee cakes saturated with fruit. A special treat was the rice cooked in milk, which we smothered with a sweet mixture of cooked prunes, home sun-dried apples, raisins, dried pears, and apricots. (We didn't call this "fruit soup," a term I learned from the Minnesota Scandinavians.)

Father always made his special and favorite "candy." After an order from Sears, Roebuck arrived in the fall, which included a good number of groceries, Father would incise the dates, remove the pits and replace them with walnuts or pecans, and then roll them in sugar.

By following the inviting aroma of sage and thyme, I was always led to the dressing ("stuffing," as we called it), or the "Wurst" (homemade sausage). Warmed "Kartoffel Wurst" (potato sausage) and "Blut Wurst" (blood sausage) were my real favorites.

Instead of butter on our homemade bread, we often used "Apfel Schmalz" (literally, apple grease), made from apples cooked with ground up cracklings. When we went to Grandmother Schmidt's house, she always seemed to have raised doughnuts to offer (in her broken English and her broken German). She was someone very special and lived to a ripe old age of ninety-six years! Also, I probably had my share of cholesterol, but we always had our oatmeal for breakfast!
(Ruben F. Schmidt--Shawano Co., WI--1920s-30s)

WELSH CAKES

This is a third generation recipe from my Welsh grandmother, Kate Lewis Davies. She was born in Rhandirmwyn, South Wales. She handed down the recipe to her daughter, Catherine Davies Thomas, born in Scranton, Pennsylvania, who then gave it to me.

Speisen-Folge

Kraftbrühe

Schleie in Butter

Kalbsrücken gespickt

Junger Gänsebraten

Eingemachte Früchte

Fürst Pückler

Butter und Käse

St. David is the patron saint of the Welsh. His feast day, March 1, is often celebrated in our house with Welsh cakes. Following is the recipe:

6 cups flour	1/2 pound butter
2 cups sugar	1/2 pound lard
1/4 teaspoon baking soda	1/2 box dried currants
1 teaspoon cream of tartar	3 eggs, beaten
2 teaspoons baking powder	1/2 cup milk
1 teaspoon salt	
1 1/2 teaspoon nutmeg	

Sift all dry ingredients together in a large bowl. Rub in lard and butter with hands. Add currants, and eggs and milk mixed together. (If you're making half the recipe, mix up 3 eggs and divide in half.)

Divide dough into 3 or 4 parts and wrap tightly with foil or waxed paper. Refrigerate several hours or overnight. The dough will keep in refrigerator nearly a month.

Roll out to 3/16" thickness. Cut out rounds with biscuit cutter about 2 3/4" in diameter. Bake on a griddle on top of the stove, adding grease only if necessary to keep cakes from sticking. Heat should be medium; the goal is to bake cakes through and brown them nicely. If the griddle is too hot, they will brown or burn before they bake through. Turn the cakes to bake both sides.

Some Welsh folks put a very light sprinkling of sugar on their Welsh cakes. We like them plain. They are perfect for afternoon tea.
(Cynthia Thomas Stuck--White Bear Lake, MN)

A BIG SLAB OF LUTEFISK!

When my boys were four and seven, I started taking an evening class at the University of Minnesota on Monday evenings. My husband was in charge of cooking on that night each week. Since he had never cooked much before, deciding what to make was always a problem.

In his job as a salesman, he traveled through the town of Day, Minnesota, a major supplier of lutefisk. There, laying in a tub, was the answer to his problem--A BIG SLAB OF LUTEFISK! The people at the store told him how to make it and what supplies were needed. He bought some cheesecloth to cook the fish in and went home early to prepare it.

The boys told me the next day how good the lutefisk was, and my husband was so proud of how it turned out. The problem was that he made it EVERY Monday night! After three months, the boys asked me if I could please quit going to school because they were getting so sick of lutefisk!
(Cindy Salberg Lerfald--White Bear Lake, MN--1978)

PETER ABRAHAMSON FARM, LANESBORO, MN, ca. 1919

TREASURES

FROM MARY B. TWAR'S DOLL COLLECTION

HEIRLOOMS, COLLECTIONS, AND HOBBIES

HEIRLOOMS FROM MY SEAFARING ANCESTORS

My Norwegian grandfathers, in keeping with Norway's seafaring tradition dating back to Viking days, went to sea. Farming and other occupations were not available to them. Their lives at sea have given me some of my most cherished heirlooms.

My maternal grandfather started as a cabin boy, and later became a ship carpenter, learning the carpentry trade that he followed for many years. When he migrated to the United States, he brought with him his handmade wooden sea chest which he had used on other voyages.

My paternal grandfather became a captain of a coastal steamship that sailed from port to port in Norway, carrying passengers and cargo. He was a smoker, and when he retired, he was given a fancy meerschaum pipe, which had a long stem with a tasseled ornament. There was a silver cap on the bowl, engraved with his name and the Norwegian word for remembrance.

The sea chest, two meerschaum pipes, a model sailing ship encased in a large wooden frame, a large framed portrait of the Captain in his uniform, one of the Captain's jackets with its brass nautical buttons, and a commemorative silver cup are prized heirlooms that remind me of my ancestors' seafaring days.
(Ole Schelsnes--WI)

MY FAMILY'S "GOLDEN BOOK OF SONGS"

My mother's old green book was the family's "Golden Book of Songs," an heirloom coveted by all. The green-covered book had many blank pages, interspersed with colored pictures of Gibson-style women in a variety of fancy dress. The book was a gift to my mother from my Norwegian immigrant father. It was used often and was prized by her. Over the years, the words of many old songs were copied on those pages--songs that had been memorized and sung by my mother and her three sisters.

Now, no blank pages remain. They have been filled with the words of many old familiar songs, and reflect memories of the past. It is a family treasure that has been used countless times, as old songs are sung by the family.
(Ole Schelsnes--WI--1910)

Many antiques grace my home. My favorite is a piece of jewelry--a watch--which was given to my mother at the time of her confirmation. It gives me comfort and a feeling of being near her whenever I wear it.

Among my antique dishes, sitting in the window because of their beautiful cobalt blue color, are Shirley Temple mugs and a cream pitcher, which were given as premiums in cereal boxes years ago. I can remember that you had to buy the large size, since the glass pieces themselves were often quite large. I think it might have been marked on the outside of the container what was inside--saucer, cup, cream pitcher, cheese plate/top, etc. I also have Shirley Temple and Little Orphan Annie spoons.
(Elayne DeZelar--St. Paul, MN--1930s)

SECRET CODE RING

I was a faithful listener of the program "Little Orphan Annie," and I could sing along with the theme song. I really didn't care for Ovaltine, but I would persuade my mother to buy it just so I could send in for the Secret Code Ring. When they gave secret messages on the program, I could use that special ring to decode the message!
(Mary Simonson Thompson--Groton, SD--1930s)

A "HOOKER" AT SIXTY

At age sixty, I became a "hooker," finally finding an instructor who taught the old art of rug hooking! I then finished a beautiful, primitive, hooked rug that my mother had left unfinished when she died. Since then, I have hooked five primitive rugs.
(Elayne DeZelar--St. Paul, MN--1980s)

A WARM QUILT FOR A COLD HOUSE

My mother often made quilts for our family to use. My father made quilt frames, which were set up in the living room, and we girls would help our mother quilt or tie the quilts. Sometimes a few neighbor ladies would come over to help. It was another way to have a good time without spending money.

My father always had sheep, and a lot of our quilts were made with our own wool used as the batting. The tops were made of wool squares and pieces, which made a very warm quilt for our cold house. There were no electric blankets in those days!
(Mary Simonson Thompson--Groton, SD--1930s)

STARRY PATH

CLOCKWORKS

PINWHEEL (2)

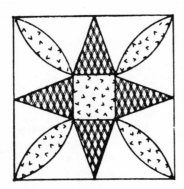

MORNING STAR

I made my first quilt in 1921, before my wedding. For many years during the Depression, I made them of pieces from cast-off clothing. After a long time, I could afford to buy new material and make some pretty ones. Sometimes it would take a year to find the material I wanted. All together, I have made about forty quilts. My seven children have most of them.

The most beautiful quilt I ever made is the "Tree of Life" quilt. It was made from a kit, and was appliqued and put together like a paint-by-number picture. It had 365 pieces and sold for $1,000. Another favorite was the "Double Wedding Ring" quilt. It was queen size and took about two years to make. I gave it to my church to sell. One of my daughters bought it for $500. I made my last quilt in 1985. I am now eighty-six years old.
(Elsie Grove--MN--1920s-80s)

"THIS IS YOUR LIFE" QUILT

For my son's graduation, I presented him with a quilt made up of thirty-five twelve-inch squares, each square representing some aspect of his life. The majority of the squares were made from his T-shirts, which I had saved since he was six years old-- from trips we had taken, sports teams he was on, etc. Other squares were made from his pajamas, sweatshirts, and miscellaneous remnants. Each piece of material was fused onto a coordinating colored background, and all the squares were sewn together and quilted. This permanent reminder of my son's childhood now hangs proudly on the wall outside his bedroom.
(Bonnie Hughes Falk--White Bear Lake, MN--1989)

"THIS IS YOUR LIFE" QUILT

My love affair with Norwegian rosemaling goes back to the days of my childhood. My grandparents came to America from Norway, and with them came the traditional Norwegian immigrant trunk which held the items needed to start life in a new country. In spite of limited space, they found room to bring with them a wood rosemaling tray, picture frame, and other small items that held a particular warm memory for them.

As a young girl, each summer I would visit my grandmother. Together, we would go through her huge round-top trunk, spending time looking at these treasures that made the journey with her from Norway. This was my first exposure to Norwegian rosemaling.

A small chest that was carried with my grandparents was used to hold their food supply. This small chest later was used by me to hold my books. When my son was about one-and-a-half years old, he had a better imagination than his mother; he used it as an imaginary boat. It is now in the process of being restored and rosemaled for my granddaughter. It will then have been used by four generations.

It seems as though I have always been familiar with the Norwegian lifestyle, and painting this beautiful Norwegian folk art is very much a part of my life.
(Marilyn Olin--St. Paul, MN)

STRAW ORNAMENTS

Christmas and straw ornaments--stars, angels, and particularly the Tomte and Julbock, were always synonymous with me as a child. Not until 1971, when surgery brought a straw mobile as a gift, did I feel I could create the ornaments myself. Then came research, creating, teaching, and the writing of two books, *Fun With Straw*, directions for the Scandinavian tied ornaments, and *More Fun With Straw*, on wheat weaving.

The Tomte, who rides on the Julbock, brings the gifts at Christmas time. In pagan times, it was the god Thor's goat. Created in straw, it would chase away the evil spirits. At the advent of Christianity, the goat lost its paganism, and was then given as a greeting card during the holiday season. It became traditional to have a Julbock at the foot of one's Christmas tree.

The Julnisse (Norwegian or Danish), or Tomte (Swedish) brought the gifts on Christmas Eve. But he is really the inhabitant of a Swedish farm (never seen, however) who watches over the animals and keeps everything going well. Thus, you must surely leave his rewarding bowl of porridge on Christmas Eve to reserve his protection throughout the year.
(Jeanette M. Starr--Minneapolis, MN--1970s-80s)

CRACKER JACK^R PRIZE COLLECTION

I had a Cracker Jack^R prize collection when I was young. I would buy a box of corn for ten cents and open the bottom, where a toy would be waiting. Usually they were plastic, which I liked the best--sometimes various people (cowboys, Indians, baseball players) or animals (fish, squirrels, lions, rabbits), and even the Cracker Jack^R boy himself. My cousin and I would play with our collections and often display them in our homes. She would line them up on the wooden ledge above the windows in her living room. I still have my collection and add to it from time to time.
(JoAnn Wanner Prom--Hebron, ND--1950s)

DOLL COLLECTION

I started collecting dolls about twelve years ago. I remember when I bought my first doll with some birthday money I had gotten, I put it in the closet for awhile because I thought people would think I was crazy buying a doll at my age! I now have eighty-three dolls. Some of my favorites are Cinderella and the Lee Middleton dolls--porcelain and musical.
(Mary B. Twar--White Bear Lake, MN--1970s-80s)

STORYBOOK DOLLS

In my small hometown, we went to many birthday parties when we were young. During my grade school years, a favorite gift was a storybook doll. At one time, I had a whole cabinet full--maybe fifty or so. I can remember an Indian, a nun, a cowgirl, and many others. A favorite was a china doll my aunt gave me; it was dressed in an outfit made from her wedding dress material.
(Vicki A. Johnson--Groton, SD--1950s)

COLLECTING STAMPS

My dad gave my older sister and me a spiral notebook to save stamps in. I had pages set aside for one-, two-, three-, and four-cent stamps, and I filled many pages of each kind. At the end of the book was a special page reserved for airmail stamps.

My sister and I looked forward to seeing what new stamps would be on envelopes that arrived in the mail each day. We took turns as to who would get the next stamp. If a package came, we were really excited, because then there would be several different stamps. I can still remember the colors and pictures of all the various stamps.
(Cindy Salberg Lerfald--White Bear Lake, MN--1950s)

FIVE-AND-DIME

We came to Aberdeen to shop every once in awhile. My favorite place was Woolworth's. They had so many things a little girl might want to buy if she had the money. I often bought a small purse with a chain handle with my ten cents, or sometimes a paper parasol, which would soon be destroyed in our South Dakota wind. We also bought small china dolls (four or five inches tall) which had movable arms; then we would sew dresses and coats for them.
(Mary Simonson Thompson--Groton, SD--1930s)

WHAT A PLACE TO BROWSE!

In our area, there were two rival five-and-dime stores--Kresge's and Woolworth's. Why were they always painted red?! Their windows were always filled with myriads of things to tempt the passersby. What a place to browse! If you were lucky enough to have a dime to spend, it required endless comparison shopping. It was definitely a major decision!
(Mae F. Hardin--ND--1920s)

THE FIVE-CENT CANDY BAR

When I was in the fifth, sixth, and seventh grades, I attended school in the small town or village of Ferney, South Dakota. At noon, we would go to the store with our penny, and buy a "B&B Bat" sucker, bubble gum, or a candy bar. A penny bought quite a lot in those days. My dream was to have a five-cent Butterfinger candy bar, as that was my favorite. A five-cent candy bar was very large at that time.

My dad told me that if I got a 95% average on my report card, he would give me a nickel. When I got the required percentage, he gave me my nickel. However, when I bought the big Butterfinger, I brought it home and divided it up among all of us, so that we each got a small piece. Consequently, I still hadn't had the pleasure of having a five-cent candy bar all for myself!
(Mary Simonson Thompson--Groton, SD--1930s)

GENERAL STORE

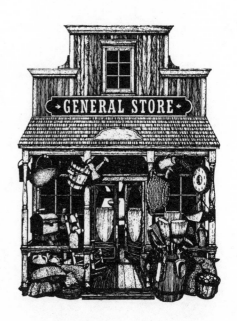

I don't suppose general stores had more in them than stores today--most weren't nearly as big--but they were so different. How long has it been since you read off your list and a clerk "waited on you?" Is there a store anyplace where you can take

170

in a case of eggs and exchange it for your groceries? Or a store where you can buy blue jeans, dress goods, or kerosene for your lamp? Today, most things come in neat little plastic packages. Sixty years ago, many things came in bulk. On the counter was a large roll of brown paper; a large spool of string hung on a spindle above it, along with a bunch of bananas just as they came off the plant. The clerk would wrap just as many as you asked for.
(Mae F. Hardin--ND--1920s)

MY GRANDPA'S CORNER STORE

Every Saturday morning in the late 1940s, I would "tag along" with my dad when he went to work at my Grandpa Bacigalupo's grocery store, which was in the basement of a large apartment building in the Midway area of St. Paul. What a thrill, as an eight-year-old, to be a part of that sales force! It was every kid's dream come true, for I was in charge of the candy counter! There in huge, wood and glass enclosed showcases, were neatly lined-up boxes of all the favorite sweets--Root Beer Barrels, Jaw Breakers, Tootsie Rolls, Snaps, Malted Milk Balls, Lemon Drops, and the list goes on and on. I spent many hours feeling important, as I arranged and rearranged those boxes of bulk penny candy, "occasionally" taking a sample or two!

Grandpa's store was much more than just candy. His daily trips to the downtown Farmer's Market provided only the freshest and best produce for his customers. An enormous white enamel and glass cooler displayed fresh deli meats and cheeses, all waiting to be sliced to perfection on the hand-operated slicer. Other large coolers featured soft drinks, dairy products and milk in glass bottles. The reach-in freezer, with the removable small lids, held more "favorites" among the frost--Cheerios, Fudgesicles, and Popsicles. Neat and stacked high to the ceiling on the surrounding walls were all the various canned goods.

Grandpa's store was sold at the beginning of the new decade, and Grandpa "Baci" left us shortly thereafter--in 1954. I often wonder what he would have to say about the supermarkets of today.
(Caroleann L. Seidenkranz--St. Paul, MN--1940s)

"SEARS AND SAWBUCK"

Sears and Roebuck (we called it "Sears and Sawbuck") got a lot of orders from my folks at Christmas time. It was sort of like writing to Santa Claus. That's where my first harmonica came from. I was pleased with it, and I've replaced it many times. I'm sure Santa brought us more useful gifts, too, like stocking caps and mittens.

Yes, the arrival of the new "Sears and Sawbuck" catalog by mail was an exciting time at our house in the country. It was full of good pictures and intriguing descriptions. There weren't many wants that couldn't be ordered--from dolls to doorknobs, towels to trowels, gramophones to grinding stones, shotguns to long johns, teddy bears to teddies, bathtubs to barbwire, story books to cornhusking hooks. Yes, it was our wishing well.
(Roy B. Moore--Central Illinois--1913-18)

THE MOST MARVELOUS PURCHASE

The most marvelous purchase I remember Mom and Dad ordering from the Sears and Roebuck catalog was a forerunner of the modern instant camera. I don't know its trade name, but we were using it in 1916. It was a black box, about 3x4x6, with a push plunger button on a line leading up to the shutter. A glass viewer was folded down on top. Fastened at the rear below was a flat metal container where some special liquid would be poured in.

To take the picture, you posed the subject as viewed through the glass, pressed the push button, reached in through the black sleeve at the back, took the front card with your hands and dropped it into the container of fluid in a slot inside, counted to thirty, slid the container back, took out the card, and--Voila! The card became a photo.

I still have some of those fading brown pictures. There is Dad wearing his black derby, looking off into the distance for effect; the 1914 Studebaker Mom bought with her chicken money; Dad pretending to drive the 1917 Dodge touring car, with Glen and me climbing across the hood (clowning as usual); Mom dressed up in a man's suit; brother Gene and nephew Don--two one-year-olds, naked as a young jaybird; and the whistle-stop station house where we lived, with the Empire sign spelled eripmE. This camera took all pictures in reverse!

The catalog also produced our gas mantle lamp, our Silvertone phonograph, our crystal tube radio, and the cavalry saddle for Old John to carry me to school. When I graduated, Mom ordered a gold pocket watch with "Roy B. Moore" engraved on the back among the flowers.

That Sears and Roebuck catalog filled our lives with many useful and joyful products, and, most of all, with many precious memories.
(Roy B. Moore--Central Illinois--1913-18)

BIG, FAT WISH BOOKS

The Sears and Roebuck catalog or the Montgomery Ward catalog--big, fat wish books full of--harness and buggy whips, clothing, heating and cooking stoves, furniture, books, records, dress material, toys, and groceries. Every fall, we sent a long grocery order to Montgomery Ward. The order was sent by freight, and Dad had to take the grain wagon to town to haul it all home--canned fruits and vegetables, 20-pound boxes of raisins and prunes, 10-pound wooden pails of apple butter, and 3-gallon kegs of vinegar. This, together with about 800 pounds of flour, 200 pounds of sugar, and about 10 boxes of apples to supplement our homegrown food, would see us through the long, cold North Dakota winter.

Ordering from a catalog was only one of its many lives. There was its life of dreams--turning the pages and wondering what it would be like to have this or that. There was also its life as a fashion magazine. The girls chose the dress style they wanted; their mother looked at the picture, ordered some material, and then made the dress. When the catalog was out of season--well, who bought paper dolls when you could cut any you wanted from the colored catalog pages! Of course, everyone knows where the catalog's last life was spent!
(Mae F. Hardin--ND--1920s)

SPORTS AND LEISURE

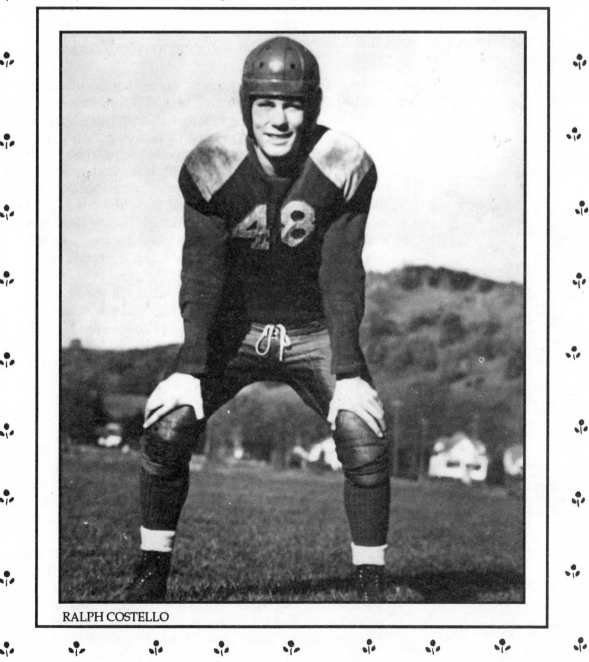

RALPH COSTELLO

THE GAME WAS PLAYED FOR FUN

When I played high school football in the 1930s, and college football in the 1940s, the game was played for fun, and it was played by "students." Today, the members of our 1947 college backfield include two doctors, an air force general, and a college math teacher. The free substitution "platooning" of players didn't exist then, which meant that most players stayed on the field for the entire game, and often for the entire season. Players then had no face mask, no mouthpiece, and less padding than today's competitors.
(Ralph Costello--Wabasha/Winona, MN--1930s-40s)

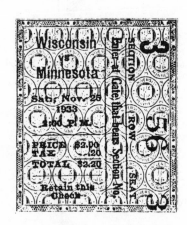

ARMISTICE DAY FOOTBALL GAME

My most memorable athletic experience occurred the day the Armistice Day killer blizzard racked Minnesota--November 11, 1940. On that day, I was quarterbacking a high school team from Wabasha, Minnesota, in a game being played at Lake City.

When the game began, there was a light mist in the air and the temperature was relatively high for that time of year. As the afternoon progressed, the mist turned to a light rain that soaked our uniforms. Then, suddenly the temperature plummeted, and a blinding, raging blizzard hit the field, freezing our soaked uniforms. Action on the field became impossible. The game was stopped by the officials, and everyone sought protection and warmth.

Many duck hunters in the backwaters of the Mississippi River could not escape the sudden ravages of the storm. The headlines in the Winona newspaper the following day very starkly read, "The Ducks Came; The Men Died."
(Ralph Costello--Lake City, MN--1940)

THE FOOTBALL PARADE

In October of 1959, everyone at Alexander Ramsey High School was anxiously looking forward to our homecoming. Our football team was having a good season, and the guys were having a lot of fun, as well as working hard. In fact, a group of juniors and seniors virtually guaranteed an entertaining time to anyone around them.

In order to assure that attention was drawn to the upcoming event, and to inform their opponents in South St. Paul of their intention to win the homecoming game, they decided to "parade" on foot from Roseville to South St. Paul. So, two nights before the game, donned in costumes of pajamas, stocking hats, and banners, they paraded through the St. Paul loop

and all the way to the opposing high school. They arrived in the South St. Paul parking lot, intending to camp there overnight and then greet their opposition as they arrived at school the next morning. However, the coaches, parents, and authorities were a little less enthusiastic about the overnight camping. So, after all of the excitement of marching to South St. Paul, and being greeted by the encouraging cheers of classmates and flashes of cameras, the guys were given a ride back home. While the game fades in our memories, the "parade" still seems like yesterday.
(Gail Westby--Roseville, MN--1959)

THE BALLAD OF THE LEFT AND THE RIGHT

The year was nineteen twenty-nine;
'Twas footeball in the Fall.
No college men did play for pay,--
They played for fun, that's all.
And patch-ed be their uniforms
And scratch-ed be their ball.

Old Normal had a new left end,--
All other ends were lame.
Spake he, Coach Joe to Moore, named Roy
"You fill that spot this game."
Eureka had a big right guard,
Ron Reagan was his name.

Pavilions pulsed with crowded verve.
Each team with valor fought.
Through flubs and flukes they struggled on,
All yardage dearly bought.
At half time ne'er a laurel won,--
The score held, naught to naught.

When once again the fray began,
No points to either came.
Then raised him up the guard named Ron
And cried with voice aflame,
"Just squeeze the ball and follow me!
Eureka is our name!"

Across the field the runner ran,
A Reagan-led stampede,--
Across the turf, across the goal!
Eureka took the lead!
Old Normal then did moan and groan
To see that team succeed.

BRIAN SCHLICHTER

But, lo! upspake that new left end,
Spake he with vocal prod,
"We must not let Eureka smash
Old Normal to the sod!
Heave high a pass,--I fain would be
A former-day Rashad!"

The clock was closing off the game
When sky-high ball was shied,
And, green as grass, the new left end
Did grasp it in full stride
And crossed the goal with wing-ed feet.
The footeball game was tied!

Aye! fifty years have flown since when
That score tied, six to six.
Now Ron and Roy play other games:
One plays at politics;
The other plays around with verse,
Like lowly limericks.

The battling of those two is done.
That age approaches night,
For Roy he is now long retired,
While Ron seeks growing might.
That once left end up-ended now,
That guard regarded right.

That fading footeball field has spread
Across the whole countree,
And Reagan has the Right to guard
By wide majoritee!
He shouts again, "Just squeeze the ball!
Eureka! Follow me!"
(Roy B. Moore--Normal, IL--1929)
(Taken from *Kindly Frost and Other Rime*, 1982)

ELEVEN OVERTIMES

Minneapolis South High School, hockey, and the Alms and Westbys were synonymous in the 1950s. There were ten boys in the two families who lived next door to each other, and all of them played hockey. South had a reputation for fine hockey, so it was no surprise to find them in the state high school hockey tournament.

South was matched with Thief River Falls in the quarter finals at 7:00 p.m. on Thursday night. Two outstanding teams took the ice. After the first period, the score was tied. Again, after the second period, it was tied. At the end of the game, the score was STILL tied, two to two.

JIM WESTBY

Then began the making of history. Overtime followed over-time, until after nine overtimes, the game was still tied. The teams were exhausted and the fans hysterical. Tournament officials decided to make ice and begin the next quarter final game, while the players rested.

Between the first and second periods of the Roseau vs. St. Paul Johnson game, the South vs. Thief River Falls teams played a tenth overtime. Still a tie! The second period of the second game got underway sometime after midnight. Between the second and third period, the eleventh overtime began. But this time, a long, hard shot from South's Jim Westby hit the net at 1:10 a.m., ending the longest game in high school tournament history. "Westby could be Mayor of Southtown" was broadcast for the rest of the weekend! South lost to Roseau in the championship game, but the quarter final game was the one people were still talking about over thirty years later.
(Gail Westby--Minneapolis, MN--1955)

BASEBALL ON RADIO

Our newspapers in the 1920s were the daily *Milwaukee Sentinel* and the weekly *County Journal*. In those days, the sports-minded of the Midwest often followed the baseball games between the Milwaukee Brewers and the Minneapolis Millers of the American Association.

Later, after we bought our first radio (a Temple), I always followed many games by listening to that radio. I would draw a baseball field on cardboard from the back of a writing tablet. Then, with the players' names written on tiny tags of paper, I would orient them appropriately on the field so that I could better visualize the plays.
(Ruben F. Schmidt--Shawano Co., WI--1920s)

HOME PLATE

The home plate from the old Lexington Ballpark is embedded in the floor of Kowalski's Grocery Store in St. Paul. That's where Babe Ruth used to stand and hit home runs. My dad even caught one there during an exhibition game with the Yankees in 1930 or '31.
(Melvin Frerck--St. Paul, MN--1930s)

ALL FOR NAUGHT

It was about six o'clock in the evening. The Minnesota Twins had just beaten the Detroit Tigers to win the American League championship. Mike, Scott, Erik, and I were on our way to Dayton's in downtown St. Paul to get World Series Tickets. Mike's car was loaded down with our supplies for camping out.

178

BRIAN SCHLICHTER

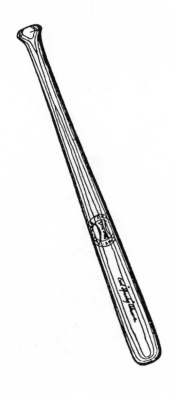

We had on several sweatshirts, heavy jackets, hats, and gloves. It was a cold day and we knew it would be a cold night.

The line was already halfway around the building when we got there. After putting our things down at the end of the line, we decided to go play football in an open area across the way. There were a few obstacles, such as trees, garbage cans, and bums, but it was a good "time killer." When we went back to our place in line, we started talking to two guys next to us. We all decided to go get something to eat at Mickey's Diner. After waiting fifteen minutes without even being given a menu, we left. Then we went back and played some more football, this time in a parking ramp. When we got tired of jumping over cars catching the ball, we decided to go rest a little. After awhile, Mike and Scott fell asleep, but Erik and I stayed up talking until about six o'clock in the morning.

At eight o'clock the line started moving, so we had to get up. We stood in line for about four hours before we finally made it into the building. At last we could see the ticket window. Anxiety was building as we slowly moved along. We couldn't WAIT to get our tickets! After all these hours, FINALLY, we were almost there.

There were about fifty people in front of us when we heard the two horrible words--SOLD OUT! We couldn't believe it! What a disappointment! After waiting in line for about eighteen hours, we came up "empty handed." Reluctantly, we picked up our gear and headed slowly out of the building and back to school. We had to settle for watching the biggest event in baseball on television.
(Scott Falk--St. Paul, MN--1987)

WHAT A SPECIAL MOMENT IT WAS!

On October 12, 1987, I was one of the 50,000 or so individuals who went to the Metrodome in Minneapolis to welcome home our Minnesota Twins from their unexpected American League play-off victory.

My husband and I were attending our son's seventh grade football game, when I heard the announcement about the homecoming celebration. I said, "Let's go!" And how glad I am we did, for we were to experience something quite phenomenal. No one expected the huge crowd that turned out that night, least of all the players. The Dome was packed with young and old alike, all there to welcome home their heroes.

The feeling that existed for both fans and players when the doors opened and the players walked out onto the field can never be replayed. The fans stood and cheered. The players hugged one another. What a special moment it was!
(Bonnie Hughes Falk--Minneapolis, MN--1987)

On October 27, 1987, Minnesota held one of its biggest celebrations ever--a ticker-tape parade for the World Champion Minnesota Twins. Schools let out and businesses closed, as thousands of people went to watch their heroes and their families parade from Minneapolis to the State Capitol in St. Paul. The sidewalks and streets were jammed. Confetti was everywhere.

My husband, son, and I were waiting on the lawn of the Capitol, clad in our Twins T-shirts, sweatshirts, caps, and other paraphernalia, waving our Homer Hankies, those "hot commodities" I had stood in line hours to get. Because of the mobs of people, the motorcade was late, but everyone waited patiently. Many climbed on light posts, trees, and anything else which would make them taller.

I can't say that I really saw them as they drove past (mostly tops of heads), but I was there! I did see and hear them as they gave their speeches on the steps of the Capitol. Too soon, it was all over, and everyone left for home. However, "We're Gonna Win, Twins" had become a reality.

(Bonnie Hughes Falk--St. Paul, MN--1987)

THE JOHN FREDERICKSEN FAMILY

American & National League Workouts

★ ★ ★ ★ ★

1985 ALL-STAR GAME

★ ★ ★ ★ ★

HHH Metrodome Minneapolis, Minn July 15, 1985

Charitable Donation for the Minnesota All-Star Baseball Fund $2.00 Suggested

Major League Baseball All-Star Workout 2:00 pm

Upper Deck Reserved

GREG SCHLICHTER

ANDY FALK

My most memorable athletic accomplishment occurred at the Fellowship of Christian Athletes Conference at St. Olaf College, in my hometown of Northfield, Minnesota, in the summer of 1981. Over 250 Christian athletes of all shapes and sizes from around the country were assembled that week for fellowship and athletic competition. We were all separated into huddles or teams of about a dozen. These teams competed in all kinds of athletic contests, some team oriented, some individual. My huddle was an odd assortment of kids, ranging from our leader who was pushing 300 pounds, to a couple of guys who had never played any sports in their lives.

On the final day of this unusual olympics, I was chosen (by a process of elimination, I'm sure) to compete in the free-throw competition. Being a squatty 5'8" hockey player, in a gymnasium packed with "real" basketball stars (several Mr. Basketball award winners from differing states were present), I didn't feel extremely confident about my chances.

I was the second in our group to take his turn at the line. Looking up at the backboard and thinking about the stories of faith I had heard throughout the week, I suddenly felt quite relaxed. I remember my first six or seven shots sailing off my fingers and sinking easily into the cylinder. Then I thought-- "Wait a second. This is too easy." My next shot shakily looped toward the basket, lacking the machine-like rhythm of my others. It bounced off the front rim and the backboard, before swirling around the rim and, luckily, falling through. I sensed the renewed belief of the true hoopsters surrounding the paint, as if they thought in unison, "This guy won't make another."

After taking a deep breath, I thought to myself, this challenge is like the game of life itself. God is most certainly testing my belief. I said a little prayer; not to make any more baskets, but to let Him let me do my best. To the surprise of everyone present, I hit all ten of my attempts. None swished after that prayer, but I had made ten of ten, nonetheless. No one in that gym, not even any of the Mr. Basketballs, made more than nine. I contributed something like fifty points (a large sum) to our team for winning that competition. My huddle members were astounded when they found out.

After the free-throw contest, I walked over to a team member who was trying to build his confidence for the football punting contest. A soccer player, he was not really sure how to go about this foreign activity of kicking an oblong ball. I remember telling him that he had the leg muscle and flexibility to do as well as anyone, and for some reason that seemed to perk him up immensely. He stepped up when his name was called and kicked that football farther than anyone else--even the ones who were kickers on their football teams--and won the competition.

In the end, our scraggly bunch made a run for overall champions. With the help of our 300-pound huddle leader, we al-

most took the tug-of-war contest, and nearly won it all. The others in my huddle elected me most inspirational, and I don't think I'll ever forget that little prayer I said at the free throw line that warm summer day.
(Greg Schlichter--Northfield, MN--1981)

FLYING DUTCHMEN-EDGERTON, MINN
MINNESOTA 1960 STATE BASKETBALL CHAMPIONS

GROTON, SD, BASEBALL TEAM, 1934

SQUIRREL HUNTING

When I was a boy, every fall we would go squirrel hunting. It was a great sport, especially where we lived. The valley of Rushford, Minnesota, is surrounded by big bluffs, which have hardwood forests on them. One could go out in the morning and never see anyone for a whole day.

There were two kinds of squirrels that we would hunt--the fox red squirrel and the grey squirrel. They were both big, but the grey squirrel had more tender meat. My friend and I would use two kinds of fire power--22 long rifle and 410 shotgun. Since some oak trees hold their leaves until spring, this gave the squirrels a chance to outwit us.
(Al Kjos--Rushford, MN--1930s)

JACK AND JOHANNA JOHNSON

YOUNG COUPLE IN A CANOE

Taking advantage of a beautiful spring day, I was fishing from the shore of a lake, when I spotted a young couple in a canoe about thirty feet from shore. The man reached into the water to retrieve a bait which was hooked on a snag on the lake bottom. The water was deeper than he thought, so he leaned over until his arm and shoulder were completely in the water. The more he leaned to one side, the more the young woman in the front of the canoe leaned to the opposite side.

When the man had the bait, he quickly sat up straight, beaming in self-satisfaction at his prize. The young woman didn't have time to react, and the canoe overturned, sending both into the lake. I will never forget the look on their faces! I didn't hear everything they said, which is perhaps for the best. However, I did hear him say that he dropped the bait. I often wonder if they ever went canoeing together again!
(Don Mockler--Patterson Lake, WI--1955)

STUFFED MUSKIE

Muskie was definitely the fish to catch! A trophy-size Muskie was the goal of the anglers staying in the cabins located around Mason Lake. If the fish wasn't big enough to mount, it still made a terrific meal. This particular Wisconsin resort specialized in preparing the "catch of the day" and serving it with all the trimmings. The kitchen staff stuffed the big fish with wild rice, using an orange to prop its mouth open.

One evening, while sitting in the dining hall, a four-year-old girl was recounting how she had dropped her orange into the lake earlier in the day. As the chef ceremoniously carried in a stuffed twenty-pound muskie on a fruit-filled tray, the child's eyes widened. Everyone laughed as she exclaimed, "I told you a fish ate my orange! Look, it's still in its mouth!"
(Steve and Doris Schmaltz--Mason Lake Resort, WI--1972)

In 1984, two transplanted Midwestern fishermen found themselves in a Tarpon Tournament taking place in San Juan Harbor in Puerto Rico. This father-son team awaited the strike with anticipation. As they looked around, their twelve-foot aluminum john boat seemed to be dwarfed by the luxury cabin cruisers surrounding it. Although their equipment was lacking, their spirit and experience made them winners.

Shortly into the contest, the rod of the fifteen-year-old angler began to bend. The stress of his twelve-pound test line was tremendous. To prevent the line from breaking, his father constantly maneuvered the boat into better position. The fight went on for seventy-five minutes. Other fishermen stopped to watch. One even managed to throw a gaff to the tiring team to help them haul the gigantic fish into the boat.

It took all of their remaining strength to pull in their prize. The father-son duo stared in amazement at the silver-scaled tarpon still thrashing around at their feet. It measured over six-feet long and weighed seventy-five pounds. That meant a pound of fish for each minute of struggle! The conquering heroes had set a new state record for twelve-pound line.

How's that for know-how? It doesn't matter if the fish is a sunny, a northern, or a tarpon. It's the savvy and dedication of the individual fisherman that makes the difference.

As for these two fishermen, they brought home to Minnesota several trophies representing the largest fish and the most pounds caught in the Tarpon Tournament. They also took home a once-in-a-lifetime memory and a whale of a fish story! (Steve and Dave Schmaltz--Puerto Rico--1984)

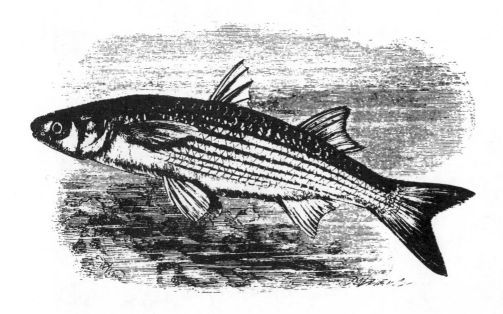

NORTHERN PIKE CAUGHT IN CROW WING COUNTY

MIKE FALK

DAVE AND STEVE SCHMALTZ

HARD TIMES

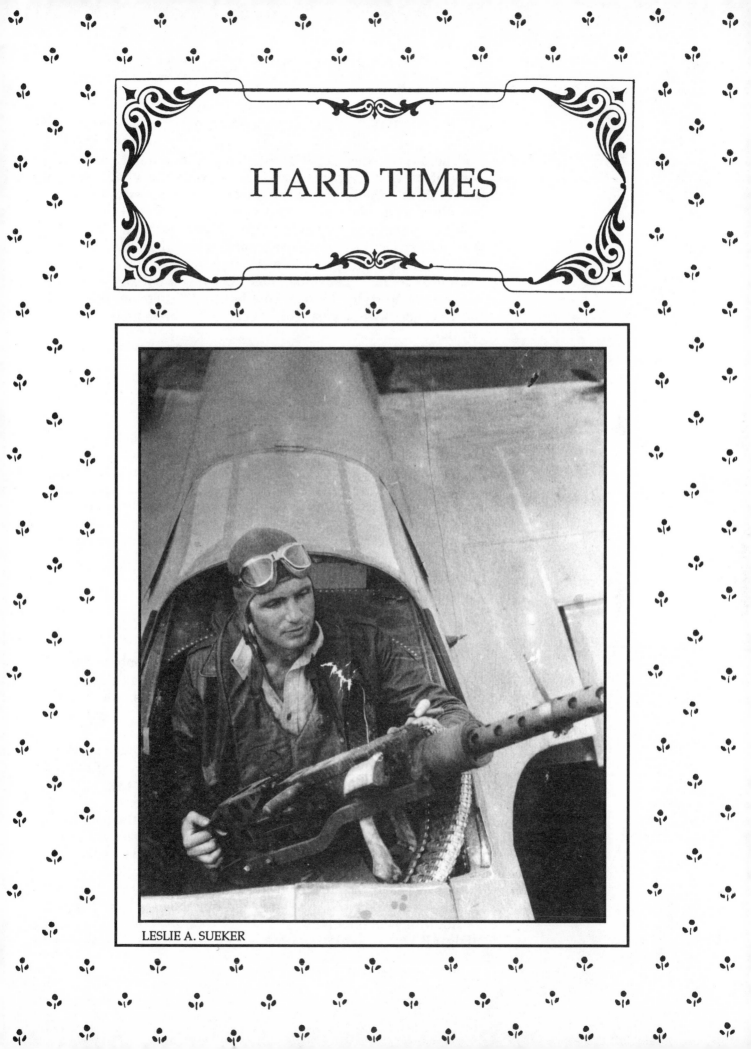

LESLIE A. SUEKER

MOTHER NATURE

THE DUST BLACKENED OUR SPIRITS

The days of the "Dirty Thirties" are in our minds forever. Any of us who lived through those terrible times will never forget them. The crop failures affected us all; poverty was everywhere. The black sky, filled with dust, also blackened our spirits, as there was very little we could do about it. It didn't do any good to clean up the house because it just got dusty all over again. With no crops to harvest, there wasn't much for the men folks to do. I remember often spending a hot afternoon in the basement, trying to keep cool by drinking homemade root beer, which wasn't very cold because of inadequate refrigeration.
(Mary Simonson Thompson--Groton, SD--1930s)

WHO CAN FORGET BLACK FRIDAY?

Brown County, South Dakota, was perhaps as bad as anywhere during the "Dust Bowl" days. Who can forget Black Friday? It was as dark as night! School was let out, and many cars were in the ditches because lights couldn't penetrate through the dust. My mom used wet towels or old rags to lay in the windowsills, but she still had to use a scoop shovel for a dustpan the next morning. Fences were buried, and the stock that was left just roamed the area looking for food.
(Lucille Blair Johnson--Brown Co., SD--1933-34)

1936--A MEMORABLE YEAR

Those of us around in 1936 remember it for a number of reasons besides our own personal lives. It was in a way a kind of last surge of the so-called "Dust Bowl" years. The summer was extremely hot and dry, and was followed by the coldest, snowiest winter in this writer's memory.

The Spanish Civil War was in progress and much in the mind of people in our government, and of citizens who cared and were aware of the almost hidden meaning of the conflict that, in a few more years, would involve us all.

Here in this country, we dealt with the heat of the summer and the cold and heavy snow of the following winter. The railroads and highways were blocked for a week, and the secondary roads were shoveled out by hand in the heavily drifted spots. There wasn't the machinery readily available then that there is now. But we survived, we lived, and our children were happy with the days of no school!
(Edgar B. Ober--Lake Crystal, MN--1936)

I was attending the University of Minnesota in the fall of 1940. Since Monday, November 11, was a holiday, I went home to Rushford, Minnesota, for the long weekend. My sister and four of her friends from Fargo were also home that weekend. They were to go back to Fargo on the morning of the 11th, so I had a chance to catch a ride back to Minneapolis with them.

It was a dreary day, with a mist coming down, but it wasn't too cold. I dressed in what I thought was suitable for a sportsman--leather high-top boots and britches, pants that fluffed out on the side (like they wear chasing fox in Great Britain), and a jacket that I considered more than adequate for the day.

As we passed through Rochester, we stopped at the Warall Hospital to visit my father who was recovering from a heart attack. A mist was still coming down when we left the hospital, and in a short time it started to snow. There was a strong northwest wind that we were driving straight into. Heavier and heavier the snow came. Each time we went through a small town or a filling station out in the country, we would vote to continue on. Cars were already being held up at many points. We, on one side of the car, would watch for the ditch, while those on the other side would watch their side and report to the driver. We were only going about five to fifteen miles per hour.

Finally, we got to Farmington. Since the car wasn't operating properly, we pulled into the first garage we saw. We got out and opened the hood. No motor! It was completely full of snow. We were told there was no way we could go any farther, so I struck out to find rooms at the hotel. It was already full, but they told me about a house down the street. Yes, they had room, so we stayed there--the three girls in one apartment and the three men in the other.

The town was completely full. Everyone ate in the restaurants and went to the movie theater to kill time. We also played cards. The only way to get a message out of town was by short wave radio. We sent a message to our mother, but she didn't receive it until a few days later.

It took the Burlington Bus Lines, with buses running around the clock, several days to get everyone out of town. When we did get out, we saw cuts in the drifts across the road that were at least fifteen feet high, and we found out about the many rescues and deaths that had occurred. We had been fortunate to make it to safety, and we even managed to have a little fun while we waited out the storm. Everyone had an experience they would never forget.

(Al Kjos--Rushford, MN--1940)

I remember the Armistice Day blizzard of 1940 very well. I was supposed to go duck hunting, but since I had been sick, I stayed home. Some hunters died that day near Hastings. The shooting was so good that they wouldn't leave, and when the storm came up, they were trapped in their boats and drowned.

I put the storm windows on that morning and then went to work at noon. I didn't get home again for two days. I worked in a filling station, and everybody kept coming in to have chains put on their tires. There weren't any snowplows like we have now. The streetcars plowed the snow, and the cars followed them.

My wife, Lydia, came home from work that day on a streetcar. After it let her off, she had to walk four blocks in snow nearly up to her waist, while wearing high heels. The storm came up so fast that no one was dressed for it. Luckily, her brother was on the streetcar after hers and was able to catch up to her to help her home; otherwise, she wouldn't have made it. When her brother found her, she said she was ready to just lie down in the snow from the cold and exhaustion.
(Melvin Frerck--St. Paul, MN--1940)

IT TOOK THE HIGH BRIDGE DOWN

My dad and his brother-in-law owned the Tivoli Theater (which doesn't exist anymore) on Wabasha and 2nd Street--at the top of the Wabasha Street Bridge. In 1904, a tornado came down the Mississippi River and Dad watched it take the High Bridge down. He then hurried inside the theater to get everyone out. They all made it except the piano player; the piano fell on him and killed him. One chair from the theater was found on Cedar Avenue, near where the Capitol is now.
(Melvin Frerck--St. Paul, MN--1904)

Minnesota Historical Society

ST. PAUL, JANUARY, 1940

THE DEPRESSION

WE LIVED THROUGH IT ALL

My husband and I were married in 1931, and the Depression started a year or so later. We lived on my husband's home farm, which he and his brother rented. Grandpa Pederson lived with us. We had cattle, hogs, and chickens, and horses to do the farm work. We churned our own butter, and had milk, cream, eggs, and meat, so we had plenty to eat. I had a big garden and did a lot of canning. We raised a few turkeys, but one year it was so dry that the turkeys even ate up the onions in the garden! There wasn't a blade of grass except some Russian Thistle, but we lived through it all and learned a great deal from it.
(Ada Ronnei Pederson--Pope Co., MN--1932-36)

POOR AS A CHURCH MOUSE

Each school was furnished with a broom, dustpan, water pail dipper, wash basin, and soap dish. One night someone entered the schoolhouse and took all of them. Because we were pretty sure who had taken them (a newly married couple, "poor as a church mouse"), nothing was done. The school board quietly replaced them and no one ever mentioned the theft.
(Dorothea Thompson--southwest MN--1932)

DANCE MARATHONS

During the Depression, they used to have dance marathons at the Coliseum Dance Hall on University and Lexington. They danced twenty-four hours a day for days on end to get money. One partner would be holding the other up, but they wouldn't quit because they needed the money so badly. Often they would dance until they fell down and had to be carried out. I went once to watch and couldn't stand it. Animals were treated better!
(Melvin Frerck--St. Paul, MN--1930s)

IT WAS A "SIN" TO WASTE FOOD

My husband worked two years in the Alden bank before he saved enough money for us to get married and buy a car. Some years later, when we felt we could take little trips, we always took our food along. Eating in restaurants was rare. We had an ice chest and a bottled gas burner in our car trunk, and at night we rented housekeeping cabins. We had some wonderful trips.

The Depression taught people to save things; we might need them some day. I still have trouble discarding old things. We were taught that we had to eat everything on our plates before we could leave the table. In fact, it was a "sin" to waste food when there were so many hungry people.
(Selma Anderson Hughes--Alden, MN--1930s)

WE ATE APPLESAUCE ALL WINTER

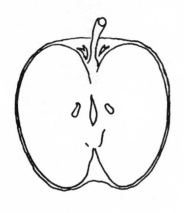

Having grown up in the "Dirty Thirties," we all went through many hard times. There never was much money, but all of us were poor, so we just did the best we could to survive. My dad and brothers milked cows, so we had a small cream check which was used to buy groceries. Also, Mother received money for selling eggs at the grocery store.

Because of the drought, gardens were never very abundant, but I think we almost always raised enough potatoes to get us through the winter, even if they were very small in size. One time we went up north of Claremont and picked apples, so we ate applesauce all winter! Wholesome and good, but we soon got tired of it.
(Mary Simonson Thompson--Groton, SD--1930s)

A DREARY TIME AT BEST, A DESPARATE TIME AT WORST

The Great Depression, the Dust Bowl, and the Grasshopper Plague all hit us at the same time; it was a dreary time at best, a desperate time at worst. You would plant a garden to help feed the family, and the grasshoppers would chew it off to the ground. Eggs were five cents a dozen and oats were five cents a bushel. If you shipped an animal to the St. Paul stockyards, you often got less than it cost to ship it!

Many lost their savings in bank closings, and farmers lost their homes and livelihood in foreclosures. In cities, thousands lost their jobs and existed by standing in soup lines. Hoboes wandered across the country, living on handouts or odd jobs. Some hitched rides on freight cars and lived in hobo jungles along the tracks or under bridges.
(Mae F. Hardin--ND--1930s)

"HOME BREW"

I didn't know about Prohibition. Everyone made "home brew;" it was a family project. My father was the one who mixed everything up. The crock sat in the back bedroom. One of my brothers would siphon it into bottles, another would cap it, and my youngest brother and I would carry it to the root cellar. Because we were good kids, Dad would make root beer for us at the same time. It was sure good! When Dad would have friends over, he would go to the root cellar to get bottles of beer to serve.

I also remember an incident involving our local moonshiner. Since I came from a strictly Scandinavian neighborhood, some of the people were very fussy about drinking. Therefore, they had the moonshiner arrested. However, when it came time for the "mash" to be bottled, the police let him out to take care of his "business!"
(Mary B. Twar--Two Harbors, MN--1920s-30s)

SPEAKEASYS

I remember there being a speakeasy in a house behind the Foot-Schultz Building in downtown St. Paul. They made "home brew" and sold it at night. It was served in the malt cans from the malt they used for the beer. When they ran out of bottled beer, they would scoop into the crocks where the malt was kept to make the brew and serve that. The drunks didn't know the difference!
(Melvin Frerck--St. Paul, MN--1920s)

MOONSHINE

Segal's Grocery used to sell sugar to all the moonshiners in town. They'd drive up in Model T Fords, and we'd put two or three sacks in the back end. Big touring cars would take fifteen sacks. My job was to stand on the sidewalk and toss the 100-pound sacks of sugar into the back seats and trunks of the moonshiners' cars. Now I can't even lift one!
(Melvin Frerck--St. Paul, MN--1927-29)

4

53|391 **BE**
UNITED STATES OF AMERICA
OFFICE OF PRICE ADMINISTRATION

WAR RATION BOOK FOUR

Issued to *Selma V. Hughes*
(First, middle, and last names)

Complete address *Alden, Minn.*

READ BEFORE SIGNING

In accepting this book, I recognize that it remains the property States Government. I will use it only in the manner and for authorized by the Office of Price Administration.

Void if Altered   *Selma V. Hughes*
(Signature)

It is a criminal offense to violate rationing regulations.
OPA Form R-145   16--85870-1

UNITED STATES OF AMERICA
War Ration Book One

WARNING

1 Punishments ranging as high as *Ten Years' Imprisonment or $10,000 Fine, or Both*, may be imposed under United States Statutes for violations thereof arising out of infractions of Rationing Orders and Regulations.

2 This book must not be transferred. It must be held and used only by or on behalf of the person to whom it has been issued, and anyone presenting it thereby represents to the Office of Price Administration, an agency of the United States Government, that it is being so held and so used. For any misuse of this book it may be taken from the holder by the Office of Price Administration.

3 In the event either of the departure from the United States of the person to whom this book is issued, or his or her death, the book must be surrendered in accordance with the Regulations.

4 Any person finding a lost book must deliver it promptly to the nearest Ration Board.

OFFICE OF PRICE ADMINISTRATION

N°. 61614 -137

WAR

ARMISTICE SIGNED

In the spring of the year that I was in the fifth grade, America entered World War I. We learned war songs, rolled bandages, bought war stamps, and engaged in other patriotic activities.

When I was in the sixth grade, the war still claimed much attention until November 11 when the Armistice was signed. I remember picking up the mail--it must have been on a Saturday--noting the streamer headline, "Armistice Signed," on the daily paper, and running out to the field with the paper to tell my dad and brother the great news.
(H. Conrad Hoyer--Clay Co., SD--1918)

PEARL HARBOR HAS BEEN ATTACKED

Whenever there is an important event, we can always remember where we were when it happened. That is true for me about Pearl Harbor. My future husband was visiting me that weekend, having been discharged from the army the week before because of a bad back. I was teaching at a rural school, and we had just gone to light the oil burner so that the schoolhouse would be warm on Monday. When we returned, the radio announcer broke in with the news that Pearl Harbor had been attacked. We were at war! What a terrible Sunday afternoon that turned out to be.
(Mary Simonson Thompson--Groton, SD--1941)

THAT FATEFUL DECEMBER DAY

"Wake up. Come listen to the radio," my mother called to me as I was sleeping that fateful December day when the Japanese bombed Pearl Harbor. I was working nights and sleeping days, when my mother awakened me with the shocking news. Only a few days before when I was discussing the Japanese war expansion with friends, I had made the rash statement that the Japanese would never tangle with the United States. How wrong I was!
(Ole Schelsnes--WI--1941)

HAWAII SEEMED SO FAR AWAY

When Pearl Harbor was bombed, I was eight years old. I remember that my family was all in the kitchen when the announcement came over the radio. It was hard to believe that anything like that could happen; Hawaii seemed so far away.
(Janice Meredith Fredericksen--Lake Crystal, MN--1941)

During World War II, Boeing geared up and worked around the clock building planes. People flocked to Seattle from all over the country to join in the war effort. A popular song was "Rosie the Riveter." When my sister got a job as a riveter at Boeing, she took a lot of ribbing because her middle name was Rose.

(Mae F. Hardin--Seattle, WA--1940s)

LETTER HOME

New Guinea, March 11, 1943
Dear Mom,

And I thought it was hot in Australia! At present it is VERY HOT here and it is raining. The mosquitoes (of which there are more and they are bigger than any place in the world) are biting like the devil! I'm writing this letter by old-fashioned lamp light in my mosquito net.

Our camp is near a small river, so we usually go swimming once or twice a day to combat the heat. We live in shorts and sun helmets most of the time, and now, after four very good "burns and peals," I think I'm going to get a tan for the first time in my life. I would certainly like to trade you some of our rather warm weather for a little bit of your zero weather and snow. Here is one guy who will never mind shoveling snow again!

Of course, the "going to town idea" has ceased to exist now, but we still do have some outdoor shows and an old phonograph in our tent. Not many new records, but it's something to listen to.

Right now in our tent we are having laundry trouble. At first, we all sent a few pieces of washing to an abo (a colored native). He charged us half a pound, which is $1.60 in our money, or about three times what it was worth. So now we do our own-- the modern way. We build a big fire under a half-barrel of water, add our clothes and a couple boxes of soap, and let them boil for an hour or so. Then we rinse them. Of course, sometimes the barrel bottom comes off and the clothes don't last so long, but the ones that DO usually come out clean.

It's getting dark now, so I must close and go to bed. Another hard day of work tomorrow. Don't worry about me. It's dangerous, I know, but at the same time, it's adventurous and a little exciting. Write soon and say hello to all.

Love,
L. A. Sueker

(S/Sgt. Leslie A. Sueker was in the Army Air Corps--a first gunner aboard one of our bombers.)

LESLIE A. SUEKER

When I was in the navy, there was an initiation while cross-ing the equator. You were then given a certificate indicating that you had been initiated into the "Order of Shellback," and it was signed by Neptunus Rex.

The process of initiation consists of rounding up any of the crew who can't prove they already have a "shellback card." Then you're generally stripped down to shorts because of the temperature, and presented to a person who represents Nep-tunus Rex. This man wears a swab (mop) for a headdress, is usually approaching 300 pounds, and wears a large diaper-like covering. His tummy is smeared with mustard, and he is seated on an elevated stage. The inductee has to approach Neptunus Rex, kiss his tummy full of mustard, jump in a can-vas container full of water; then, as he leaves this tank, the other shellbacks hit him with paddles.

There is another ceremony when you cross the International Dateline, where you are given a card indicating that you're a member of the "Realm of the Golden Dragon." I crossed the equator at the International Dateline, so these two installations were combined.
(Emmett D. Salberg--Equator--February 29, 1944)

THE BOYS ARE COMING HOME!

The town went mad! It seemed like everyone, in spite of gas-oline rationing, drove downtown to yell, honk their horns, and throw things out their car windows. What a traffic jam! But no one cared if they couldn't move, because they were wild with joy. The boys were coming home!
(Mae F. Hardin--Minneapolis, MN--1945)

"FELLOW AMERICANS LOOKED SO GOOD!"

V-E Day was one of the best days of my life.

I was one of many prisoners of war in Germany. We had been herded along by our guards for some 60 days and 300 miles. The last days and weeks of April 1945 were pure sur-vival for us. We ate what we could find along the way: frozen turnips, potatoes, grass, snails, anything.

We were "liberated" on April 27, 1945, by the 3rd Infantry Division. Never did fellow Americans look so good! We were given food rations and grave warnings to stay where we were, as battle reports indicated strong and concentrated SS troops all around us. Our liberators then left to continue their part of the war.

Because we didn't know whether we would be recaptured, the 11 days between April 27 and May 8 were excruciatingly long.

CHIC BLAIR
JUNE TOTZKE
JACK JOHNSON

When May 8 arrived, with the realization the war was over, I felt an euphoria as great as I have ever known.
(Guy Fisher--White Bear Lake, MN--1945)

VICTORY OVER JAPAN DAY

After serving in the Pacific Theater for a couple of years, I was stationed on Treasure Island in San Francisco Bay, waiting for a new assignment in the OGU (Outgoing Unit). On this particular day in August, I was in Oakland on liberty, and was returning to Treasure Island on the "A" train when the siren went off, horns blew, etc., signaling the end--Victory over Japan! Rather than getting off the train at Verna Buena or Goat Island (as it was sometimes called), I stayed on the train and went to Frisco, since I knew if I went back to the station, I would be restricted to base.

San Francisco was a charged-up place on this day. Impromptu parades started up and down Market Street. Streetcars couldn't move. As the excitement built, there wasn't any resemblance of law and order. Booths which were formerly used for selling war bonds were moved to the street and burned. Army and naval officers were relieved of their caps which designated rank. As the day wore on, liquor stores were required to close one hour after the signal was given. As a result, the wild crowd started to kick in the windows, and liquor was given to one and all. As windows were smashed in, the mannequins with fur coats were left naked. Many girls, consequently, had new fur coats!

Later in the evening as we were leaving to return to base, we noticed quite a change on Market Street. Paper and debris was over a foot deep. All servicemen were picked up and hauled to any base to get them off the street. In the midst of all the paper, etc., you might find a drunk person sleeping, covered with debris. The newspaper the next day reported over 300 injured and 5 killed.
(Emmett D. Salberg--San Francisco, CA--1945)

RATION COUPONS--WHAT A PAIN!

Ration coupons--what a pain to keep track of! There were separate stamps for gas, sugar, canned goods, meat, shoes, and coffee. Not only did you have to keep track of all the different stamps, but also the dates when each was valid and when they would expire. If you bought something that didn't use the full value of the stamp, you got a little blue or red token, a little smaller than a dime.

Some things were scarce but not rationed; you just couldn't find them. Candy, chocolate, and camera film I could easily do without, and electric appliances I couldn't afford on a serviceman's allotment, but elastic I REALLY missed. Would the tiny

DAWN, LYLE, AND KATHY BLAIR

WE MUST GET ALONG WITH LESS SUGAR THIS YEAR BECAUSE—

1. Military needs are high. Each soldier actually consumes twice as much sugar a year as the average civilian now receives
2. Ships which otherwise might be bringing sugar into the United States are hauling supplies to the battle fronts
3. Manpower is scarce at sugar refineries and shipping ports.
4. Beet sugar production last year was 500,000 tons short, making the stock of sugar smaller for this year.
5. Last year many people over-applied for canning sugar. We used so much sugar that stocks at the beginning of this year were abnormally low.

DO NOT APPLY FOR MORE SUGAR THAN YOU ACTUALLY NEED FOR HOME CANNING — HELP MAKE OUR WAR SHORT SUGAR SUPPLIES LAST ALL YEAR

bit of rubber used in a child's training pants have really made a difference in the war effort?! Most two-year-olds don't have much in the way of hips, and the ties were a real headache. Tie them comfortably, and they ended up around the ankles; tie them snug enough to stay up, and they hurt. No two-year-old has really mastered knots, and by the time mother got there to untie them, it was usually too late!
(Mae F. Hardin--Minneapolis, MN--1940s)

RATIONING WAS NECESSARY

During World War II, I worked after school and on weekends in a small grocery store. Because of the war, there were shortages of many things. Therefore, rationing was necessary.

Coupons were needed to buy butter, sugar, certain meats, and even canned vegetables. We made frosting from white syrup because sugar was so scarce. When a box of bananas arrived, all the neighbors came running in hopes of buying some. Gasoline was also rationed, so it was almost impossible to take any long drives. If you did go for a drive and had a flat tire, you were really in trouble. There just were no new tires available anywhere. Another item in short supply was nylon hosiery. We used make-up on our legs to make it look like we were wearing nylons. Sometimes we even drew lines on the back of our legs for seams!
(Shirley Raines--Hastings, NE--1943)

WAR BOND DRIVE

"Who's on First?" That baseball comedy skit was performed in our city by the movie team of Abbott and Costello during a War Bond Drive. They delighted a large crowd that had gathered in front of the local Greek temple-style post office, since then demolished for a modern crackerbox.

As I had not entered the service at that time, I was in the crowd that saw Abbott and Costello. I laughed at their funny baseball routine, and took a picture of them with my Kodak box camera while they were performing. My picture was not like the "choice one" in the city newspaper, but it was a prized momento for me.
(Ole Schelsnes--WI--1940s)

READ BEFORE USING 5-POUND HOME CANNING SUGAR COUPONS

Before the attached coupons are used for the purchase of sugar *for home canning*, you or any member of your "family unit" listed on the application must sign each home canning coupon (OPA Form R-342). The person signing must enter the serial number of his War Ration Book Four thereon.

For the purpose of identification, it will be necessary for the signer to take his War Ration Book Four with him when he purchases the sugar.

These coupons are not transferable.

NEVER BUY RATIONED GOODS

WITHOUT RATION STAMPS

NEVER PAY MORE THAN THE LEGAL PRICE

United States Office of Price Administration

IMPORTANT: When you have used your ration, salvage the TIN CANS and WASTE FATS. They are needed to make munitions for our fighting men. Cooperate with your local Salvage Committee.

<u>July 29, 1968</u>

We arrived at the Seattle airport at 6:30 p.m. and went right to Fort Lewis to get our jungle gear, flight number, and barracks. The next morning, we left for Vietnam. There were 164 men on our plane. We stopped in Hawaii, Clark AFB in the Philippines, and finally Cam Ranh Bay, which is about three quarters of the way up the coast and is sort of an island--a big sandbox. The bay area is a huge supply depot. It is quite secure; only four shells have hit there, and that was last year during the Tet Offensive.

<u>August 3, 1968</u>

As we approached the Vietnam coast, the first thing I saw were tree-covered slopes--a different kind of tree that I have never seen before. As the plane came down, I could see the villages, which were shoddy and close together. The air strip here at Cam Ranh Bay is one of the busiest in the world.

After we landed, we were bussed to the 22nd Replacement Company. This whole area is comprised of huge hills of sand. It is really hot here and just breathing is difficult. Now was the first look I had at the barbed wire barriers and bunkers. We processed in, had our money changed to M.P.C., and had our bags inspected for drugs. Then we went to the barracks, which had only roofs, half sides, and screens. For the next year, I will have access only to cold water and no flush toilets. The waste is collected in half-barrels, and each morning it is burned.

Things here are quite well-developed; someone is making money at home because of what is built and used here. After formation, I went to sandbag bunkers. It's so hot here that you're sweating continually. We wear our jungle fatigues, which are light, with the sleeves rolled up.

At our later formation, we got our orders from MACV. I go to An Khe, which is in the Central Highlands. It is a base camp for the 1st Cavalry Division, of which I am now a member. When we first arrived, we had details for two days. Then we left for four days of training for infantry action at Camp Evans, which is only about twelve miles from the DMZ. It was really hot there--120 degrees in the sun. There were only tents to live in, and sandbags everywhere. When we flew up there, we could see bomb craters and shell scars all around. We made a quick landing on a hastily-built dirt runway.

On Tuesday we marched to the rifle range to zero our weapons. We wore flack vests weighing about twenty-five pounds, which are supposed to stop fragments of shells and rockets. There were no trees at Evans and the sun really beat down. My face burned and my lips cracked and bled. The only water to drink was purified warm water, which tasted awful. We had to dig fox holes and set up a perimeter for the night, and it was pouring rain at the time. There were five men try-ing to sleep in a hole for three, so it was very cramped. Also, the bugs were terrible. We were shown an assault on a hill us-

TOM FALK

ing five choppers. One fires 78 rockets at the hill, and another shoots 4,000 shells a minute. Then we had to repel from a forty-two foot tower.

August 12, 1968

I was glad to leave Evans and return to An Khe. It is cooler here, and we live in wooden buildings with cement floors. Things here are dirty, but Evans was unbelievable! I will be working in the Finance Office, since I have had college accounting. The 1st Cavalry is the first in the army to go all computer in finance, so the job should be interesting. I will handle the payrolls--taking the vouchers and money to the different units at Evans and outposts.

August 23, 1968

We went on full alert on Wednesday night. An infantry company had been overrun about five miles from here; radar picked up some movement, so they took half the men to the perimeter. We were looking at the casualty list tonight. Many men are getting killed. Last week there was a mortar attack at one of the outposts, and that list was four pages long. A lot of officers on the front lines get it. It's so bad in the field now that many are re-enlisting so they can come to the rear.

There has been a lot of action here this week. This morning at 2:00 the siren started blaring, so we got all our gear on and picked up ten magazines of ammo, ready to go to the perimeter if needed. We sat and waited at the bottom of the hill, but by 4:00 it was all over.

It had started when mortars hit the airfield and a couple guys were hurt. The VC overran a place about seven miles from here. Our artillery was firing heavily; the helicopters were in the air in no time, dropping flares which lit up the whole countryside.

August 30, 1968

Last night the LZ about ten miles from Camp Evans was hit and nearly overrun--fourteen killed and over forty wounded. Our artillery is firing now--normal harassment to the VC. The rounds land anywhere from the perimeter to five miles out. When the gun fires, you can hear the shells flying overhead. Last night I was on guard duty on Tower 6, which is on top of Hong Kong Mountain. One side of the road coming up to the tower is completely wild, with many snakes, lizards, and some baboons, so we don't get out of the truck until we get near the top.

As of October 1, I will be the chief payroll clerk in charge of correlating 18,000 pay vouchers and getting them and the proper amount of money to the units--about one million dollars worth. I will go to Evans every month for nine days to distribute the payroll.

September 5, 1968

The monsoons have started; it has been dreary and has rained for three straight days. The runway at Evans washed out, so the planes are having trouble getting in and out. Also, there have been very strong winds, so that has presented a problem.

September 15, 1968

I'm at Evans now. Our plane trip here (in a Caribou) was really something--everything from oil coming from one of the engines, to landing with a flat tire. On guard duty at An Khe last night, I had quite an experience. I sat in the tower with a Vietnamese man. We struck up a conversation in our limited tongues. I found out he is fifty years old, has been married twice, and has twelve kids. Two of his boys are fighting now. He told me where the Viet Cong are and then asked if I was Catholic. When I told him I was, he made the sign of the cross and pointed up. Then he grabbed my hand, got on one knee, said a prayer or something, and got up with a nod and an approving smile. I didn't know what to think!

October 30, 1968

Last night I got back to An Khe and had guard duty on the green line. We had an attack; there were helicopters flying all around, dropping flares. We found out the next morning that the other side of the mountain got hit pretty bad. The mess hall had a side blown out and one of the officer's hutches had a huge hole in the roof. A mortar went through the barracks next to mine and exploded just outside the barracks, throwing metal chunks into the other end of my barracks. Also, a tower and oil tank were blown up. About thirty Viet Cong made it inside the wire; they're here somewhere, but no one knows where. Now we carry our weapons and have our flack jackets and steel pots on.

November 15, 1968

I'm in Phuoc Vinh now, about twenty-five miles north of Saigon. The camp is on a rubber plantation, and the area kind of reminds me of a resort in northern Minnesota.

We got hit again last night. I was working late, when I heard an AK47 (a Russian-made rifle) fire near the artillery battery about two blocks from here. The ammo dump blew up. There were VC inside who set off the charge. I saw the fire and went to the bunker at the office, which is one of the best around. It has concrete walls about ten inches thick and railroad ties for a roof--with sandbags on top. After they knocked out our artillery, they could mortar us at will.

November 21, 1968

Only thirty-four days until Christmas and ninety-four until R & R. Our chopper ride today to Tay Ninh was really wild. We took off, just missing a power wire. We flew at treetop level, tilting from side to side. Then we flew at about ten feet at 130 miles per hour along this road, trying to scare people and making the water buffalo run.

January 3, 1969

Yesterday we went to "Sin City." There were lots of shops, but we didn't buy anything. Kids grab you and try to exchange money, sell stolen watches, etc. It is quite a sight to see the tribesmen from the hills selling their wares. It is sad to see the kids not knowing what is in store for them.

(Tom Falk--Vietnam--1968-69)

MERRY
CHRISTMAS

THIS 'N' THAT

Minnesota Historical Society, Harriet Friedman Schmidt Schroeck photo

HANS CARL SCHMIDT AND GRANDPARENTS, ca. 1905

ST. PAUL WAS A HAVEN FOR GANGSTERS

St. Paul was a haven for gangsters during the 1930s. My dad ran a saloon downtown on 8th and Cedar, and he was a friend of the police chief, O'Connor. He always said that gangsters had to register when they came to town, and O'Connor promised that they would not be bothered as long as they stayed "clean." This must have been true, because when John Dillinger (who was hiding out in West St. Paul or somewhere on the West Side) went to a party that got a little wild, somebody called the police. When they got there, Dillinger said, "What's going on? I paid for protection!"

Dillinger had an apartment on Lexington Avenue, near Grand. The Feds found out about it and went to get him, but he escaped. Some time later, in Chicago, he got mixed up with "The Lady in Red." She was the one who gave him away to the Feds, outside a theater. My wife, her brother, and their cousins from Chicago were at the theater the night he was shot. They were inside watching the "Manhattan Melodrama" when Dillinger was killed. They didn't even know anything was going on outside until they actually left the theater.

Homer Van Meter used to hole up in a house on Aurora, west of Rice Street. One afternoon I was driving down University Avenue toward Rice Street, when I saw men who looked like Feds running between a couple of houses and jumping over a wooden fence. Soon I heard the sound of shooting, and I found out that they had shot Van Meter. As I recall, J. Edgar Hoover was there when it happened.

I used to work in a filling station on Rice and Wheelock Parkway in St. Paul. Baby Face Nelson used to stop for gas occasionally. He was real nice and never caused any trouble. One day he stopped in with some girl, and after getting gas, drove up Rice Street. Somehow, he tipped over in a ditch, and that's how the police caught him.
(Melvin Frerck--St. Paul, MN--1930s)

THERE REALLY WERE GANGSTERS

When I was growing up in Two Harbors, we had heard about gangsters down there in the big city of St. Paul. I kind of believed it, but wasn't really sure. Well, one day when I was in St. Paul visiting my mother in the Frogtown area, we heard loud noises; someone said the police were shooting. We ran outside to see what was happening. Through all the commotion and confusion, we found out that Homer Van Meter, one of the Dillinger gang, had just been shot in an alley off of University Avenue. We saw them take his body away.

Boy, did I have something to tell when I went back home to Two Harbors! There really WERE gangsters down there in the big city! It wasn't just something our parents had made up to scare us.
(Mary B. Twar--Two Harbors, MN--1930s)

OUR PLACE WAS MARKED

After World War I, tramps were very much in evidence in the rural areas. We would often see one coming up the road. Since our home was close to the main road, we could see for a long distance. When the tramp came closer to the house, he would have a very noticeable limp or maybe an arm inside his coat. Usually, he would have a little book in his pocket which he would hand to my mom or dad to read about his handicap. Later, we would see him walk up the road as well as anybody!

Mom would always tell him to sit on the back steps; then she would fix him a very substantial lunch. We always thought our place was marked--that they knew they would be fed there. Since there wasn't any welfare in those days, these tramps did a lot of begging.
(Ada Ronnei Pederson--Pope Co., MN--1920s)

BEN SELZER

THE FIDDLER

Our house was about a city block from the railroad track at the edge of town, and it was the handiest place to "hit" for those who "rode the rails." During the Depression days, there were a lot of men who did just that. They would jump off the freight car just as it hit the edge of town and walk across the field to our back door, where Mother would always cheerfully give them a good meal. Sometimes they would offer to split wood or do some other chore in payment for food. Dad would often let them sleep on a bed we had put up in the garage behind the house.

I remember one elderly fellow in particular. He had a long white beard, and he seemed somehow different from the general run of individuals who came to our door. He carried a violin case and was cleaner than most. Mother's opinion was that he was a man who was "well bred." He had a nice smile and his voice was soft and gentle. After he ate supper with the family (which was a bit unusual), Dad told him he could sleep at our place that night. The man then pulled out his fiddle and played for us. My father played the violin, too, and we really had a wonderful evening of "fiddling." I never forgot that old man and have often wondered just what his story was.
(Marian Quam Stoneback--Lansing, MN--1920s-30s)

We had many bums or hoboes coming to our house asking for food. One Sunday morning, my brother Clair and I didn't go to church with the folks, so we decided to get some green apples off the tree in the back yard. While Clair was up in the tree, I stood in the doorway with the door open so he could run right in. All of a sudden, a bum came around the corner of the house and scared me half to death! When the folks got home from church, Clair and I were under the bed eating our apples! (Janice Meredith Fredericksen--Lake Crystal, MN--1938)

OUR TOWN'S MOST UNFORGETTABLE CHARACTER

Every town or community has a most unforgettable character. In my hometown, it was the local druggist, Bill Deutsch. His drugstore was like a museum. There were animal heads from his hunting trips mounted all over the store; a huge gun collection and other collectibles (including old musical instruments) in the basement; and hundreds of bottles of all types in the back of the store. No matter what ailment people came in with, he would whip up something that would usually do the trick!

For over thirty years, Bill hosted a May Day party for all twelve-year-olds in the community. Bill also was Santa Claus each year at our local theater and at our church Christmas program. He wasn't the greatest looking Santa, and everyone knew who he was, but, nevertheless, we all looked forward to his visits!

Another recollection I have of Bill is when he served as our one and only church usher for many years. He wore the strangest clothing combinations. Some Sundays he would have a clothespin attached to his tie instead of a tie tack! I often wondered what anyone visiting our church must have thought.

Everyone who grew up in my small hometown has a Bill Deutsch story. My husband remembers often going to the drugstore to get an ice cream cone. No matter what flavor he ordered, he always got "rainbow,"-- a little of each flavor stuck to the scoop! My cousin remembers roller skating uptown. If she fell and scraped her knees, she would go to Bill at the drugstore and he would "doctor" the scrapes with Mercurochrome and Band-aids.
(Bonnie Hughes Falk--Lake Crystal, MN--1940s-60s)

BILL DEUTSCH AND
SHIRLEY HUGHES SELZER

DO YOU REMEMBER?

--Standing in line at the J. C. Penney Store during World War II, hoping to buy a pair of silk hose.

--Searching in the big crock for a dill pickle, with all that dusty scum on the surface of the vinegar.

--Using a cup or big spoon to skim the frozen cream from the top of the can of cream that was ready for town.

--Cleaning and packing eggs for town, saving the cracked and odd-shaped ones for family use. Groceries were usually bought with the egg and cream money; shopping was "skimpy" or "splurging," depending on the price and amounts of produce brought in.

--Hundred-pound bags of sugar and flour piled in a spare room for use in the winter.

--A jar of yeast starter on the back of the kitchen range or on the top of the warming oven.

--Using used rubber jar rings to sew on the back of crocheted rugs to make them skid proof.

--Nailing bottle caps to a board for a handy foot scraper.

--Making Christmas tree ornaments by covering walnut shells with bits of foil from gum wrappers.

--Frying pork sausage and then layering it--pork patties and fat-- in a two or three-gallon crock for later use. We had no refrigerator or deep freeze.

--Getting lamps and lanterns cleaned and filled before dark--or wiping a barn lantern globe with crumpled newspaper.

--Wearing mittens and/or slippers made from sheepskin saved from the lining of an old coat.

--Riding to town in a straw-filled sleigh, huddled under a horse-hide robe, with warm bricks by your feet.

--Sugar sold in paper bags during World War II--or laundry soap in a paper bag.

--The newness of jeans or slacks for women.

--Garter belts for children (and maternity wear).

--Rolling your stockings.

--Using kerosene for furniture polish (a minute amount).

--Grating P&G or Fels Naptha bar soap, covering with water, and then simmering slowly, to make soap easy to dissolve in the washing machine.

--Ironing a big basket of clothes--starched with boiled Argo.

--Churning butter in a wooden churn, or a Daisy churn.

--Bringing in a wooden clothes rack filled with frozen clothes.

--The wonderful days when chicken feed came in the brightly colored sacks that could be used for the little ones' dresses or pajamas.

--Having large flour sacks to make and embroider in sets of seven dish towels to give as gifts.

--Eating a ten-cent malt at the wire tables and chairs in the back of Setter Drug, while the big ceiling fan blew that delightful breeze.
--Girls becoming WAC's during the war.
--Country school programs where every child took part and the whole family came.
--Making cottage cheese.
--Mother polishing the top of the black kitchen range.
--Bread sponge set the night before.
--Making a placket instead of buying a zipper.
(Margaret Seeger Hedlund--MN)

DO YOU REMEMBER?

--Evening in Paris perfume in the blue bottle with silver print.
--Old Spice aftershave cologne for guys.
--Brylcream--"A little dab with do ya!" All the guys I knew dripped with it. Also, crew cut butch wax stuff that made their hair stand up straight!
--Crew cuts and ducktails (DA).
--Vinegar rinse for hair.
--Bubble bath (green stuff from the Jewell T).
--Baking soda for toothpaste and tooth powder in a can.
--Wave set, bobby pins, and pink plastic curlers.
--White margarine with a color capsule.
--Fresh farm cream and homemade cranked ice cream.
--Push lawn mowers.
--Rain barrels (That's how my grandma raised a huge garden.)
--Saturday night movies for twelve cents.
--Roasting marshmallows over burning leaves.
(Vicki A. Johnson--Groton, SD--1950s)

DO YOU REMEMBER?

--Going to the spring rummage sale to get great formals for five or ten cents each, in which to play dress-up.
--Picking blackberries in the woods behind our house.
--Throwing the hose over the clothesline so we could run under it on a hot summer day.
--Filling an old metal tub with water so we could sit in it to cool off.
--Having to take the youngest sibling outside and sit with him on a little blanket; this got boring fast!
--Neighborhood outdoor ice rinks. All the kids dragged their old Christmas trees there to place around the rink after the holidays.
--Having the milkman leave a block of ice on a warm summer day for us to chip at and suck on.
--Being able to leave our bicycles ANYWHERE and never even think that someone might steal them!

--Mom wearing "house dresses," aprons, and cut-off rolled down nylons and "orthopedic" shoes; these moms were only in their thirties!
--Babysitting for thirty cents an hour.
--Entering EVERY pony giveaway contest, just hoping I'd win. In one name-the-pony contest, I submitted the name "Tinker Toy" and was SURE I'd win!
(DeeDee Purcell Valento--White Bear Lake, MN--1950s)

DO YOU REMEMBER?

--Stiff, net strapless formals that didn't move when you did!
--Pedal pushers, anklets, saddle shoes, penny loafers, poodle skirts, little collars worn with sweaters, rayon Hawaiian shirts, argyle socks, jeans--rolled up at the bottom.
--Sadie Hawkins Day Dance (girls asked guys), dressed up like "Dogpatch."
--Chubby Checker and "The Twist."
--Cherry Cokes.
--Wearing a boy's class ring or football on a chain.
--The Edsel.
--Roller skating; the guys who always hung out at the roller rinks were called "rinks" (the ones who wore black leather jackets and had greasy hair).
--Root beer stands and carhops.
--Elvis Presley--and the sensation he caused swirling his hips!
--Movie magazines (*Photoplay*, *Modern Screen*, etc.). I used to have my nose in one of them all the time reading about Debbie Reynolds, Eddie Fisher, Tab Hunter, Rock Hudson, James Dean, Paul Newman, Pat Wayne, Kim Novak, etc.
--Flagpole sitting. The year I was in college (1959-60), one Mankato State student set a record during spring break in Florida for flagpole sitting the longest.
--Homecoming in high school--the big bonfire, the snake dance, the parades with floats, etc.
(Norma Hughes Schlichter--Lake Crystal, MN--1950s)

DO YOU REMEMBER?

--Going to drive-in movies with excess people in the trunk of the car so we didn't have to pay admission for everyone.
--Sock hops every Friday night in the high school gym. My steady and I often won dance contests; we ALWAYS won if they played "The Naughty Lady of Shady Lane" or "Moonlight Serenade," which was "our song."
--Girls in their ankle-length skirts and cardigans worn buttoned down the back, usually with tie-on angora collars!
--Guys in their crew cuts or the "hoody" ducktails; white socks, and white buckskin loafers.

--Big time TV shows, such as "Your Hit Parade" (top songs of the week), with Snooky Lanson and Gisele McKenzie; also, "Texaco Show of Shows," a forerunner of the variety shows. One of the first hosts was Milton Berle.

--"American Bandstand" with Dick Clark. No teenager missed it for the latest hits and ratings.

--Howdy Doody, Clarabelle, and Buffalo Bob.

--The "in" magazines, such as *True Confessions* (to be hidden from your parents or confiscated), or any one of the movie magazines which kept you up-to-date on all the latest Hollywood scandals.

--My boyfriend's 1950 Chev (my favorite car); my least favorite was a friend's 1939 Ford, which spent more time being pushed than it did in operation!

(Mary Price--North St. Paul, MN--1950s)

EXCERPT FROM 1941 DIARY

March 4--Went to the dentist; had teeth cleaned--$1.00

April 29--Mother came over to help clean the chimney and pipes. We papered the ceiling, painted the little kitchen, and put linoleum down.

May 3--Got first ice for the icebox.

May 6--Set up the brooder stove.

May 12--Got a permanent in New Ulm (23 curls)--$3.75.

May 13--Went to first free outdoor show in Cambria.

May 15--Bought a baby buggy--$8.85.

May 16--Got a car at Clements--$337 plus old car.

June 3--Planted 210 pounds of potatoes.

June 9--Planted peas for the third time.

June 10--Went to the show, *Joe E. Brown*.

June 16--Went to Mankato and got 307 chickens that were hatched June 5; cost $10.40 a hundred.

June 18--Put up hay. Mother stacked and I drove the team.

June 21--First hollyhocks opened.

June 23--Got diapers washed and ironed. Sprayed the cabbage.

June 24--Ironed. My water broke and pains started.

June 25--Norma born at 11:24; Doctor bill=$25; hospital bill=$35.

July 13--Norma baptized.

August 1--Threshers for lunch and supper.

August 18--Canned corn and tomatoes; threshed flax.

August 27--Cleaned fruit cellar.

September 17--Sold 56 roosters=$15.68.

September 18--Canned 11 quarts of pears=$1.23 a lug.

September 19--Went to Mothers' Club; everyone fussed over cute baby.

September 20--Norma laughs and talks. Weighs 14 pounds. Eats cereals, fruit juice, Jell-O, and cod liver oil.

October 21--Russell went to corn husking contest at Walters.

(Mae Hanson Hughes Kjos--Lake Crystal, MN--1941)

REFLECTIONS

WE LEARNED NATURALLY

In the 1920s and 1930s, we were poor in material things but rich in imagination, yet based on a reality; rich in new ideas, often demanded by necessity; rich in a sense of self-sufficiency, yet tempered with an interdependence of family and neighbors. We didn't have much by today's measurements, but we had close community. We learned to dream, to do, and to care for ourselves and others. Values and ethics impregnated our being as by osmosis!

We spontaneously learned to conserve and recycle because we wanted to keep and make do with what little we had. Consequently, we learned naturally a sense of reverence and discipline--a sense of caring for things, nature, and community. We, rather subconsciously, felt a stewardship responsibility. (Ruben F. Schmidt--Shawano Co., WI--1920s-30s)

THE FINISH LINE

Perhaps our life is like a race,
With training ere we toe the mark--
The mental set, the practiced pace,
The tinder waiting for the spark.

We're off! and all around we see
A hundred million legs that flash,
All vying to the same degree
To head the pack with pounding dash!

But as we race we feel within,
As on we haste with pumping heart,
That running will not help us win
Unless we know the courses' chart.

Each forking of the racing trail
Will force a choice of ways to go.
That one may reach elusive grail,
The other lead to naught but woe.

With luck, we find at turning lane
A guide to point, explain, advise--
We list with ears and heart and brain
And, with God's grace, our choice is wise.

So through the dale and o'er the hill
And past the crowds that wave and cheer,
We pass the mileposts stark and still,
Each marking one more passing year.

210

The beauty of the way beguiles
And oft we wish to stop and rest--
But onward stretch the future miles
Of twists and turns to give us test.

And then, at last, we see afar
The finish line among the trees--
And high above--the evening star--
And singing of doxologies!

And when we reach the race's end
And comrades cry "Good race! Well run!"
We say to each supporting friend--
The Race of Life is never done!
(Roy B. Moore, from *Sparks from the Embers*,
1976)

PEACE ON EARTH

In my lifetime, I have come from Model T cars to seeing man
walk on the the moon. Electronic devices have changed so
many things, with computers taking the place of hand labor.
And we thought the first ballpoint pens were miraculous!

I am glad to have seen so much progress in my lifetime, but
our biggest hope and dream for the future is still "PEACE ON
EARTH."
(Mary Simonson Thompson--Aberdeen, SD)

Allen, Jo Cutler, 56
Bishop, Gail, 25, 29, 31, 143, 155
Blankenburg, Brian, 74
Boerboon, Rose Grozdanich, 45
Brueck, Konnie George, 39
Buck, Anita Albrecht, 53, 72
Carr, Florence H., 13
Chelberg, Merideth Allen, 51, 99, 134
Costello, Ralph, 174
Cunion, Jill Allen, 16
Degnan, Allan, 19, 22, 64, 80, 81, 83, 93, 94, 95, 109, 123, 125
DeZelar, Elayne J., 95, 101, 123, 165
DiIoia, Joanne Strong, 105, 121, 126
Drake, Timothy A. H., 155, 158
Eugster, Lois, 31, 131
Fabyanske, Ida Posteher, 24, 25, 48, 81, 93, 94
Falk, Bonnie Hughes, 8, 32, 42, 51, 56, 68, 88, 106, 115, 133, 148, 149, 166 178, 179, 204
Falk, Mary Paré, 27
Falk, Mike--60, 61, 67
Falk, Scott, 115, 177
Falk, Tom--68, 157, 197
Falk, Vernelle Sueker, 44
Feller, Wayne, 8, 79
Felsch, John L., 73, 132
Fisher, Guy, 136, 194
Fredericksen, Janice Meredith, 102, 192, 204
Fredericksen, Mark, 120
Frerck, Melvin, 58, 124, 143, 177, 188, 189, 191, 202
Grace, Susan M., 13, 100
Gronquist, Hazel, 53, 137, 159
Grove, Elsie, 166
Guenther, Thelma, 121
Gullikson, Dawn Blair, 20, 54, 71
Hansen, Marcile, 61
Hanson, Patricia McClure, 134
Hanson, Raymond, 130
Hardin, Mae F., 9, 19, 64, 114, 139, 142 169, 171, 190, 193, 194, 195
Hedlund, Margaret Seeger, 14, 37, 43, 96, 205
Hibbard, Clare, 18
Hoyer, H. Conrad, 78, 192

Hughes, Alice C., 20, 52, 138, 154
Hughes, David Wendell, 112, 123, 153
Hughes, Selma Anderson, 9, 29, 30, 116, 120, 153, 189
Hughes, Tom, 20, 119
Johnson, Buster, 70, 101
Johnson, John W., 15, 139
Johnson, Lucille Blair, 9, 99, 155, 186,
Johnson, Vicki A., 58, 62, 87, 89, 98, 100, 102, 108, 111, 131, 154, 168, 206
Juhl, Elizabeth, 60, 145, 146, 153, 155
Kjos, Al, 23, 128, 144, 182, 187
Kjos, Mae Hanson Hughes, 4, 5, 10, 14, 103, 208
Kostroski, Julie, 37
Kuehn, Karen, 156
Kuehn, R., 129, 137
Lee, Elaine, 105
Lehman, Loretta C., 46, 110, 139, 144
Lerfald, Cindy Salberg, 99, 110, 161, 168
Lerfald, Edith Tannahill, 25, 50
Liberda, Joy, 40, 95, 104
Mart, Red and Betty, 48
McKee, Eileene Barry, 43, 147
Meredith, Clair, 30
Meredith, Walt and Grace, 46
Meyer, Amy Frederickson, 30, 143
Mockler, Don, 182
Moore, Roy B., 149, 170, 171, 175, 209
Morse, Ella M., 28, 54
Ober, Edgar B., 186
Olin, Marilyn, 167
Pederson, Ada Ronnei, 20, 67, 146, 189, 203
Philiph, Darlene Lonneman, 12, 83, 130
Price, Mary, 207
Prom, JoAnn Wanner, 77, 98, 147, 148, 168
Rabe, Betty Johnson, 87, 146
Raines, Shirley, 196
Salberg, Beatrice, 8, 50
Salberg, Emmett D., 51, 194, 195
Schelsnes, Ole, 18, 56, 76, 164, 192, 196
Schlichter, Gary, 76, 132
Schlichter, Greg, 180
Schlichter, Norma Hughes, 21, 38, 45, 84, 122, 145, 207

212

Schmaltz, Dave, 183
Schmaltz, Doris, 182
Schmaltz, Steve, 182, 183
Schmidt, Ruben F., 24, 59, 78, 82, 121
    122, 130, 160, 177, 209
Seidenkranz, Caroleann L., 58, 97, 98,
    103, 158, 159, 170
Selzer, Ben, 16
Selzer, Nikki, 119
Selzer, Shirley Hughes, 39, 48, 62, 64,
    87
Snider, Terri Ball, 111, 152
Starr, Jeannette, 167
Steinwall-Ahrens, Jerrie, 64, 76, 77,
    80, 84, 97, 102, 136
Stoneback, Marian Quam, 33, 34, 92, 93,
    102, 122, 203
Strong, Mary E., 19, 25, 29, 31, 46, 49,
    64, 103, 111, 125, 134, 137, 152

Stuck, Cynthia Thomas, 160
Sueker, Leslie A., 193
Sutliff, Jerome D., 41, 125, 152
Swanson, Allan F., 157
Thompson, Dorothea, 49, 55, 147, 189,
Thompson, Mary Simonson, 19, 21, 33,
    45, 49, 51, 101, 113, 123, 129, 165, 169,
    186, 190, 192, 210
Twar, Chris, 70
Twar, Mary B., 27, 50, 115, 131, 135, 157,
    168, 190, 202
Valento, DeeDee, 34, 206
Warren, Ferne R., 95
Westby, Gail, 174, 176
Winter, Mabel, 82, 114, 142
Zappa, Helen K. Giannini, 89, 111, 159
Zappa, James C. Sr., 22, 59, 108

COVER PHOTOS
Front Cover
Bonnie Hughes Falk, 1952
Horses (Bill and Dick), Russell Hughes and Bonnie Hughes Falk
Scott Falk
Russell and Mae Hughes, 1937

Back Cover
Russell Hughes and his grandmother
Minnesota Historical Society Photo--Teen Towner's Club Dance at
    Ramsey School, St. Paul, 1950
Susan Herman, Tom Falk, Mike Falk, Dennis Herman

The artwork in this book is from the following sources: *The Clip Art Book, A Compilation of More Than 5,000 Illustrations and Designs,* Research and Introduction by Gerard Quinn, Crescent Books, New York, 1990; *New Calligraphic Ornaments and Flourishes,* by Arthur Baker, Dover Publications, Inc., New York, 1981; *Christmas Designs,* Designed by Ed Sibbett, Jr., Dover Publications, Inc., New York, 1979; *Old-Fashioned Illustrations of Children,* Edited by Carol Belanger Grafton, Dover Publications, Inc., New York, 1989; *Old-Fashioned Romantic Cuts,* Edited by Carol Belanger Grafton, Dover Publications, Inc., New York, 1987; *Graphic Trade Symbols by German Designers,* F. H. Ehmcke, Dover Publications, Inc., New York, 1974; *Food and Drink Spot Illustrations,* Designed by Susan Gaber, Dover Publications, Inc., New York, 1982; *Old-Fashioned Floral Illustrations,* Selected and Arranged by Carol Belanger Grafton, Dover Publications, Inc., New York, 1990; *Victorian Spot Illustrations, Alphabets, and Ornaments,* Edited by Carol Belanger Grafton, Dover Publications, Inc., New York, 1982; *1,001 Advertising Cuts from the Twenties and Thirties,* Compiled and Arranged by Leslie Cabarga, Richard Greene and Marina Cruz, Dover Publications, Inc., New York, 1987; *Floral Spot Illustrations,* Designed by Stefen Bernath, Dover Publications, Inc., 1989; *Early American Patchwork Quilt Designs,* by Susan Johnston, Dover Publications, Inc., New York, 1984.

Potpourri of Nostalgia, a collection of stories blending the "spices" of life.
Cost: $14.95, plus $2.00 shipping per order (add 6% sales tax if Minnesota resident).

Country School Memories, a collection of stories from individuals who experienced the one-room school as a teacher or pupil.
Cost: $7.95, plus $2.00 shipping per order (add 6% sales tax if Minnesota resident).

"Country School Memories fascinated me, and I read it almost from cover to cover without putting it down. The one-room school was a significant phase in our American culture, and Bonnie Hughes Falk has rendered us all a service by assembling and publishing these anecdotes of country school life." Dr. H. Conrad Hoyer.

Forget-Me-Not, a collection of autograph verses from the 1880s-1980s.
Cost: $9.95, plus $2.00 shipping per order (add 6% sales tax if Minnesota resident). Second printing available December 1, 1990.

"I love your book *Forget-Me-Not.* The verses, the art work, the colorful pages--it is precious! Thanks a million for having it published so everyone can enjoy it." Ellen Rufsholm

----

ORDER FORM

Mail order form to: BHF Memories Unlimited
3470 Rolling View Court
White Bear Lake, MN 55110
(612) 770-1922
(Please make checks payable to Bonnie Hughes Falk)

Please send____*Potpourri of Nostalgia* at $14.95 each.   _____
Please send____*Country School Memories* at $7.95 each.   _____
Please send____*Forget-Me-Not* at $9.95 each.   _____
                                  Subtotal   _____
         (6% sales tax if Minnesota resident)   _____
         Shipping (all orders) $2.00
                              Total   _____

Name_____

Street_____

City/State/Zip Code_____

THANK YOU FOR YOUR ORDER!

ABOUT THE AUTHOR

Bonnie Hughes Falk was born and raised in rural southern Minnesota, near Lake Crystal. She and her husband, Tom, also a native of Lake Crystal, moved to White Bear Lake, Minnesota, in 1970. They have two sons--Scott, a sophomore at St. Cloud State University, and Andy, a sophomore at White Bear Lake High School.

Bonnie has published two other books--*Forget-Me-Not*, a collection of autograph verses from the 1880s-1980s, and *Country School Memories*, a collection of stories from individuals who experienced the one-room school as a teacher or pupil. She enjoys writing about the past, and specializes in helping others tell their stories. She has facilitated two Elderhostel classes through Lakewood Community College, both of which dealt with the life and lore of yesteryear.

NOTE FROM THE AUTHOR

I am in the process of collecting stories for two more books: *Fashion, Fads, and Fun in the Fifties*, and *Memories from the Porch*. If you have one or more stories to share on either of these subjects, feel free to submit them. Since I won't be able to return the stories, be sure to make a copy. Also, if you have a good photograph to go along with your story, send a photocopy. If I am able to use your material, I will contact you. Please keep your stories SHORT--half a page or so. I will do any necessary editing. Thanks for your help!